Lacan and Psychoanalyt. Obsolescence

This book explores the importance of Lacan's role as an irritant within psychoanalysis, and how Freud and Lacan saw that as key to ensuring that psychoanalysis remained fresh and vital rather than becoming obsolescent. Drawing on Freud's thinking as well as Lacan's, Rabate examines how Lacan's unwillingness to allow psychoanalytic thinking to become stale or pigeonholed into one part of life was key in his thinking. By constantly returning to psychoanalytic ideas in new and evolving ways, Lacan kept psychoanalysis moving and changing, much as Socrates did for philosophical thinking in classical Athens. This 'gadfly' or irritant role gave him free reign to explore all aspects of psychoanalytic thinking and treatment, and how it can permeate all aspects of life, both in the consulting room and beyond. Drawing on a deep understanding of Lacan's work as well as Freud's, this book is key reading for all those seeking to understand why Lacan's work remains so important and so challenging for contemporary psychoanalysis.

Jean-Michel Rabaté, professor of English and Comparative Literature at the University of Pennsylvania.

Lacan and Psychoanalytic Obsolescence

The Importance of Lacan as Irritant

Jean-Michel Rabaté

Routledge
Taylor & Francis Group

LONDON AND NEW YORK

Front cover image: © DTaggart84319/Getty Images

First published 2025
by Routledge
4 Park Square, Milton Park, Abingdon, Oxon, OX14 4RN

and by Routledge
605 Third Avenue, New York, NY 10158

Routledge is an imprint of the Taylor & Francis Group, an informa
business

ISBN: 978-1-032-71582-7 (hbk)
ISBN: 978-1-032-71579-7 (pbk)
ISBN: 978-1-032-71583-4 (ebk)

DOI: 10.4324/9781032715834

Typeset in Sabon
by SPi Technologies India Pvt Ltd (Straive)

Contents

Preface

In this book, I present a systematic view of Lacanian psychoanalysis both as a discourse in relation to society at large and as a praxis, an intervention in subjective positioning, which will be exemplified by theses presented in a non-dogmatic manner. The first one is that, in order to understand psychoanalysis as a coherent discourse, we need to read Freud and Lacan together, even though we know that, while Lacan insisted that he was reading Freud literally, he was taking huge liberties with Freudian dogma. This paradox begs the issue of the function of the Author in psychoanalytic discourse. Finally, one cannot understand psychoanalysis if one reads it abstractly, detached from one's personal investment, for psychoanalysis turns readers into active agents who take into account desire, sexuality, and the body. Readers get surprising insights into how they are enmeshed with a language shaped by affective responses, which will bring about the tricky issue of affects. I will deal with it later and include themes like irritation and anxiety, both linked with cruelty and the death drive.

I will read Lacan next to philosophers like Heraclitus, Plato, Kant, Nietzsche, Hegel, Heidegger, Derrida, Nancy, and Deleuze. I will focus on the debate with Derrida and look closely at the work of Jean-Luc Nancy who situated himself between Derrida and Lacan. Like Niklas Luhmann, Nancy pays attention to the role of writing in psychoanalysis. We will try to understand the idea of an "autopoiesis," that is, a discourse that renews itself constantly by absorbing "irritations." The concept of "autopoiesis" was developed by Luhmann in his sociology of society and my theoretical point of departure consists in splicing Luhmann and Michel Foucault when they describe the logic of social discourse.

A second point of departure is more trivial. I respond to a reproach I have often heard among English-speaking readers who complain that Lacan is hard to read and feel frustrated and irritated. Whenever I am told that Lacan is irritating, I answer: "So much the better!" This brought me to develop a meta-biological concept of irritation. For Jean-Baptiste Lamarck, irritability was the only criterion that distinguished between life and non-life. As soon as there is a reaction to a stimulus, there is life and "irritability." Hegel and Nietzsche inherited this concept from nineteenth-century biological discourse.

The term "*irritation*" will provide a red thread that links the question of authority to critique, a critique including self-criticism in a conversation that places Lacan between Foucault and Luhmann. All three considered psychoanalysis as a discourse, which means an archive in constant revision or translation. The issue of translation looks all the more urgent as we are expecting the publication of the revised Standard Edition of Freud's collected works in 2024. Translation will provide a first key and will allow us to understand what Foucault means when he calls Freud an "inventor of discursivity," someone who has shaped our own responses to his discourse and influenced our views of interwoven themes like life, death, and society at large. This imbrication generates a constellation of concepts with their attendant rhetorical questions, their discursive modes, and their styles of thinking.

When Lacan endowed Freud with the distinction of being the main "author" of psychoanalysis, it was to act in a militant manner and combat the danger he saw in the rapid obsolescence of psychoanalytic discourse. Lacan had perceived that psychoanalysis was declining philosophically as it gained in popularity in developed countries. Lacan accomplished this program of rejuvenation by irritating psychoanalysis as a discourse. His wanted to galvanize it, to force it to react, become more alive, dynamic, unpredictable, and also more politically responsible. In a counterintuitive manner, such a rebirth of psychoanalysis entailed that the concept of the "death drive" should be given pride of place in the system. After World War II, it had been relegated to a distant past, a hangover from an alleged Mittel-European pessimism. In the course of his wide-ranging crusade, Lacan was to address the issue of style and writing: insisting on the non-transparency of language, he paid attention to the role of fiction in theory. He stressed the agency of symbolic death in writing one decade before Jacques Derrida who nevertheless asked sharp questions that I will echo.

Irritated by Derrida and his followers like Philippe Lacoue-Labarthe and Jean-Luc Nancy, Lacan ended up considering writing as a way of reaching what he called the Real, which was not to be confused with "reality." Because writing works with letters and not just signifiers, Lacan discovered in their loops a mode of access to a knot uniting speech and writing, discourse and text, body and symptom. If, as Dante had stated in his *Banquet*, authors tie themselves to their work via a type of knot,[1] Lacan combined the logical time of the letter that always arrives at its destination, and the vital insistence of a restless gadfly of culture. Since his metapsychology was founded on the death drive, which provided an ontological foundation for irritation understood as a provocative incentive, his activity as a teacher was an invigorating and often humorous stimulant, an incitement to work with passion and with the passions. Lacan introduced a principle of style, hence also of tact and taste, in issues that have to do with ethics and politics. However, his irritating strategies stopped short of insulting or offending people. And if an analysand was not satisfied, he advised his disciples to give back all the money that had been invested without any question or hesitation. The motto I deduce from Lacan's example, a motto that gains in relevance today given our culture wars and the exacerbation of sensitivities, a loaded situation in which everyone can feel offended by someone else at some point, is something like "Always irritate, never infuriate!"

Note

1 I am alluding to Dante's theory of authority, which would require ampler developments. At this point, I am pointing to the question of poetry as discussed at the end of the book. See Alighieri, *Convivio*, Book 4, chapter 6: "This word, namely 'auctor' without the third letter *c*, has two possible sources of derivation. One is a verb that has very much fallen out of use in Latin and which signifies more or less 'to tie words together,' that is, 'auieo.' Anyone who studies it carefully in its first form will observe that it displays its own meaning, for it is made up only of the ties of words, that is, of the five vowels alone, which are the soul and tie of every word, and is composed of them in a different order, so as to portray the image of a tie. For beginning with A it turns back to U, goes straight through to I and E, then turns back and comes to O, so that it truly portrays this image: A, E, I, O, U, which is the figure of a tie. Insofar as 'author' is derived and comes from this verb, it is used only to refer to poets who have tied their words together with the art of poetry..." **The Convivio, Book 4—Digital Dante—Columbia University.**

Acknowledgments

Parts of some chapters have been published in collections, albeit entirely modified and rewritten for this book.

Two sections of chapter 1 were published in "Translation and Psychoanalysis: *Kulturarbeit* as transliteration" in *Translation: Crafts, Contexts, Consequences*, edited by Jan Steyn, Cambridge, Cambridge University Press, 2022, p. 126–139.

A section of chapter 2 was published in "Psychoanalysis: from *Degeneration* to *Regeneration*" in *The Oxford Handbook of Decadence*, edited by Janes Desmarais and Dadi Weir, Oxford, Oxford University Press, 2022. p. 649–665.

Chapter 3 was published as "Jacques Lacan's Evanescent Affects" in *Affect and Literature*, edited by Alex Houen, Cambridge, Cambridge University Press, 2020, p. 116–132.

Parts of chapter 4 were published in "Cruelfictions of Psychoanalysis: Freud, Derrida, Mignotte" in *Lacan's Cruelty: Perversion beyond Philosophy, Culture and Clinic*, edited by Meera Lee, Cham, Palgrave-Macmillan, 2022, p. 15–39.

A part of chapter 6 was published in "Close Relations: Nancy and the Question of Psychoanalysis" in *Understanding Nancy, Understanding Modernism*, edited by Cosmin Toma, New York, Bloomsbury, 2023, p. 147–161.

A part of the Conclusion was published as "I am a Poem, not a Poet: Jacques Lacan's philosophy of poetry" in *Philosophy and Poetry: Continental Perspectives*, edited by Ranjan Ghosh, New York, Columbia University Press, 2019, p. 97–112.

I am grateful to the editors for granting permission to use these passages.

Introduction

Irritations

Lacan irritates you? So much the better! This is how I summarize conversations that took place with North American psychoanalysts of various persuasions over decades. Thirty years ago, I would be told that Lacan was "arrogant," which meant obscure, incomprehensible, or dangerous. Now that he is read by a larger audience of students and intellectuals, another reproach recurs: Lacan is interesting but "irritating." The more he appeals to students, the more he irritates clinicians. His audience is made up of young people devoted to psychoanalysis or social work, those under forty who find in him an alternative to the sexist and apolitical ideologies dominant in bastions of traditional psychoanalysis in the United States.

I must confess that I, too, find Lacan irritating, given his dense, allusive, and poetic style, his cryptic interventions in clinical debates, or even his main invention, the practice of variable-length sessions. That was enough to brand him as a "heretic" (he compared himself to Spinoza and Joyce) who jeopardized the fundamental financial contract marked by payment for an immutable fifty-minute session, thus opening the door to all kinds of abuses. On top of that, Lacan irritates because he sounds like a Freudian literalist although often contradicting Freud in spirit. At times, he looks closer to Jung given his symbolist side, he can lean toward Melanie Klein or Donald Winnicott in his theory of the partial object or stand out as a "French Bion." Like the British psychoanalyst whose language could be obscure, Lacan encumbered his seminars and texts with a profusion of abstruse graphs, letters, and abbreviations, even if he resorted to "mathemes" instead of Bion's idiosyncratic grid of Greek letters (see Bion:1963).

Most of the time, these conversations are held in pedagogical and academic contexts. Even though I have been invited to give lectures by IPA-affiliated groups in New York and elsewhere, my main investment has consisted in presenting Lacan's thought in English (Rabaté: 2000, 2001, 2003, 2014, 2020). After the huge backlash that swept psychoanalysis out of teaching and research institutions in the United States in the 1980s, psychoanalysis is coming back into fashion, not least because of the psychic havoc

DOI: 10.4324/9781032715834-1

that the Covid pandemic has wreaked on young people, and all those patients unwilling to be treated only with drugs.

My university, the University of Pennsylvania in Philadelphia, a member of the Ivy League group, was home to a dominant American psychoanalytic school in the middle of last century, at a time when Philip Rieff taught Freud (see Rieff: 1959). Following an inevitable pendulum swing, the university saw the emergence of the cognitive therapy school launched by Aaron Beck, who was a professor of psychiatry. In the 1970s, Beck replaced a Freudian model deemed too "pessimistic" (the term will recur in these pages), with an uplifting form of psycho-therapy closer to self-help. He was followed by Martin Seligman who launched "positive psychotherapy," a therapy countering Freud's alleged pessimism by enhancing constructive values and attitudes and was meant to restore hope, faith, and resilience, aiming at developing altruism, tolerance, and responsibility. These aims are indeed highly commendable; however, in practice, they fail to address students' anxieties when they are invaded by irrational and uncontrollable worries and once in a while develop suicidal ideation.

This contextual survey explains why it was a general surprise when in 2015 the University of Pennsylvania launched a "minor" in psychoanalytic studies; this "minor" complemented the "major" curricula and enabled students from all the university's schools to explore the intersections between psychoanalysis and culture. Bringing together professors from the Departments of English, German, Economics, History, Anthropology, Urban Planning, and Psychology, it usually couples academics and clinicians from the Psychoanalytic Center of Philadelphia. One of the standard books used for the introductory class is *Freud and Beyond: A History of Modern Psychoanalytic Thought*, which is used as a guide for the general introductory course, taken by an average of seventy students. It includes a decent chapter on Lacan (see Mitchell and Black:1995, pp. 193–205). English-speaking readers new to Lacan's thought can now use a solid, detailed annotation of *Ecrits* in four volumes, (see Hook et al.: 2019, 2020, 2022, and 2024). Commentators provide line-by-line glosses on all the essays collected by Lacan in his 1966 compendium. The equivalent does not exist in French, which testifies not only to increased visibility but also to a wish to read more deeply and completely founding texts of Lacanian psychoanalysis.

As a sign of the changing times, I would quote a novel by the British artist Susan Finlay, *The Jacques Lacan Foundation*. With an enticing photo of Kate Moss on the cover, Finlay tells a crazy story with chapters dotted with epigraphs reproducing the graphs of Lacan's "discourses." We find in succession the discourse of the master, the discourse of the university, the discourse of the hysteric, the discourse of the analyst, and even the discourse of capitalism (Finley: 2022, pp. 9, 47, 77, 121 and 151). The names of Kate Moss and Melanie Griffith mingle with those of Melanie Klein and Georges Bataille. The plot takes place in a Texas university. Nicki, who has been hired by the

Foundation Jacques Lacan, has to translate the master's unpublished note-books. Unfortunately, the only French words she knows are L'rigine-du-monde, the title of Courbet's notorious painting of his lover's vagina, once owned by Lacan. This light-hearted comedy poking fun at the intellectual pretensions of academic milieus reveals a new Anglo-Saxon familiarity with Lacanian terms, even if they contribute to the general sense of a farce.

If Lacan's name entered Anglo-Saxon popular culture with certain delays followed by an increased visibility, it is above all due to his reputation as a rebel, a protester, a theoretical troublemaker. Lacan, a French joker who rudely interrupted the satisfied purr of the post-Freudians, was ahead of the times when he presented Socrates as the first psychoanalyst. This was his thesis when in a seminar on transference (Lacan: 2015) he gave a sustained commentary of Plato's *Symposium* in which he alluded to Socrates as the inventor of psychoanalysis. Socrates would parade his ignorance in the well-known tactical display of irony but he also stated clearly that there was one type of knowledge he possessed: he knew something about love. More tanta-lizingly, he explained to his audience that this specific knowledge had been imparted to him by a woman, Diotima. For Lacan, Socrates discloses the mainsprings of the dialectic of erotic transference upon which Freud therapy rests. It might be useful to recall that Socrates would also compare himself to a "gadfly." This occurred in a dramatic moment when he was pleading with his judges who had decided to condemn him to death. The sentence had to do with accusations of immorality and impiety: Socrates would have been a bad model for his students, among whom was the notorious Alcibiades. When he compared his role in Athens with that of the insect that stings horses, Socrates was not making things easy for him. Indeed, such a self-appointed role of perpetual irritant hesitates between the comical and the ludicrous. Socrates takes pride in the critical function he has taken in the city: he wanted to wake up his fellow citizens by biting or stinging them:

> For if you put me to death, you will not easily find another, who, to use a rather absurd (*geloioteron*) figure, attaches himself to the city as a gadfly (*múops*) to a horse, which, though large and well bred, is sluggish on account of his size and needs to be aroused by stinging. I think the god fastened me upon the city in some such capacity, and I go about arousing, and urging and reproaching each one of you, constantly alighting upon you everywhere the whole day long.
>
> (Plato:1966, 30 e–31 a)

There is no doubt that Plato's Socrates was aware that the image sounded funny, ridiculous, or even grotesque. The term *múops* Plato uses can refer to a "spur" as well as to a "gadfly," although the context spells out that the image is silly or absurd: it is called *geloioteron*, meaning something that makes you laugh. Curiously, the laughable trope of Socrates as a horsefly also taps an older tragic tradition. The image of the biting insect stinging relentlessly its victims comes from Greek myth. We encounter it in Aeschylus' *Prometheus in Chains*, a tragedy written a century before Socrates was condemned to death. *Prometheus in Chains* presents the titular hero sadistically tortured by Zeus. Then he gets the visit of Io, a young girl who has been metamorphosed into a heifer constantly bitten by a gadfly sent by Hera. The goddess was jealous of Zeus' sexual attentions. Seeing Prometheus chained to the rock, the unfortunate girl exclaims: "Oh, oh! Aah! Aah! A gad-fly, phantom of earth-born Argus is stinging me again! Keep him away, O Earth!" (Aeschylus:1926a, l. 566). Hera had enlisted Argus to find the sting that hurts the animal most, this *oistros*, another type of gadfly literalizing the frenzy of mad desire. Io must move on, spurred by pain, fleeing in mad wanderings. Prometheus recognizes Io and calls her simply *oistrodinetos*, "driven by the gadfly."

Another tragedy also by Aeschylus, *Suppliant Women*, offers more details about Zeus' fateful passion for Io. The god metamorphosed her into a heifer and then impregnated her. Argus was supposed to watch on her but was killed by Hermes. The image returns here, linked with an allusion to Egyptian mosquitoes and gadflies:

Chorus: What manner of all-seeing herdsman with a single duty do you mean?
King: Argus, a son of Earth, whom Hermes slew.
Chorus: What else did she contrive against the unfortunate cow?
King: A sting, torment of cattle, constantly driving her on.
Chorus: They call it a gadfly (*oistros*), those who dwell by the Nile.
(Aeschylus: 1926b, l. 300–308).

The same insect that bites or stings so horribly that it maddens its victims exemplifies a universal drive quite close to the Freudian drive to which we will return. Why this stinging horsefly, why this turmoil, these tortures, why this overwhelming delirium? Whether the rhetorical filter is tragic or comic, the biological simile defines a certain relationship between gods and men, between the *polis* and the philosopher, who like a tragic hero, suffers but will never yield.

By comparing himself to a horsefly, Socrates admits that he is a kind of parasite; he needs to draw blood from the Athenian horse, just as much as the horse needs to be irritated, pushed forward, awakened from its torpor. His younger follower, the wayward disciple who was also an anti-Platonician rival, the Cynic philosopher Diogenes, chose another animal as his totem. The trope of the dog who barks at the citizens defined his role in Athens. Diogenes who had withdrawn from "normal" social exchanges by sleeping in the open like a homeless vagrant was dependent on charity and the attention of passers-by: they had to lend an ear if he was to keep on teaching.

In the convergence between tragedy and comedy, the Greek words translated as "gadfly," *muops* and *oistros*, display metaphorical meanings suggesting the sting, the spur, irritation, or the sudden stimulation of impulse. In English, the term "*gadfly*" refers to annoying critics, people who mean well but provoke by their barbs, attacks, and snide remarks. When Socrates calls himself a gadfly, his image betrays his reluctance to leave Athens even to save his life, as his friends urge him to do. In the end, he obeys the death sentence and refuses the easy exile they had advised, for it is his own death alone that can ensure the perpetuation of his sting. Choosing death, Socrates remains an eternal *muops*, a formidable gadfly who retains his critical, ethical, and political dimension. Two features are of interest in this trope: first, it sends us into the biological realm, and then it presupposes the substance needed for the insect, that is blood, a basic substance to which I will return in a later chapter.

What links Lacan to Socrates and Diogenes is that Lacan was not just a famous psychoanalyst who revised Freudian theory to render it up to date but also a self-appointed pedagogue. His teaching mattered most for him, all the more so as he felt acutely that he had been excluded from the main psychoanalytic associations, as the novelist Philippe Sollers recounts in his freewheeling and irreverent chronicle, *Women*. In the book, Lacan is called Fals:

> Fals even claimed to be a heretic who'd eventually be proved right... (...)
> It was a merciless settling of scores between the Freudian church and himself... The weapon he relied on most was his "teaching"... "Yes, I know
> the word makes you laugh," he'd often say to me dryly... And the
> "Lectures"! ... In them, Fals can be said to have created a new genre...
> They were solemn, hermetical, logical, apocalyptic and comic... Great
> art... Oration, peroration, grandiloquence.
>
> (Sollers: 1990, p. 80)

I will discuss Lacan's distinctive style in the seminars here called "lectures" and his writings. Another link with Socrates is that they were not compensated financially for their teachings, unlike the Sophists who, in Athens, were quite greedy, and unlike today's professional academics teaching in universities or institutes.

All this suggests that the image of the theoretical gadfly all too eager to wake up dormant institutions has not lost its relevance in the modern world. This is the contention made by Olivier Postel-Vinay in his book *The Gadfly in the City*, a careful re-reading of Socrates' activity and death. In his final chapter, Postel-Vinay advocates the Socratic model while denouncing modern medical science as racist or eugenic (Postel-Vinay: 1994, pp. 126–127). Moreover, he denounces the racism of Plato's idea of a superior type of humanity and thinks that Plato had perverted Socrates' original insights, thus paving the way for Friedrich Nietzsche. We know that Nietzsche, indeed, preferred Plato to Socrates. For Nietzsche, Socrates announced a Jewish and Christian morality that he despised. I will return to Nietzsche's theses on morality and biology—their links are multiple and complex, as Barbara Stiegler has shown (Stiegler: 2001, 2021). Socrates' self-definition as a gadfly incites us to revisit critically these seductive but risky biological metaphors. Freud, who had read Nietzsche carefully and always felt a deep proximity in their approaches, resisted the drift that might lead to racism and would uphold the myth of a noble race. As we will see in his conversations with Georg Viereck, Freud quoted Nietzsche's critique of values freely, while being very proud of his Jewish heritage.

On the whole Freud acknowledged that he was a disciple of Darwin. Behind Darwin, one glimpses the ghost of Jean-Baptiste Lamarck who had anticipated his ideas about inheritance. Lamarck stressed the acquired changes that later generations inherit. One can revisit his theories in a socio-logical manner. I will show that in a systemic vision of the body and the social body, the concept of irritation provides a productive link. Indeed, Freud betrayed Lamarckian leanings in his very first theoretical text, his *Project for a Scientific Psychology*. When he introduced a "quantitative" approach, he wrote: "If we look still further back, we can in the first instance link the neuronic system (as inheritor of the general susceptibility of protoplasm to stimulus) with the irritable outer surface of protoplasm which is interspersed with considerable stretches of non-irritable substance" (Freud:1954, p. 357). The three main functions ensuring the continuation of life, hunger, respiration, and sexuality, would this be predicated upon the basic irritability of the neuronic system.

Freud echoes the thesis that Lamarck developed in 1809 in his *Zoological Philosophy*. For Lamarck, the most general definition of life means for animals is a capacity to react to stimuli coming from the physical environment. Here is what "irritability" means. This feature is the most distinctive character of animals; it is more fundamental than the faculty of voluntary movements, of feeling, and of digesting. Irritability serves as a criterion that allows one to distinguish animals from plants. Animals are living and organized bodies endowed with parts that are irritable. If they digest food and move, these movements may not be determined by a will, but they always signal a response to an excited irritability (Lamarck:1809, p. 127). The science of life takes irritability as a key concept. The idea recurs in Freud's attempt at combining Lamarckism and Darwinism. In fact, the two doctrines clashed over the possibility (or not) of a generation bequeathing acquired characteristics to its descendants. This poses the interesting question of deciding whether Freud, the biologist of the psyche, was closer to Lamarck or to Darwin, as Frank Sulloway did brilliantly (Sulloway:1979, pp. 274–275).

Freud's initial biologism receded slowly to give birth to a theory of language. We can verify this in a later essay like the "Magic Writing Pad."

Freud describes the psychic apparatus as excited by stimuli coming from the outside; it keeps a certain opacity or resistance to irritation in some neurons that will be able to inscribe traces. A pure irritation would entail a simple discharge losing itself; its sheer intensity would leave no durable trace. This point is a key for Jacques Derrida who sums up Freud's comparison of the psychic apparatus with a "magic" or "mystic pad," that *Wunderblock* in which words can be inscribed and erased by pulling a separating sheet. What matters is the alternation between excitation, the moment of irritation of the system, and the erasure accompanying the inscription of the trace. Such a double activity generates a space for writing, as Derrida puts it cogently:

> If there were only perception, pure permeability to breaching, there would be no breaches. We would be written, but nothing would be recorded; no writing would be produced, retained, repeated as legibility. But pure perception does not exist: we are written only as we write, by the agency within us which always already keeps watch over perception, be it internal or external. The subject of writing does not exist if we mean by that some sovereign solitude of the author. The subject of writing is a *system* of relations between strata: the Mystic Pad, the psyche, society, the world."
>
> (Derrida:1978, pp. 226–227)

To this list, one can add the sense of time, which does not refer only to individual time, for it extends to a social time mediated by writing systems: "The 'origin of our concept of time' is attributed to this 'periodic non-excitability' and to this discontinuous method of functioning of the system Pcpt.-Cs [Perception-Consciousness]. Time is the economy of a system of writing" (Derrida:1978, p. 226). Derrida's analysis of writing ends up highlighting the link between writing and death, or, better put, the unity of death and life gathered in the notion of the death drive. Derrida's interpretation of the Freudian program is announced earlier in his essay: "Life must be thought of as trace before Being may be determined as presence. This is the only condition on which we can say that life is death, that repetition and the beyond of the pleasure principle are native and congenital to that which they transgress" (1978, p. 203). Freud's insights generate the notion of a general archive that includes social discourses. If Freud's Lamarckism led him to envisage a theory of social systems, it was because he saw human language as retaining a sense of time and memory, even when life and death are intertwined in it. This is the social landscape explored by the sociology of Niklas Luhmann. My main contention here is that Luhmann's work parallels and redoubles the social epistemology deployed by Freud, but once rethought by Foucault and Lacan.

Freud insisted that psychoanalysis completed two previous revolutions, the Copernican revolution that replaced geocentrism with heliocentrism and made humanity aware of its decentered position, and the Darwinian revolution that pointed to the links between human and animal species. Freud was to usher in a third revolution when he posited an unconscious that abolished the centrality of consciousness. Lacan meditated these lofty claims and added that they all had to be made consistent by the creation of a new discourse. Luhmann agrees when he provides an original way of understanding psychoanalysis as an evolving biological or eco-system, all the while retaining the features of a discourse.

What is meant when one speaks of psychoanalysis as a discourse? I refer to the term *discourse* as it appears in Foucault's analysis of the author-function in a lecture given in 1969 and attended by Lacan. At the end, Lacan intervened and praised Foucault because he had recognized himself when Foucault mentioned his slogan of a "return to Freud" as a good way to understand the function of an author. Foucault was asking: "What is an Author?" (Foucault:1977, pp. 113–138) after Roland Barthes had announced the "death of the Author" in a famous 1968 essay. For Barthes, the "Author" had died or was to be abolished as an institution in which the ultimate source of truth and knowledge resided. The Author was to be replaced by a Reader who would be granted license to deploy batteries of codes and autonomous reading grids. There was no need to ask whether the result was in line with the Author's intentions.

Having completed his ambitious theoretical compendium in *The Order of Things*, Foucault intended to restore the author's place even if he, too, denied to authors the position of moral supremacy imposing meaning from above on the works. Foucault understood the need to retain authors as names for the names of authors allow him to provide a necessary tabulation of historical knowledge. In a second moment, the concern for the elaboration of a structural chronicle led him to distinguish a general "author-function" from a more complex or loaded category, that of the "founders of discursivity." Foucault cites two such initiators of new discourses, Marx and Freud, both authors of abundant works, both producing texts and concepts that gave rise to new possibilities of discourse. Each of them produced concepts, hypotheses, and analyses that were then developed to create a specific discourse within a given epistemological formation. Whether a particular commentator is faithful to the author's spirit can only be judged in relation to the foundational theses. The "founders of discursivity" cannot be treated like Galileo or Newton when they revolutionized physics. Indeed, "the work of these initiators is not situated in relation to a science and in the space it defines; rather, it is science or discursive practice that relate to their works as the primary points of reference" (Foucault:1977, p. 134).

Foucault deduces from his analysis a need for a constant "return" to the works of such founders, by which he alludes both to Louis Althusser who was then re-reading Marx and to Lacan who was re-reading Freud. What does such a "return" imply for authors of this type? Their texts are read in relation to the present, that is, recursively, with a view to find gaps or omissions, holes in knowledge. The result is an incessant back-and-forth for the return belongs to the discourse while never ceasing to modify it from within. The return to the text is not a historical supplement that would add more discursivity or redouble it in an ornamental manner, for it is "an effective and necessary means of transforming discursive practice" (Foucault:1977, p. 135). Thus, re-reading Galileo's texts will not change the foundations of contemporary physics whereas re-reading Freud's texts can change psychoanalysis as it is practiced. The discovery of unpublished texts by Freud would modify his theoretical stakes and redraw the limits of the field. "In saying that Freud founded psychoanalysis, we do not simply mean that the concept of libido or the technique of dream analysis reappear in the writings of Karl Abraham or Melanie Klein, but that he made possible a certain number of differences with respect to his books, concepts and hypotheses, which all arise out of psychoanalytic discourse" (Foucault:1977, p. 132).

Such feedback removes those foundational texts from the criterium of truth defined by empirical verification. Since the work is textual in nature, it is both unverifiable and interminable. Accepting fully the definition of his own role, Lacan appreciated the theoretical justification given to his slogan of a "return to Freud." His "return to Freud" forbade him to be an "author" and confined himself to the position of the commentator, which did not prevent him from modifying or displacing Freud's concepts. Refusing to play the part of an author, Lacan preferred to negotiate differently, signing a discourse caught up between oral performance and writing, taking a paradoxical position that I will analyze later.

If what constitutes psychoanalysis as a discourse and as a practice eludes scientific verification of the kind provided by laboratory testing or quantitative statistics, if the "founders of discursivity" cannot be accused of factual error, their theories demand a constant reactivation, which means a practice of retranslation—hence I will begin with a chapter devoted to translation in psychoanalysis. Freud's works should neither be considered as a sacred origin, a vatic source of truth, or as a scientific document whose accuracy can be tested by truth procedures or protocols of verification. Their textual origin cannot help being porous, full of gaps, knotted, dotted with idioms specific to one language, semantic riddles that constitute points of resistance. Returning to these texts, we will all be engaged in a program of perpetual translation. Lacan's program thus did not entail respectful imitation but a literalist reading that, paradoxically, doubles as creative rewriting. By applying the practice of reading to the obscure productions of an unconscious made up of signs, barely legible signs on a palimpsest, psychoanalysis testifies to a need for endless literalizations that are as many retranslations.

I will flesh out Foucault's theory of discourses by placing it next to Luhmann's systems theory. Foucault's position on discourse had an impact on Luhmann who, like Foucault, rejected humanism and saw subjects as determined by linguistic and social structures, but preferred not to stress the issue of power. Luhmann added that the structures that make up a system are constantly self-correcting. The only difference is that Luhmann rejected Foucault's agonistic or politicized thesis that ended up considering that everything revolved around the relationship between knowledge and power. Luhmann explains this difference in the English preface to his book on *Love as Passion*, a book whose object is the historical codification of love, not a genealogy of sexuality, a favorite field of Foucauldian archaeology. Like Foucault, Luhmann starts from the rejection of humanism but replaces the analysis of power patterns with considerations of how systems interact with the environment (Luhmann:1998, pp. 2–4). What is proposed by Luhmann is a general theory, both abstract and detailed, of the cultural mechanisms accounting for variations in social values. These values are constantly evolving and can be exemplified by his analysis of the morphological changes in the discourses on love along with the emergence of a conception of love as passion marking the transition between the classical and the modern age. Luhmann's conception of information is inspired by cybernetics, structuralist epistemology, and evolutionary theory. This is the convergence that enables him to introduce the concept of systemic irritation.

For Luhmann, social communication is organized rigorously and results from progressive adaptations that are capable of metabolizing irritations coming from the environment. Language, given its slow rate of evolution, resists the potentially destructive character of such irritations, it absorbs and perpetuates them: "… language has the peculiar ability to convey irritations to communication without breaking down" (Luhmann:2012, p. 58). Luhmann does not understand communication as an exchange between one consciousness and another, as we might be tempted to think, for he sees no direct access from physical, chemical, or biological processes to communication, except when there is material destruction. This dialectical relationship is captured by a striking image: noise, distance, lack of air can prevent communication, but fire, however, cannot by itself make a writer: "Books can burn or be burned. But no fire can write a boo or even irritate the author strongly enough to cause him to write differently while the manuscript burns than had there been no fire" (Luhmann:2012, p. 63). What does this example suggest? First that consciousness remains in a privileged position in the production of the autopoiesis of the social system but works not as the agent or "subject" of communication, but rather as a cog in the machine of the system. The structural coupling of consciousness and communication solves the apparent paradox whereby each system appears self-determined yet develops in relation to its environment.

Consciousnesses are mediations through which systems produce their auto-irritations, and further what Luhmann calls the "autopoiesis" of systems. Systems reconstitute themselves through a constant self-creation, which presupposes an element of destruction filtered by protective layers. Not all irritations penetrate the system, for usually the systems choose their own irritations; this is true in ecology as well as social interactions. Psychic structures, even if there are differences in size and regime between individual organisms and social codes, progress by managing their auto-irritations. While organisms can only react to irritations on their external surfaces (regardless of how they then interpret these irritations internally), communication systems increase their irritability by replacing spatial boundaries with meaning and new distinctions. A whole array of boundaries, irritations, and digestions of the senses is deployed by Luhmann, whose theory of irritation parallels Lacan's theory of the signifier. If Lacan repeated that "a signifier represents a subject for another signifier" (Lacan:1979, p. 207), in the same way, for Luhmann, human beings are not communicating between themselves: only communication systems communicate with each other.

Like Lacan, Luhmann accepts the "linguistic turn" that emphasizes the power of language over subjectivity while refusing to reduce reality to a language effect, as some postmodern thinkers have done. He writes: "We follow the 'linguistic turn,' which replaces the transcendental subject by language—now we say by society" (Luhmann: 2012, p. 131). Society stabilizes an imaginary space by successive projections to which it adds symbolic values. These recursive applications create "autopoiesis," a mechanism by which the system protects itself from noise and selects its own irritations, a concept that I will apply to Lacan in the last part of this book. Communication begins to work when systems increase their response to irritations, be they significant events or ancillary factors treated as coincidences. Systems build their own complexity and its irritability, which then increases their autopoiesis when they differentiate between self-reference and hetero-reference.

Tackling the issue of evolution, Luhmann notes that Lamarck had inherited the term *irritability* from Renaissance biology, as we will see. He mentions the historical controversy between Lamarck and Darwin in those terms: "Lamarck called the most important structural characteristic of all living being that replaced fixed type characteristics *irritabilité*. This characteristic also described the relation of the system to the environment. Nothing has since been changed" (Luhmann:2012, p. 304). Luhmann was committed to a sociocultural Lamarckism because he analyzes structural transformations through learning and collective memory.

On this point, Luhmann evinces affinities with Freudian thought, which leads him to stress the function of forgetting as an integral part of memory. For him, the function of memory is to guarantee the boundaries of possible consistency checks while at the same time freeing up information-processing capacities, which allows systems to open up to new irritations. It is not a paradox to assert that the main function of memory lies in forgetting. Forgetting prevents the system from clogging by sifting through the results of its previous observations. Forgetting generates the regular re-imprinting of the system. This calls up Freud's image of the Unconscious as a writing machine we glimpsed earlier; the machine keeps stratified written traces that pass through differentiated layers of neurons all the while erasing parts of these continuously.

If the idea of the unconscious emerged in the nineteenth century, Luhmann links its emergence with a new concept of the individual, both accompanying a diminution in the social and political role of religion. When individualism was on the rise, its darker double was the unconscious, which brought about a subversion and even a negation:

> With the help of the Freudian theory of the unconscious, the individual found this counter-concept *in itself*, and it was only this development that completed the semantics of individuality. The individual could be understood as *in distinction to himself*—and could leave the concept of society to ideologization.

> (Luhmann:2013, p. 296)

Luhmann refers here to Marx's definition of ideology while taking into account Freud's critique of society seen as a "culture" or "civilization" (*Kultur*): *Kultur* only brings acute discontent or constant irritation to the subjects it regulates.

Luhmann's main theoretical aim was to reconcile constructivism and deconstruction, hence his frequent allusions to Derrida with whom he had one contentious exchange at the Cardozo Institute in New York in the early 1990s. Halfway between the negativism of the Frankfurt School, for whom the issue is to relentlessly criticize the ideology of advanced capitalism, and the American optimism that reduces social critique to the efforts of Hollywood heroes fighting for an ideal of social justice, Luhmann elaborates a description of society by society: society projects and renews meanings endlessly. These meanings cannot be abstracted from recent events, like the changes brought about by history, the problems caused by globalization, the digital information revolution, the degraded environment, the return of a cold war that was thought to have been forgotten, and so on.

Luhmann does not want to throw a backward gaze on a past understood once it has been fulfilled, as Hegel saw and expressed in the famous "owl of Minerva" metaphor (Hegel:2001, p. 20). The redistribution of categories of meaning and discourse that he promotes accounts for an autopoietic evolution in progress; these dynamic concepts enable us to better understand Lacan's position on the links between psychoanalytic discourse and the social bond. Lacan's concept of the social bond can be understood as a series of knots that are psychically, politically, historically, and legally interrelated. These knots shape subjectivity. Lacan's theory of the four social discourses, Freud's concept of civilizations and group psychology, the psychoanalysis of individual and collective power, the unconscious workings of ideology, all these knots determine the social bond. The social bond shapes subjectivity by demanding specific modes of subjection, submission, and treatments of jouissance. It is in this social context that Lacan can appear as an irritant, that is, someone who never ceased irritating psychoanalysis insofar as it involves a group constituted by the concepts of a founder. In fact, as whoever has read him knows, his return to Freudian texts involved major shifts.

A telling example can be found in Lacan's reading of *Hamlet*. In his seminar on desire and interpretation, Lacan flatly contradicts Freud's central intuition about Hamlet as Oedipus. The seminar *Desire and Its Interpretation* goes against the classical Freudian reading according to which Hamlet was a modern version of Oedipus. According to Freud, Hamlet cannot kill his uncle because the uncle has realized his own unconscious murderous wish, his desire rooted in the Oedipal structure to kill his father and marry his mother. Lacan questions this idea and calls it "non-dialectical" (Lacan:2019, p. 278). He objects that Hamlet might just as well have wanted to kill a man he would consider as a happy rival. Lacan's reading dismantles the psychology of imitation on which Freud's reading had been predicated. Like all psychological readings, it remains at the level of the imaginary and thus can easily be reversed into its opposite. The Oedipal pattern is not sufficient to account for Hamlet's inaction. Lacan shows that a number of Freudian concepts like desire, castration, and the phallus have to be brought into play. Above all, there is the thesis of mimetic desire.

Lacan had been working on the mirror stage since the 1930s. In his "mirror stage" essay from 1949, Lacan pointed out that any imaginary identification entails a form of aggression, "an aggressiveness deriving therefrom in all relations with others" (Lacan: 2006, p. 79). If one wishes to overcome the logic of identification, one needs to change the grammar, hence move from an objective genitive to a subjective genitive: what will be determining will not be the desire for the mother but the mother's desire. That desire, in which Hamlet sees an excessive jouissance playing with death, remains Gertrude's enigma. In fact, according to Lacan, Hamlet is paralyzed because he cannot solve the riddle of maternal desire. He only frees himself through the intermediary of a second feminine desire that he contributes to kill. By engineering Ophelia's suicide, Hamlet finds a way back to his own desire, and puts himself in a position to die as well. This summary of a long section of the seminar shows how Lacan was Freudian: he would read him carefully, point to weaker points in the logic, follow the strong concepts, and deploy a creative critique that manages to "irritate" Freud in a positive sense.

With *Hamlet*, we verify that Lacan remained within the terms of Freud's discourse but innovated by twisting its grammar: a shift from the objective genitive (love of the mother) to a subjective genitive (a mother's love) is sufficient to irritate the Freudian analysis of the Oedipal solution to *Hamlet*'s riddle. Here is where the analyses of Foucault, Lacan, and Luhmann converge. Psychoanalysis is both a discourse taken from the field of the human sciences that tackles sexuality, desire, the cleaved subject of the unconscious, the function of subjecthood split by desire, the drives, etc., and an archive of texts that need to be compared, re-read, rethought. The consequence is an autopoietic system constantly being revised, a text full of gaps and holes that must be carefully parsed. Lacan returns to Freud because Freud is the unique Author of psychoanalysis, and he renders his position stronger by tapping other discourses like those of cybernetics, biology, ethology, mathematics, not to mention the philosophies of Plato, Aristotle, Kant, Hegel, and Marx. Freud retains the status of initiator of discursivity: he is fully an Author, but an author who needs to be translated.

Bibliography

Aeschylus (1926a). *Prometheus Bound*. Perseus Digital Library, transl. Herbert Weir Smyth.

Aeschylus (1926b). *Supplicant Women*. Perseus Digital Library, transl. Herbert Weir Smyth.

Bion, Wilfred R. (1963). *Elements of Psycho-Analysis*, London, Heinemann.

Derrida, Jacques (1978). *Writing and Difference*, trans. Alan Bass, Chicago, Chicago University Press.

Finley, Susan (2022). *The Jacques Lacan Foundation*, London, Moist.

Foucault, Michel (1977). *Language, Counter-memory, Practice*, trans. by Donald Bouchard and Sherry Simon, Ithaca, Cornell University Press.

Freud, Sigmund (1954). *The Origins of Psychoanalysis, Letters to Wilhelm Fliess*, trans. Eric Mosbacher and James Strachey, New York, Basic Books.

Hegel, G. W. F. (2001). *The Philosophy of Right*, trans. S. W. Dyde, Kitchener, Batoche Books.

Hook, Derek, Neill, Calum and Van Heule, Stijn (2019). Editors of *Reading Lacan's Écrits*, From "Signification of the Phallus" to "Metaphor of the Subject," =, New York, Routledge.

Hook, Derek, Neill, Calum and Van Heule, Stijn (2020). Editors of *Reading Lacan's Écrits*, From "The Freudian Thing" to "Remarks on Daniel Lagache," New York, Routledge.

Hook, Derek, Neill, Calum and Van Heule, Stijn (2022). Editors of *Reading Lacan's Écrits*, From "Logical Time" to "Response to Jean Hyppolite," I, II, III and IV, New York, Routledge.

Hook, Derek, Neill, Calum and Van Heule, Stijn (2024). Editors of *Reading Lacan's Écrits*, From "Overture to this Collection" to "Presentation of psychic causality,", Routledge.

Lacan, Jacques, (1979). *Seminar XI, The Four fundamental concepts of Psychoanalysis*, translated by Alan Sheridan, New York, Penguin Books.

Lacan, Jacques (2006). *Ecrits*, translated by Bruce Fink, New York, Norton.

Lacan, Jacques (2015). *Transference, Seminar VIII (1960–61)*, translated by Bruce Fink, London, Polity.

Lacan, Jacques (2019). *Desire and its Interpretation, Seminar VI*, translated by Bruce Fink, Cambridge, Polity.

Lamarck, Jean-Baptiste (1809). *Philosophie zoologique*. https://ia801004.us.archive.org/28/items/LamarckPZ/Lamarck_PZ.pdf

Luhmann, Niklas (1998). *Love as Passion: The codification of intimacy*, trans. Jeremy Gaines and Doris L. Jones, Stanford, Stanford University Press.

Luhmann, Niklas (2012), *Theory of Society*, Vol. I, translated by Rhodes Barrett, Stanford, Stanford University Press.

Luhmann, Niklas (2013). *Theory of Society*, vol. II, trans. Rhodes Barrett, Stanford, Stanford University Press.

Mitchell, Stephen A., and Black, Margaret J. (1995). *Freud and Beyond: A History of Modern Psychoanalytic Thought*, New York, Basic Books.

Plato (1966). *Apology*, Perseus Digital Library. http://www.perseus.tufts.edu/hopper/text?doc=plat.+apol.+17a

Postel-Vinay, Olivier (1994). *Le taon dans la citÉ: actualitÉ de Socrate*, Paris, Descartes & Cie.

Rabaté, Jean-Michel, editor (2000). *Lacan in America*, New York, The Other Press.

Rabaté, Jean-Michel (2001). *Jacques Lacan: Psychoanalysis and the Subject of Literature*, London, Palgrave.

Rabaté, Jean-Michel, editor (2003). *The Cambridge Companion to Lacan*, Cambridge University Press.

Rabaté, Jean-Michel (2014). *The Cambridge Introduction to Literature and Psychoanalysis*, Cambridge, Cambridge University Press.

Rabaté, Jean-Michel, editor (2020). *Knots: Post-Lacanian Psychoanalysis, Literature and Film*, New York, Routledge.

Rieff, Philip (1959) *Freud, the mind of the moralist*, Chicago, Chicago University Press.

Stiegler, Barbara (2001). *Nietzsche et la biologie*, Paris, PUF.

Stiegler, Barbara (2021). *Nietzsche et la vie*, Gallimard, Folio.

Sollers, Philippe (1990). *Women*, trans. Barbara Bray, New York, Columbia University Press.

Sulloway, Frank (1979). *Freud, Biologist of the Mind*, New York, Basic Books.

Chapter 1

Psychoanalysis as irritant translation

One of Lacan's insights was that psychoanalysis was only a language therapy. Freud defined its limits by refusing to use hypnosis as the French schools of Charcot in Paris and Bernheim in Nancy did, and thus implied that one would also eschew the use of medication. What is more, Lacan generalized the insight by presupposing a linguistic unconscious, or as he kept repeating, one has to understand that the unconscious is structured like a language. This entailed a theory of translation of a special type, as Lacan suggests in an early seminar when he states that the translation must be made in a language one does not fully understand:

> Translating Freud, we say—the unconscious is a language. Its being articulated doesn't imply its recognition, though. The proof of this is that everything proceeds as if Freud were translating a foreign language, even carving it up and reassembling it. The subject is, with respect to his own language, quite simply in the same position as Freud. If it's ever possible for someone to speak in a language that he is totally ignorant of, we can say that the psychotic subject is ignorant of the language he speaks.
>
> (Lacan:1993, pp. 11–12)

One simple way of summing up the work of psychoanalysis is to say that it is a process aiming at making the unconscious conscious via a certain use of language that foregrounds its opacity, even when it comes to translation. We can infer from this that if psychoanalysis implies some form of translation, the process is not predicated on one-to-one correspondences. This tends to make translation dynamic, complex, and dialogical. Let us explore its manifold uses and functions.

1.1 Retranslating psychoanalysis

Excellent scholars have pointed out the abundant use of terms that evoke translation in Freud's texts; they have analyzed their links with two related technical terms, transference and interpretation (see Mahony:1982, 2001,

DOI: 10.4324/9781032715834-2

Benjamin:1992, Basile:2005). As Derrida had noted in a more critical mode, the omnipresent concept of translation is not without dangers: "… and yet Freud translates all the time" (Derrida:1978, p. 210). Derrida's attention was attracted by Freud's comment in his *Interpretation of Dreams* on the analogy between dream-images and "'grammalogues' in short-hand," an analogy that might seem to fix oneiric meanings by giving stable interpretations (Freud:1965, p. 386). In this passage, Freud alluded to the way whole words tended to be represented by a single dream symbol as it used to be done in shorthand writing. The analogy with shorthand is crucial: this method of rapid writing using conventional symbols and abbreviations was meant to go as fast as speech in dictation to a secretary. Here, although Freud has rejected systems of linear equivalences, he nevertheless implies an interpretive machine that offers equivalents for symbols and images. In that sense, interpretations of dream symbols, images meaning this or that, could be questioned, as Derrida does, or seen as a regression to medieval allegories. Here is the root of objections to psychoanalysis as one finds in Vladimir Nabokov's numerous attacks (see Rabaté:2014, pp. 1–3, and Kwon:2019).

On a plane that is more topical, the issue of translation looms larger today in the domain of psychoanalytic theory because of the forthcoming revised version of Freud's collected works in English. We will now have a new "standard edition" of Freud, which reminds us that we read him in translation. The same hurdle awaits non-French-speaking readers of Lacan. Lacan began his work of revision by stressing burning issues of translation that derived from the "return to Freud" that he advocated, as we have seen.

In one of his *New Introductory Lectures on Psycho-Analysis*, Freud concluded a discussion of "the dissection of the psychical personality" by offering a telling image, an allegory one might say, of the therapeutic effect of psychoanalysis. He stated that the intention of psychoanalysis was to strengthen the ego by making it more independent of the super-ego; this would entail an effort to broaden its scope and "enlarge its organization, so that it can appropriate fresh portions of the id." Freud then adds the unforgettable sentences: "Where id was, there ego shall be. It is a work of culture—not unlike the draining of the Zuider Zee" (Freud:1989a, pp. 99–100). Freud's original text had a different layout for the last sentence; it began a new paragraph to add more emphasis:

Wo Es war, soll Ich werden.
Es ist Kulturarbeit etwa wie die Trockenlegung der Zuydersee.
(Freud:1933, np)

If one searches the web for translations of the famous sentence "*Wo Es war, soll Ich Werden*," a rather typical commentary will explain it in these terms:

Freud hoped that, by bringing the contents of the unconscious into consciousness, he could minimize repression and neurosis. The English translation of "Wo Es war, soll Ich werden" is "Where It was, shall I be." In other words, the "it" or "id" (unconscious) will be replaced by the "I", by consciousness and self-identity. Freud's goal was to strengthen the ego, the "I" self, the conscious/rational identity, so it would be more powerful than the unconscious. (No Subject:2019)

This gloss is not bad; we learn that there is a difference between Freud's "Ich"/"Es" and the translation by "Ego"/"Id." However, the shift from "Ich/I" or "Ich/Ego" to the self, then to a consciousness equated with a "rational identity" yields the picture of a poor ego battling against the encroachments of the id, which suggests a vision of the unconscious as the enemy within.

In fact, Freud's idea is that the ego struggles mostly against the super-ego, in which he sees the severe or even cruel introjection of parental laws, whereas the ego's task is to appropriate as much ground as possible from the id. The "it/id" is compared with inundated terrain that can be reclaimed from the sea, much as what the Dutch were achieving at the time when they enlarged their country. Freud was giving his lectures in 1932, which is the moment the Afsluitdijk was finished. The new dike transformed the Zuiderzee into the Ijsselmeer, which rendered large areas of land under the sea level available for farming and housing. The historical and geographical reference reminds us that the domain of the id as "Es" should be considered as potential farmable terrain and not a dark dungeon filled with monsters.

The commentary I quoted fits theories that my students find everywhere and then repeat with assurance. Freud's doctrine would try to prevent rational consciousness from being invaded by uncontrollable urges stemming from the "Id." The topology of the I/ego, the It/Id, and the Super-ego turns into a Walt Disney cartoon: a super-egoic Jiminy Cricket, who in Collodi's *Pinocchio* was called *Grillo-parlante*, a "talking cricket" (Collodi:1949, p. 11)—helps a Pinocchio-like Ego to become human by avoiding metamorphosing into a braying Id-ass. In an effort to introduce some nuance, I usually send my students to the dissenting voice of Bruno Bettelheim. His spirited refutation of the translation of "Es" by "Id" and "Ich" by "Ego" dates from 1982. Bettelheim renders the sentences as: "Where it was, there should become I," and "It is a cultural achievement somewhat like the draining of the Zuyder Zee" (Bettelheim:1984, pp. 61–62). He explains that the sea represents the natural world more than the unconscious and definitively rejects an earlier translation in the Standard Edition of *Kulturarbeit* as "reclamation work," a symptomatic blunder silently corrected in later editions. The contention is that the Standard Edition of Freud's works does "standardize" by distorting the meaning of psychoanalysis, which turns into a dry, abstract, and pseudo-scientific doctrine. Bettelheim, who came from the same Viennese culture as Freud but fifty years later, noted with dismay how current German words like *Besetzung* or *Fehlleistung* had been rendered in English by importing Greek terms like "cathexis" and "parapraxis." And whenever Freud mentioned *die Seele* (the soul), it was translated as the "mind."

More than twenty-five years earlier, and in Vienna too, Jacques Lacan discussed "*Wo Es war, soll Ich werden*" in his essay "The Freudian Thing." In that lecture given in German in November 1955, Lacan insisted that Freud's sentence should not be construed as meaning "where the id was, there the ego shall be" but should keep its homely and demotic feel. Like Bettelheim, Lacan rejected the imposition of a static topology on a dynamic grammar. If the subject's "I" turns into "the Ego," if the "it" one grapples with becomes "the Id," one loses this mobility. Even if these terms are capitalized by Freud (which had not been the case in a first version), one should keep the flexibility of Freud's spoken syntax. Thus, Lacan highlights the modal value of "*sollen*," a verb indicating an ethical imperative and announcing a duty: there is a duty to speak that defines the emergence of "I" as a speaking subject, as we will see in Chapter 3. Only by continuing to use language well will I overcome the limitations of my structure and truly "become." Punning on a French syntax distorted via a shift from "*là où c'était*" (where it was) to a reflexive "*là où s'était*" (literally: "where it was for itself"), Lacan expands the sentence and makes it say: "Where (it) was itself, it is my duty that I come into being" (Lacan:1966, pp. 347–348).

Later, Lacan rewrote the sentence as: "Where it was, there must I come to be as a subject" (Lacan:2006, p. 734). In all these cases, Freud's syntax is taken literally: what matters is to render adequately the movement leading from an undefined neuter to a first-person utterance of "I." Meanwhile, the verb "*soll Ich*" introduces a paradoxical injunction to be myself, as in a double bind order like: "Be more spontaneous!" Lacan comments: "… the 'must I' of Freud's formulation, which, in inverting its meaning, brings forth the paradox of an imperative that presses me to assume my own causality. // Yet I am not the cause of myself, though not because I am the creature" (Lacan:2006, p. 734). Quite logically, Lacan compares Freud's sentence with Descartes' foundational "Cogito ergo sum." Thus, in different and almost opposite manners, Lacan and Bettelheim agree with Freud's account of his terminology. Parodying Wallace Stevens, one could say that Freud gave us three main rules for his archive's translation: it must not be abstract; it must change; it must tackle the issue of pleasure.

When he wanted to remind his readers that he aimed at simplicity, Freud took as an example the crucial concepts of "*Es*" and "*Ich*" in *The Question of Lay Analysis*:

> You will probably protest at our having chosen simple pronouns to describe our two agencies or provinces instead of giving them orotund Greek names. In psycho-analysis, however, we like to keep in contact with the popular mode of thinking and prefer to make its concepts scientifically serviceable rather than to reject them. There is no merit in this; we are

obliged to take this line; for our theories must be understood by our patients, who are often very intelligent, but not always learned. The impersonal "it" is immediately connected with certain forms of expression used by normal people. "It shot through me," people say; "there was something in me at that moment that was stronger than me." "*C'était plus fort que moi.*"

(Freud:1953, SE/XX, p. 195)

If it seems curious to see Freud illustrating German idioms with a French phrase, his choice is, nevertheless, justified by his quoting the common phrase, "*C'était plus fort que moi,*" for in this case, the French elides a "C'..." that stands for "*Ça*" or "*Cela.*" At the time, Freud had just borrowed from Georg Groddeck the concept of the "*Es,*" the "It," as we will see later. In German, the elided 'S for *Es*, as in the usual greeting: "*Wie geht's?*" can be used in the past ("Wie ging's)." However, this cannot be repeated in English with the past tense: a sentence beginning with "t' was" remains poetic or archaic. In French, the full form ("*Cela était plus fort que moi *)*" would sound wrong; here, an elision is required, which renders the subterranean impact of the *Ça* all the more invisible and powerful. All those who attended Lacan's seminars, as I did for a while, were struck by his tendency to elide most mute "e"s, which made him say "*l' pot d' moutard'*" for "*le pot de moutarde*" (the mustard pot). I have analyzed this idiosyncratic feature in "Lacan's turn to Freud" (Rabaté:2001, pp. 2–3). Lacan would pronounce "*s'técritur'*" ("that writing") instead using the full form standard in French, *cette—écriture.* In the Postface to his Seminar XI, he systematized his idiosyncratic mannerism by referring to his own writings as an unreadable rebus, punning on the same word: "*Vous ne comprenez pas stécriture. Tant mieux, ce vous sera raison de l'expliquer*" (Lacan:2001, p. 505). ("You don't understand that-writing. All the better, this will give you some ground to explain it.") Unlike Freud, Lacan taunted his readers and paraded his strategic display of opacity.

"*C'était plus fort que moi*" was Freud's first approximation of the work of the Unconscious: a driven "*Ça*" (the term would later translate "das Es" into French) pushes the envelope in the subject's realm; this "*Ça*" forces the self as *Moi* to do things that ought to be avoided, as we see in the annals of French psychopathology in which patients confess to their irrepressible and forbidden urges. This subterranean reference calls up Freud's justification for using blunt sexual terms in conversations with hysterical women, as was the case with the young woman he called Dora. To explain why he had to be that explicit, Freud quotes French sayings, "*J'appelle un chat un chat,*" and "*Pour faire une omelette il faut casser des oeufs*" (Freud:2013, p. 41). This testifies to his fidelity to Charcot whom, he saw as a "Master" who regularly used them and allows him to introduce covert sexual metaphors. The French slang of "*chat(te)*" is a common euphemism for feminine genitals, while "*oeufs*" can allude to the testicles. These sayings combine sexual literalism with the breaking of word shells that will have to be rearranged and produce substantial meaning: this is how you make the desired "omelette" of sense appear in order to serve it to patients and readers alike. Following similar associations, Lacan punned on "omelette" when he wanted to give an ironical portrayal of a little man as less than an "*homme*" (see Marini:1992, p. 73.)

Freud justified his preference for demotic expressions by an argument of accessibility—the point was not simply to convey meanings to his readers, but also to convince analysands of the correctness of the theory. Analysands should be able to use theories explained to them and apply the main terms to gain a new understanding of their symptoms and lives. It is no wonder to see that the main conceptual choices of psychoanalytic terms were discussed with passion by the first British translators. James Strachey gave an egregious example of his resistance to the translation of "*Es*" by "*Id*." He states that he fears that such a term will be misunderstood; he sees it distorted in a racist manner, as he tells his wife in 1925:

> They want to call "das Es" "the Id." I said I thought everyone would say "the Yidd." So Jones said there was no such word in English: "There's 'Yiddish,' you know. And in German 'Jude.' But there is no such word as 'Yidd.'"—"Pardon me, doctor, Yidd is a current slang for the word for a Jew—"Ah! A slang expression. It cannot be in very widespread use then.
> (Strachey:1985, p. 83)[1]

Happily, few people made that racist slur in England at the time; we'll to come back to the sensitive issue of Jewishness in the next chapter.

What one gathers from the letters exchanged by James and Alix Strachey is that the first English translations were a collaborative affair. Ernest Jones exerted, at times abused, his authority when it came to tricky terms. At some point, James Strachey jokes about the *Id*: "I find it terribly difficult to follow the modern, fashionable, what they call 'Iddish' conversations..." (Strachey:1985, p. 17). He alludes to the explosion of sexual innuendoes brought about by the discovery of Freud's theories; their impact was huge in the Bloomsbury group. All at once, one could talk about semen and ejaculations in polite society. Strachey remains professional, of course, and helps with the composition of an international glossary. In 1924 already, Adolf Storfer began a *Wörterbuch der Psychoanalyse* (dictionary of psychoanalysis), which included forty-eight languages. Even though this never materialized, the first realization was a *Handwörterbuch der Psychoanalyse* that Richard Sterba published in 1936, a glossary of 160 pages (see Strachey:1985, p. 178). Meanwhile, Strachey agonized over each tricky decision; what should be the correct verb translating the repeated couple of *betsetzen/ Besetzung*, the latter rendered as "cathexis"? Should it be "cathectize," "cathectize," "cathexise," or "cathect"? (Strachey:1985, p. 237). In the end, quite logically, a shorter form prevailed: "to cathect" was chosen, although most writers tried to avoid it by using periphrases.

According to Freud's wishes, therapy and theory were to illuminate each other, both being founded upon a simple vocabulary. The clinic would be linked with current language use, even when some technical terms could be required in an effort to formalize and systematize the discourse of psychoanalysis, an insight shared by Lacan and Bettelheim. Both knew that Freud listened to what his patients had to say and then proposed elements of the theory allowing them to interpret dreams and symptoms. The process entailed a double translation, first a linguistic synthesis produced by the unconscious, an initial translation of dreams or parapraxes provided by the analysand, followed by the intervention of the psychoanalyst who may or may not interpret, but nevertheless sends back to the analysand a part of the initial message. A delay, which often results in silence, marks the second moment: Freud listened less in order to translate than to let analysands learn how to translate freely and autonomously.

Sharing Freud's basic principles, Lacan and Bettelheim criticize the Standard Edition's choices in similar ways; however, the similarities end there. Bettelheim rages against Strachey's pseudo-scientific medicalization, which as he states transforms a supple and idiomatic German text into an ossified doctrine that loses its spontaneity; for him, psychoanalysis should be less concerned with a scientific terminology and pay more attention to immediate engagements with the affects of the "soul" presented by patients. On the other hand, Lacan aims at being rigorous, which at times makes him sound more "scientific" than Freud; he never avoids the technical vocabulary, he often resorts to Greek and Latin terms, and he punctuates his essays and seminars with algebraic "mathemes," graphs and schemata. Lacan rejects the ideology of the boosted autonomous ego that Strachey and the first translators promoted and sold to the American psychoanalytic diaspora to insist upon a dynamic engagement with Freud's texts.

1.2 He Do the Psyche in Different Voices: Freud's talking dogs[2]

Mobility, the ability to shift between different idioms, styles, and linguistic registers, is a key when it comes to translation. The psychoanalytic experience consists in rendering banal words and sentences different, foreign; they will have to be interpreted over and over. Thanks to psychoanalysis, we learn to speak in a foreign language, an insight that came early to Freud. We discover a typical blend of creativity, word play, and fanciful use of translation in Freud's letters to his friend Eduard Silberstein. That epistolary exchange began when he was fifteen and lasted ten years. Many of these letters are written in a fanciful Spanish idiom replete with mistakes, personal allusions, and grandiose schemes. Freud and Silberstein had discovered Cervantes's

"*Coloquio de los perros*" ("The Dialogue of the Dogs") from the 1613 *Exemplary Stories* when reading a primer of Spanish literature. Their enthusiasm made them invent a "Spanish Academy" of which they were the only members. Neither knew Spanish well, which did not prevent them from writing to each other in garbled but fluent enough Castillan. Freud chose the persona of Cipion, leaving Silberstein the role of the other dog, Berganza when he arranged an epistolary pact entailing weekly confessions, but "in the spirit of romanticism" (Freud:1990, p. 58).

In these letters, Freud betrays his love of the German Romantic tradition marked by wit, humor, fantasy, and whimsy. One of his models was E. T. A. Hoffmann whose "Sandman" story would provide evidence for the Uncanny. Indeed, Hoffmann had published a sequel to Cervantes's *Coloquio de los perros* in 1814 (Hoffmann:2006, pp. 101–177). In Hoffmann's version, a first-person narrator listens to Berganza who narrates fanciful adventures. In Freud's letters, a similarly jocular tone dominates. Freud also displays his adolescent infatuation for a pretty young neighbor from Freiberg, his hometown, Gisela Fuss, whom he calls "Ichthyosaura" because of an obscure association with a poem by von Scheffel staging a lover's first kiss. Burlesque and satire abound, as in Cervantes's tale. Freud as Cipion is endowed with an authoritative voice; he interjects witty comments while his friend Silberstein (Berganza) spins endless yarns. This interaction cannot but evoke the setting of the forthcoming psychoanalytic cure, with the qualification that here we have a "writing cure" fully outlined. Berganza is a *pícaro* whose adventures end in catastrophe, and Cipion the philosopher who meditates on them. Cipion knows Greek as Freud did, thus can give the correct etymology for "philosophy." At some point in their exchange, Silberstein forgot who he was; he began mixing up their aliases, signing a letter "Cipion." Then Freud rebuked him in his strange Spanish:

> Parece, que no sabeis, Señor Don Berganza, como os habeis de llamar, pues que á vestra carta del 2. Junio subscribes Cipion, lo que es usurpacion de mi nombre. Pero si quieres, que mudemos de nombre, como Jean Paul dice, que Siebenkäs y Leibgeber hicieron, consiento y espero vuestro arbitrio. // El que hasta alli se llama Cipion.
> (Freud:1990, p. 118, and Freud:1989b, p. 134)

Freud berates his friend for having forgotten his alias; he pretends that they want to play the part of Siebenkäs and Leibgeber, characters from a novel by Jean Paul. In his novelistic trilogy, Siebenkäs and Leibgeber change their names. Siebenkäs, unhappily married, agrees to a trick suggested by Leibgeber, whose name means "body-giver": he fakes his own death to be released from his marriage vows. When he meets Natalie, his true love, he marries her after his death, in a sense. Freud saw his friend's role as that of a *Doppelgänger*, but insists playfully on the theme of the double to introduce issues of life and death. Here is how Freud managed to sublimate his homosexuality, as he kept on doing with later male correspondents like Wilhelm Fliess.

Freud's letters to Silberstein state the wish that, under the aegis of the Academia Española, the friends should send to each other a detailed account of their day-to-day lives by the intermediary of a language that neither masters fully. Intimacy will be regulated by an idiom in which they are not proficient, because the detour via a foreign literary language provides a filter for introspection and exchange. Often Freud struggles to find adequate Spanish equivalents, thus misremembers a passage from a play by Cervantes and writes *cerro gordo*, which means "fat hill," and takes *cerro*, rather than *gordo*, to mean "fat." Finally, he wrongly feminizes the word as "Cerra," then retranslates it as *"Dicke"* (fat) (Freud:1990, pp. 98–99). The layering of languages can be baffling, even daunting as in one crazy letter in which Freud sketches an imaginary house that Silberstein should visit. Here, Freud sounds drunk with languages, being at the time under the influence of Carlyle's *Sartor Resartus*, a book in which the author pretended to translate the works of an invented German philosopher looking like Kant. The "Third floor" (the title being in English) contains long snatches of Spanish, of Greek in the original alphabet, of German and Latin (Freud:1989b, pp. 60–61). Here is why Freud states that he will let all the "other nations" speak in their own idioms and mentions Italian, French, and English (Freud:1990, p. 47). A passage in Greek characters explains how he has no news from another friend; Latin is used to mention Silberstein's letter; he reverts to Spanish when offering to send books by Shakespeare; German describes a shower of meteors; finally, Spanish is again the filter when he jokes about Gisela, that "not long extinct Cretaceous," continuing the private joke. Gisela Fluss's nickname, "Ichtyosaura," would place her as an inhabitant of the Cretaceous period. Mistakes abound, for "greda" does not mean "Cretaceous" but "clay." Freud invents Spanish words out of mere assonances and explores boldly the polysemic possibilities offered by different languages.

Freud knew Greek and Latin well enough to use them correctly, which he did in a 1871 postcard complaining about his bad teeth (Freud:1990, pp. 1–2). Freud's English was better than his Spanish, his French quite fluent had improved while he lived in Paris. He translated all these languages: from the English John Stuart Mill's twelfth volume and an interesting section on Samuel Butler in Israel Levine's 1923 book *The Unconscious*, from the French, Jean Martin Charcot's volumes of *Leçons sur les maladies du système nerveux* and *Leçons du Mardi à la Salpêtrière*. Freud also translated Hippolyte Bernheim's *De la suggestion et de ses applications à la thérapeutique* and *Hypnotisme, suggestion et psychothérapie*.

A point worth stressing is that Freud was allowed to work closely with Charcot when he heard that the professor was looking for a German translator, the previous one having disappeared. Freud offered his services and immediately was invited in Charcot's home. His first translation, published in

German before the French original was out, was appreciated, and then had the opportunity to stay longer in Paris. When translating Charcot, Freud attempted to render the master's inimitable style, giving a faithful equivalent of a delivery based upon inspired improvisations: "These lectures present so accurate a picture of Charcot's manner of speaking and thinking that, for anyone who has once sat among his audience, the memory of the Master's voice and looks comes alive" (Freud:1953, SE/I, p. 135). Translating one of these lectures, Freud quotes a remark that Charcot had made to him—Freud having insisted on the need to have a theory of the origin of hysterical symptoms like hemi-anesthesia. At the time, Charcot was still looking for traces of hysteria in the brains of his patients. Freud asked why. Charcot replied to him with a witty dismissal: "*La théorie c'est bon, mais ça n'empêche pas d'exister*" (Theory is fine and all, but *that* does not prevent *it/us* from existing) (Freud:1953, SE/I, p. 135). We can leave the rather enigmatic expression resound: *ça n'empêche pas d'exister* would condense a lot, for thanks to it, one can anticipate a clash between a not-yet born *Ça* and the ego or the object, none of them named yet. Indeed, Freud quoted the famous saying several times; he added wryly to the first occurrence: "If one only knew *what* exists! ..." (Freud:1953, SE/I, p. 139.) His question ("What exists?") announces new dialectical elaborations to come in which the *Id* is pitted against a "*what?*" that includes both the ego and its objects.

The repeated use of French idioms in Freud's first texts betrays the lasting impact of Charcot's teaching, even though he quickly rejected the Master's theses, such as a search for a localization of hysteria in the brain, and the idea that heredity had a role to play. Against this, Freud stressed the impact of an embodied language that had turned into symptoms by conversion. The neurotic symptom was presented as an undelivered letter, or, as Poe would say, a "purloined letter" that had to be deciphered with the help of the psychoanalyst until the all too powerful affect could be tamed and subjected to a translation: "The task which the ego, in its defensive attitude, sets itself of treating the incompatible idea as *non arrivée* simply cannot be fulfilled by it. Both the memory-trace and the affect which is attached to the idea are there once and for all and cannot be eradicated" (Freud:1953, SE/III, p. 48.) The phrase *non arrivée* in the feminine suggests that its subject, the idea, is also a letter that has been sent and not delivered; at least it has not been acknowledged by the recipient. However, the affect that was attached to it cannot be denied. This introduces the domain of what Shirley Sharon-Zisser, following Derrida and Lacan, calls an "unconscious grammatology,"[3] and I will discuss it as an interplay of traces in a chapter on affects.

At the end of his life, Freud returned to translation when he helped his daughter Anna translate Marie Bonaparte's memoir about her dog. Topsy, Marie Bonaparte favorite chow dog, was diagnosed with mouth cancer, but when treated with radiation, he survived. While Freud and his family were waiting anxiously for the visa that would allow them to leave Vienna and settle in London and were prevented from seeing patients because of the new racial laws, he translated Bonaparte's *Topsy, chow chow au poil d'or* (1937) as *Topsy, der goldhaarige Chow* (1939). He wanted to thank his devoted supporter and express love for their pets. His daughter began translating a manuscript given in December 1936. Soon Freud took over. The translation was finished in April 1938. This story begins with despair at the announcement of a fatal disease and ends with a passionate affirmation of life: "Topsy, who has reconquered life, is for me a talisman that conjures away death" (Bonaparte:1994, p. 164). As Freud had understood through the ventriloquism of Cervantes's dogs, survival in spite of all odds is also an effect of translation. Moreover, such exercises in translation are transferential: Marie Bonaparte and Freud shared and exchanged their love of furry pets. Bonaparte could not think of Freud's jaw cancer caused by smoking when evoking the cancer of the jaw that almost killed Topsy. Once more, this interaction confirms the proximity between terms like "transference" and "translation."

The epistolary exchange with Silberstein anticipates insights Freud had deduced thanks to his friend Breuer when the latter worked with the young Viennese hysteric he called "Anna O." Her contribution to psychoanalysis was to coin the English phrase of the "talking cure" at a time when her hysteria prevented her from using German. She spoke a medley of four or five languages, which rendered her incomprehensible for her maids and guardians. A slightly archaic English ended up prevailing, for like Freud, she had read Shakespeare assiduously (Freud and Breuer:2004, p. 29). Then she developed an uncanny ability to translate any language into English immediately. One day, a consultant was brought in and Breuer made her "read a French text aloud in English." Translating perfectly, she laughed, adding: "That's like an examination" (Freud and Breuer:2004, p. 31). Through hypnosis, she was able to talk things through, thus coining two expressions for the same process, the "talking cure" and "chimney sweeping" (Freud and Breuer:2004, p. 34). One night, when her father was still alive but very sick, she was sat next to his bed and hallucinated a black snake that was coming to bite him. Her hands refused to work—her fingers had turned into small snakes. She wanted to pray to overcome the terror but found she could not speak. She was saved when a little English ditty came back to her. After that, she was able to pray, think, and speak, but only in English (Freud and Breuer:2004, p. 42).

Anna O's "talking cure" capitalized on her speaking in tongues, which streamlined the linguistic process. Like her, Freud systematically hystericized language by estranging it from its usual consensual function. Thanks to the use of an estranged language, the cure in words replaced hypnosis, which did wonders for Anna O before becoming the trademark of psychoanalysis. Translation presides over the origins of psychoanalysis; it links the interpretation of texts with the act of reading the unconscious as a foreign language one is merely learning. Hence the importance of today's debates about revising the versions of Freud's texts that we are reading.

1.3 Revisionism and Freud in translation

As most commentators agree, the Standard Edition of Freud's collected works in English is a monument; one can cavil at individual faults but, on the whole, the translations remain consistent, robust, and well organized. As Darius Gray Ornston and Mark Solms agree, the translation of Freud's collected psychoanalytic works was a huge achievement historically (see Ornston:1992; Solms:2018). However, even those who want to respect the integrity of this historical monument of translation acknowledge the need for a revision. Newly discovered linguistic difficulties have given rise to different attitudes facing the translation of Freud's works. These positions are usually buttressed by different editorial attitudes. Freud's text can be treated as an evolutionary archive requiring new, modernized, more rigorous systematic ordering of the concepts. This was the position of the group of translators in the French version of *Presses Universitaires de France* under the guidance of Jean-Baptiste Pontalis.

In England, a less systematic attitude prevailed when Adam Phillips invited different translators to render different volumes of Freud in new Penguin translations. Thus the "New Penguin Freud" has taken more liberties and found a precursor in the pioneering work of Joyce Crick, a gifted Germanist who published her *Interpretation of Dreams* in 1999. Finally, the position adopted by Solms and his team was a third one—they held that they should not retranslate the individual texts but would revise passages that posed problems. They felt that the whole series of "collected works" had been so "standardized" already that they belonged to a given cultural moment that could not be obliterated. In spite of James Strachey's worries, no-one imagines changing the "Id" back into the "It" today: it is undeniable that the term *Id* is embedded in our culture.

In 1999, Joyce Crick published a translation of *The Interpretation of Dreams* that relied on a simple idea: not only was it important to retranslate the *Interpretation of Dreams* in a more literary mode, but also it made sense to look at the first edition of the *Traumdeutung*. It was a slim volume once shorn of its numerous later additions. This yields a text about the half of the length of the usual editions, and it sounds more writerly and more direct in its theorization. Reading Freud's 1899 version, one realizes that the *Interpretation of Dreams* is a stylistic masterpiece that can double as an engrossing autobiographical novel. Crick reproduces its fluid style. We sense the urgency, the excitation of an exploration much more than the wish to build a system. One comparison can suffice. Here is a passage in Strachey's version in which Freud concludes that his notion of the Unconscious differs from those that preceded:

The fact that excitations in order to reach consciousness must pass through a fixed series or hierarchy of agencies (which is revealed to us by the modifications made in them by censorship) has enabled us to construct a spatial analogy. We have described the relations of the two systems to each other and to consciousness by saying that the system *Pcs.* stands like a screen between the system *Ucs.* and consciousness. The system *Pcs.* not merely bars access to consciousness, it also controls access to the power of voluntary movement and has at its disposal for distribution a mobile cathectic energy, a part of which is familiar to us in the form of attention.

(Freud:1965, p. 653)

In Crick's version, this paragraph becomes:

The fact that, in order to reach consciousness, the excitations have to make their way through an immutable sequence of agencies, which we discovered from the changes imposed by the censorship they exercised, enabled us to set up a spatial analogy. We described the relations of the two systems by saying that the *Precon.*-system stood like a partition-screen between the *Uncon.*-system and consciousness. The *Precon.*-system did not only block access to consciousness, we said, it also governed access to voluntary movement and directed the transmission of a mobile energy-charge (*Besetzungsenergie*), a part of which is familiar to us in the form of attention.

(Freud:1999, p. 407)

Crick, more idiomatic and precise, renders *Besetzungsenergie* with all its force. Indeed, we should distinguish between terms that seem untranslatable because they have no equivalent in English, and terms for which a simpler or homelier equivalent can be found. I used "homely" pointedly because I am aware of the difficulty of rendering "*das Unheimliche*" into English. This being of one Freud's most quoted texts, one will remember that Freud takes the time to walk us though several dictionaries before concluding that the term condenses two opposite meanings, the familiar and the opposite of familiar. Barbara Cassin has a detailed analysis in her entry on "*Das Unheimliche*" in *Dictionary of Untranslatables: A Philosophical Lexicon* (Cassin:2004, p. 432). The German etymology is "*Heim*," an equivalent of "home": why not render the concept as the "Unhomely"? David McLintock, the translator of the new Penguin version, did not resist the temptation: "... we can understand why German usage allows the familiar (*das Heimliche*, the 'homely') to switch to its opposite, the uncanny (*das Unheimliche*, the 'unhomely')" (Freud:2003, p. 148). The term, meaning roughly "uncomfortably unfamiliar," had been introduced by Ernest Jentsch in 1906, but it was expanded and systematized by Freud so as to make sense of a variety of psychic manifestations, from the fear of dead people, ghosts, and doubles, to the involuntary repetition of certain actions. It is deployed in fantastic literature.

Freud's 1919 essay, acting upon Jentsch's prompt, culminates with a detailed close reading of E. T. A. Hoffmann's short story "The Sandman." However, we should resist the temptation to leave the term in German. The "Uncanny" is also a key concept of the younger Heidegger, and an excellent book by an American philosopher proves that one can keep on thinking with the concept in its English form (see Withy:2015).

A different position from Crick's rejuvenation of the text by a new translation is held by Mark Solms. Solms, the general editor of the *Revised Standard Edition of the Complete Psychological Works of Sigmund Freud* (Freud: 2024), combines a new perspective with a respect for the cumulative impact of Strachey's previous translation. His revised edition in twenty-four volumes reveals a different Freud less by changing conceptual keywords, or by giving us a sense of Freud's varied styles, than by adding to the already huge corpus letters, unpublished fragments, interviews, and short texts that had been omitted from the canon. His decision was to keep the "standard" version while revising a few crucial terms whenever he felt that a critical consensus prevailed.

One important change is the decision to replace "instinct" with "drive" as a translation of *Trieb*, which had become a major theoretical issue. As commentators have noted after Bettelheim, Freud used both *Instinkt* and *Trieb*, and understood different notions under each of them. This should be sufficient ground to choose two different words in English. Moreover, Freud was not very pleased by Strachey's choices. For instance, this was the case of "cathexis," a Greek work that he did not like. However, some of his own choices have been unfortunate. His proposal to render *Fehlleistung*, a term glossed by Bettelheim as meaning "faulty achievement," indeed not well rendered by Strachey's Greek term *parapraxis*, as "defective act" (Bettelheim:1984, p. 87), would not pass muster in today's English. In the same short text directly written in English, his "Introduction to J. Varendonck's *The Psychology of Day-Dreams*" (Freud:1953, SE/XVIII, p. 271), Freud believed that one should replace the "preconscious" with "fore-conscious thinking." He also glossed the meaning of "daydreaming" (*Phantasieren*) as "freely wandering or phantastic thinking," not the most concise translation indeed, however quite suggestive.

Solms provides useful discussions of tricky concepts like *Nachträglichkeit, Enstellung, Schaulust, Kultur, Angst,* and *Verneinung.* One term stands out as offering intractable difficulties, that of *Witz,* which is usually rendered in English as "joke." *Mot d'esprit*, the usual French translation, works better because it keeps "*esprit*" while adding "*mot*"—alluding as much to funny stories we like repeating as to one-liners. *Witz* links Freud to the Romantic tradition that anticipated a knowledge of the Unconscious, because as with Freud's *Unbewusst, Witz* derives from *Wissen* (knowledge) to allude to a different knowledge, a knowledge that is always "other": the witty knowledge that does not know itself, as demonstrated by dreams, slips of the tongue, "defective acts" and other unconscious manifestations.

This unknown knowledge bypasses discursivity to emerge as the underside or reverse of Reason. In Romantic *Witze*, bizarre or baroque verbal forms lead one to glimpse higher knowledge, perhaps reaching the infinite: "*Witz* is an immediate, absolute knowing-seeing; it is sight regained at the blind spot of schematism and, consequently, sight gaining direct access to the productive capacity of works" (Lacoue-Labarthe and Nancy:1988, p. 52). Freud's debt to German Romanticism has been explored by Jean-Luc Nancy among others, and I will discuss him more fully later. If Freud's "*Witze*" are often untranslatable, they deploy themselves on the background of a practice of translation that could be called "transliteration" to suggest a play on literalism.

The idea of transliteration suggests that even if we are aware that signs need to be translated, we must resist the impulse to treat them as transparent. A transliterated sign keeps a part of its original opacity. It should be deciphered as slowly as possible so as to leave more chances of expression to the hidden suggestions it contains, whether at a material or at a semantic level. The interpreter works like Champollion and invents a new dictionary for each text. This slow, tentative, hesitant, practice is similar to the creative process involved when one attempts to render a pun in a different language. The key is to find a prompt in apparently random associations of related signifiers; one mobilizes them in a new series of signifiers, before returning to the original phrase in its common signification. Hopefully, one can be both literal and creative at the same time.

No doubt, Freud was aware of the slipperiness of his major concepts. This forced him to retranslate his terms time and again; in the end, most of his texts appear as layered archives. Here is a simple example, at the beginning of one of his most influential essays, the *Three Essays on the Theory of Sexuality* dating from 1905. Here is what we find in the translation provided by the Standard Edition:

> The fact of the existence of sexual needs in human beings and animals is expressed in biology by the assumption of a "sexual instinct" (*Geschlechtstrieb*) on the analogy of the instinct of nutrition, that is of hunger. Everyday language possesses no counterpart to the word "hunger," but science makes use of the word "libido" for that purpose.
>
> (Freud:1962, p. 1)

This passage confirms that the choice of "instinct" to translate "*Trieb*" is wrong. Freud postulates a *Geschlechtstrieb*, a sexual drive on the analogy with the hunger drive, a drive that tells us that we have to eat, and what. If animals know how to get food immediately, for all they need to do is follow an instinct that instructs them what to eat and how just after they are born, this is not the case with human beings. There is a need generating a wish to satisfy it, which entails that the drive is a force motivating humans to satisfy their needs. The clinic of anorexia, for instance, shows that hunger is never a need that will be satisfied mechanically by more food. Even with breastfeeding, the baby's desire appears as caught up in the mother's desire, which can lead to a rejection of the breast's primary function on both sides.

Boasting of his simple word-choice, Freud opposes *Trieb* to a more rigorous term coming from "science," as he puts it, to introduce the Latin word "libido." In fact, what he calls "science" refers to his own texts dating from 1894. In his letters to Fliess, Freud included "Draft E" in which he discussed anxiety as produced by the accumulation of undischarged sexual energy; from this, he deduced the existence of a "psychic libido" (Freud:1985, p. 80). "Libido" corresponded to a measure of sexual excitation, for this quantitatively measurable force functions like any type of energy: it can be dammed, strangled, or fully released.

In 1910, Freud revisited the opposition between *Trieb* and *Lidido* in a footnote in which he considered the word *Lust*. He regretted that the word *Lust* was "unfortunately ambiguous," because in German it means both need and gratification, a point made in the first version (Freud:1962, p. 1). In the third version, Freud added the idea that *Lust* indicated both desire and tension. The phrase "*Ich habe Lust...*" means "I would like to..." However, *Lust* also suggests the satisfaction of desire, as in Rilke's famous epitaph: "*Rose, oh reiner Widerspruch, Lust, niemandes Schlaf zu sein unter soviel Lidern*" (Rose, O pure contradiction, pleasure of being no-one's sleep under so many lids.) Soon after, Freud constructed a metapsychology founded on the opposition between the pleasure principle (*Lustprinzip*) and the reality principle, and then would want to go "beyond."

A last revision of the *Three Essays* was made in 1920. Freud added a new preface in which he countered the attack against psychoanalysis deemed to be obsessed with sexuality, the prey to a vaunting pan-sexualism. Freud found allies in philosophers: first in Schopenhauer, the first thinker who had an insight of the Unconscious as a global force traversing Nature that he called "Will," a force determined at root by sexuality (Freud:1962, p. xviii). Then the last word was left to Plato; Freud reminded his readers that his enlarged conception of sexuality "coincides with the Eros of the divine Plato" (Freud:1962, p. xviii). One might be tempted to read here "the divine Eros of Plato." By such a neat hypallage, Freud points to the fact that Eros is a god, which explains not only sexual desire but also all the vagaries of object choice in human erotic interactions.

Plato's name was not mentioned when Freud presented the notion of bisexuality in his analysis of "sexual deviations" but alluded to via the playful model of "sexuation," as Lacan would have it later, provided by Aristophanes. In the *Symposium*, Aristophanes explains the essence of love by imagining that Zeus had cut in two original human beings who had two bodies. Each would then pine for the other half, irrespective of whether it was of the same or other sex (Freud:1962, p. 2). This locus classicus allows Freud to state what matters most for him: "deviation" as such does not exist because the polymorphous perverse disposition of all human beings *is* the norm. Hence the need for translations shifting from concept to concept, from one idiom to another, here Latin with Libido, Greek with Eros, German with *Lust*. A generalized translatability recognizes that concepts are as mobile as sexual objects. This mobile epistemology required not only a new philosophy of language but also an original discourse while carrying a burden linked with translation, the risk of obsolescence.

1.4 Translation and obsolescence (Marcuse and Lacan)

One of the most striking differences between an original text and a translation is due to historicity: whereas original texts do not change over time, except when manuscripts or alternative versions are discovered, even if they sound more foreign as time passes, which explains the glosses, modernized spellings, or rewritings in contemporary English that we use for Renaissance plays for instance, unhappily, translations do betray their age; soon, someone will produce a new one. Important texts need to be retranslated every twenty years or so. Jorge Luis Borges has played on this problem in his "fiction" about Pierre Ménard who, he claims, was the "author of *Don Quixote*" because he copied the Spanish text verbatim (Borges:1999, pp. 88–95). In this deliciously subversive story, Borges quotes two identical passages and concludes that Pierre Ménard's version is better—Cervantes was expressing banalities of his times about truth and history. Pierre Ménard, supposed to be familiar with Symbolism and Paul Valéry, had to traverse innumerable philosophical layers before rethinking the original platitude and enriching it. What Borges accomplishes in this tale is to give us a solid philosophy of translation, in which one can "translate" even when copying an original text without changing one letter.

Lacan's critical insight that Freud needed to be reread, hence retranslated, was shared by Herbert Marcuse. Marcuse reached similar conclusions when he criticized the obsolescence of Freudian theory in the 1960s. Marcuse gave a lecture on "The Obsolescence of Psychoanalysis" in 1963 at the annual meeting of the American Political Science Association that he published as "The Obsolescence of the Freudian concept of man," later included in *Five Lectures* (Marcuse:1970, pp. 44–61). Marcuse identified the main changes in the concept of the ego and the role of the Father. Contemporary society would be marked by the atomization of individuals, which entailed that the powerful castrating Father of Freud's times was a dated hangover. Because psychoanalysts refused to see that social and political evolution in the 1960s, its unseen obsolescence makes it pander to the status quo. As Marcuse writes, psychoanalysis now "seems to help the Establishment rather than the individual" (Marcuse:1970, p. 44).

When Marcuse returns to Freud's statement about the id and the ego, glossing it as "The id shall become the ego" (Marcuse:1970, p. 45), he states that this would hold the key to Freud's rationalism: the aim is to conquer the Id and manage "impossible" drives located in the Unconscious. What has changed, according to Marcuse, is that the conflict between individuals and society cannot be explained by the resistance to the authority of the Father. The evolution of the family throughout the world in the twentieth century has shown a steady decline in the father's power and authority (Marcuse:1970, p. 46). For advanced or industrial societies, this irreversible decline happened between the two world wars. Today, Marcuse claims, people's egoes cannot be measured by the family structure; they are shaped by mass media, sports teams, gangs, and cliques. State administrations are the only agencies capable of dealing with those new masses.

To buttress his observations on the decline of the role of the father, Marcuse quotes a collection of essays in which he had participated, the huge volume of more than 900 pages in German entitled *Studies on Authority and the family* (Horkheimer:1936). The volume, published in Paris in 1936 by the exiles of the Frankfurt school, analyzed multiple links between authority, submission, rebellion, and domination. It was edited by Max Horkheimer and began with an essay by Marcuse that surveys the philosophical conceptions of the family from the Renaissance to modern times, moving from Luther and Calvin to Kant, Hegel, Marx, Sorel, and recent sociologists. Recently, Juan Pablo Lucchelli (2017, p. 81–90) has shown that Lacan not only read it but quoted the volume in a bibliography that he appended to his essay "The Family Complexes in the Formation of the individual." This essay begun in 1935 was published in 1938 in the eighth volume of the *Encyclopédie Française*. Because the bibliographies were gathered at the end, the reference to the German collection was not mentioned when Lacan's essay was republished in *Autres Ecrits* (Lacan:2001, p. 23–84).

In the "Family Complexes," we meet a newly Freudian Lacan; however, one passage quotes literally Horkheimer about the decline of the paternal imago and the way this disappearance impacts totalitarian societies. From the same collection, Lacan must have seen the French abstract of a chapter by Alfred Meusel on "The family in the social doctrines in Germany since 1933" (Horkheimer:1936, p. 894–895). Lucchelli has provided evidence of the convergence between the views of Lacan and those of the Frankfurt school, a parallelism already explored by Peter Dews in 1995 (Dews:1995, pp. 215–235). I cannot add anything to these two excellent analyses and simply insist that Lacan and Marcuse shared a certain neo-Marxism with which they criticized the obsolescence of psychoanalysis. Both planned to overcome obsolescence by offering new and different translations of Freud's main concepts.

Lacan's extensive essay on the Family eloquently condenses Freudian doctrine, albeit harking to a traditional language; for instance, he still speaks of the "death instinct." The original ideas he had introduced himself, like his analysis of the "mirror stage," are inserted in a broader social context. The "mirror stage" included an analysis of the brother's jealousy about sharing the mother's breast; such an archaic hatred felt for the rival also structures sociability as such. Lacan writes: "Jealousy is revealed as the archetype of social feelings" (2001, p. 43). One perceives some critical remarks about classical Freudianism, but they are muted, even if Lacan then reproaches psychoanalysis for avoiding sociological analysis. The indictment is more severe when Lacan perceives that classical Freudian psychoanalysts downplay the theory of the drives and "neglect structure to focus only on dynamism" (Lacan:2001, p. 51). The essay announces Lacan's attention to social structures, whose insights will be systematized with the emergence of structuralism and the important contribution of Claude Lévi-Strauss a few years later.

Lacan distinguishes between vulgar Freudianism and Freud's texts, praising his "admirable case studies" (Lacan:2001, p. 77). He expresses his admiration for Freud's treatment of affects, a point to which we will return, and mentions Freud's accurate interpretation of how repressed affects turn into anxiety. The essay ends with a brief discussion of homosexuality still presented as an "inversion" but extolled as offering a key to social antinomy. Homosexuality would announce a new social paradigm and give access to a deeper understanding of general issues like "forms of culture, morals, the arts, struggles and thought in general" (Lacan:2001, p. 84).

The common element that links the analyses of Marcuse and Lacan when they translate Freud, both wishing to be as literal as possible, is a wish to obviate the consequences of the obsolescence of psychoanalysis. For Marcuse, obsolescence can be turned against itself and yield new perspectives, which leads to this optimistic conclusion: "Thus psychoanalysis draws its strength from its obsolescence: from its insistence on individual needs and individual potentialities which have become outdated in the social and political development. That which is obsolete is not, by this token, false" (Marcuse:1970, p. 60). Here, one sees clearly that their solutions diverge: Marcuse wants to recapture a conception of man capable of resisting the violence of a repressive society, which means putting an end to the domination of death instincts. Lacan chooses the opposite direction, as we will soon see, for indeed he seems to stake everything on the potentialities of the death drive. What might reconcile them is the moment when Marcuse states: "The truth of psychoanalysis lies in its loyalty to its most provocative hypotheses" (Marcuse:1970, p. 61). If Lacan endorses this idea, he chooses a different site for his own provocations, even though this site is linked with a similarly Marxist critique of capitalism.

At the end of Seminar XVIII, Lacan examined Freud's 1913 *Totem and Taboo*, stating that one should not "psychoanalyze" this text or any other work by Freud: such a gesture would be silly or misplaced. Freud's texts are here for us to "criticize them" (Lacan:2007, p. 161). Indeed, Lacan immediately criticizes not only *Totem and Taboo* but also a confusion he finds to be prevalent in psychoanalytic literature; it would hinge around the idea that the murder of the father, a murder that Freud sees as the root of civilization, would reenact the Oedipus myth, or be an earlier version of it. On the contrary, Lacan says, there is a "split" (*une schize*), a huge gap, a hiatus, a veritable epistemological break that separates the Oedipus myth from the founding legend of *Totem and taboo* (Lacan:2007, p. 158).

For Lacan, the two myths follow a different logic according to the position of the Law. In the "myth" of *Totem and Taboo*, Freud presents a domineering Father, a tyrant who enjoyed the undisputed possession of all the women of the horde; the rebellious sons then unite against him and slay him. Such a primal murder takes place after the sons agreed to a new rule: no one should follow the primal Father in his "gluttony for enjoyment" (Lacan:2007, p. 159). After this initial pact, the sons devour the dead father. Each eats a part of his body, which creates a "first" communion. Then the dead Father returns in an idealized or deified form: he becomes a god. This arranged murder is the starting point for any subsequent social contract; in this unwritten contract, no male will touch the mother and the father's wives.

This myth cannot be aligned with the Law that Freud presents as underpinning the Oedipus legend; in the Greek drama, the Law prevents incest with the mother, and such a law provides the foundation of psychoanalysis. In the Oedipus myth, the Law of prohibition comes first; it is primordial in that that it punishes anyone contravenes it, even when the guilty party has done the deed innocently. In the Oedipus myth, the murder happens without the knowledge of the murderer who does not recognize that he is attacking the father. What the myth suggests is that the place occupied by the generating father, Oedipus's father in fact, is problematic. In the myth of *Totem and Taboo*, one observes a reversed logic: enjoyment is posited at the origin; then comes the Law whose function is to limit or prohibit jouissance. A sacred cannibalism accompanies the fact that all the women are prohibited, in principle. They are untouchable for the community of the males, a community that transcends itself in a ritual communion. Lacan concludes thus:

> *Totem and taboo* is a neurotic product (...) which does not mean that I question the truth of the construction. That is how it bears witness to the truth. One does not psychoanalyze an oeuvre, that of Freud no less than any other, is that not so? One criticizes it, and far from the idea that a neurosis would render its solidity suspect, it is the very thing that solders it...
> (Lacan:2007, p. 160)

Freud's fascination for the murder of the father, from Oedipus to Moses, makes him appear as neurotic, but he was able to transform his neurosis into a productive agency. What does Lacan mean by "criticizing" in this context? Soon after, in the last session of seminar XVIII, he put his cards on the table when he names Karl Marx as the true inventor of the notion of symptom

(Lacan:2007, p. 164). Indeed, the passage quoted cannot but evoke Marx's famous eleventh thesis on Feuerbach: "The philosophers have only interpreted the world, in various ways; the point is to change it" (Marx:1977, p. 158). In the aftermath of May 1968, Lacan elaborated his version of Freudo-Marxism by formalizing social bonds as made up of four "discourses," in which the "discourse of the Master" could be understood as "the "discourse of the capitalist," but then he added a fifth discourse for capitalism. Lacan was combining Althusser's influential readings of *Capital* as having launched "symptomatic readings" of society and Foucault's critical historicism, also known as "genealogy." Lacan needed to insert what he called "surplus jouissance" (*plus de jouir*), a synthesis of Freud's *Lust* and Marx's *Mehrwert* (surplus value). In this coined *Mehrlust*, we have a good example of a "translation" that is both a Freudian condensation and a precise political intervention.

1.5 Lacan translates, from Freud to Heidegger

Lacan translated only one text by Freud in his whole career. It was a tactical choice, for he was to use these analyses as he completed his doctoral dissertation. Lacan chose to translate Freud's 1922 essay *"Über einige neurotische Mechanismen bei Eifersucht, Paranoia und Homosexualität"* (Freud:1973b, pp. 219–228). Lacan's translation (Freud:1932, pp. 391–401) came at a crucial moment, for it helped him elaborate a vocabulary with which he could make sense of Aimée, the woman whose treatment was the focus of the thesis on paranoia. Indeed, Aimée's case exemplified a "projective jealousy" outlined in Freud's essay. The same essay is quoted twice in the dissertation (Lacan:1980, pp. 229 and 264). In her biography, Elizabeth Roudinesco (Roudinesco:1997, p. 32) astutely points out that Lacan remained faithful to Freud's text to the point of not changing the dominant code in French psychoanalytic circles. He stuck to standard translations: *Trieb* was "instinct," *Trauer* (mourning) was "tristesse" (sadness), and *Regung* (impulse) was "tendance" (tendency). In spite of these semantic blinders, there is much to admire in Lacan's effort. He renders Freud's style elegantly. Here is a passage in which Freud mentions a jealous man who developed delirious associations with Prometheus in Lacan's rendering:

> Je sais un homme qui souffrait très fort de ses accès de jalousie, et qui, selon son dire, traversait ses tourments les plus durs dans une substitution imaginative consciente à la femme infidèle. La sensation qu'il éprouvait alors d'être privé de tout recours, les images qu'il trouvait pour son état, se dépeignant comme livré, tel Prométhée, à la voracité du vautour, ou jeté enchaîné dans un nid de serpents, lui- même les rapportait à l'impression laissée par plusieurs agressions homosexuelles, qu'il avait subies, tout jeune garçon.

Literally:

> I know of a man who suffered greatly from his attacks of jealousy, and who, according to him, went through his harshest torments in a consciously imaginative identification to the unfaithful wife. The sensation he then felt of being deprived of any recourse, the images he found for his state, depicting himself as delivered, like Prometheus, to the voracity of the vulture, or thrown chained into a nest of snakes, he himself would relate them to impression left by several homosexual attacks that he had be subjected to as a young boy.

If one compares Lacan's rendering with a more recent French version by D. Guérineau, one notices that in order to gain in clarity, Guérineau had to lose Freud's stylistic ease and fluency. Moreover, a clumsy parenthesis breaks the flow of Freud's sentence: "*... les images qu'il trouvait pour son état (c'était comme s'il avait été livre tel Prométhée à la voracité d'un vautour, ou jeté enchaîné dans un nid de serpents)...*" (Freud:1973a, p. 272). Worse, the term used by Freud to call up the imaginative identification of the husband to his allegedly "unfaithful" wife, *bewußten Versetzung*, is translated literally as "*permutation consciente avec....,*" a phrase that is less evocative than Lacan's "*substitution imaginative consciente.*" If Lacan did not modify the accepted equivalents used in translations of Freud at the time, he would later rail all the more violently against those limitations and conceptual misunderstandings.

Lacan translated Freud just when he became truly "Freudian," which happened during the composition of his dissertation; we see him move from Spinoza to French psychiatry and then to Freud. Later developments entailed shifting from Freud to Hegel via Kojève in the 1930s; then he grafted Martin Heidegger and Ferdinand de Saussure after World War II. The new program appeared when Lacan launched his own psychoanalytic review as Lacan translated Heidegger's essay "Logos." "Logos" was published in the first issue of his journal *La Psychanalyse* in 1956. Roudinesco documents the personal interaction between Lacan and Heidegger and shows how their meeting took place in a particular cultural context, the French re-discovery of a philosopher misunderstood by Sartre and the Existentialists. Heidegger was taken as a guide by a few younger philosophers at a moment when phenomenology took a different turn, a theological turn as Dominique Janicaud has argued when he examined how Emmanuel Levinas and Paul Ricoeur found inspiration in Heidegger after the war (see Janicaud:2015).

Roudinesco's chapter "A Resounding Tribute to Martin Heidegger" highlights the role of Jean Beaufret as a mediator. Beaufret was emerging as the leading specialist of Heidegger in France; Beaufret knew Heidegger personally, having had the distinction of triggering Heidegger's 1947 *Letter on Humanism*, a text that answered to Jean-Paul Sartre. Beaufret had asked Heidegger whether he could be called an "existentialist" and whether existentialism was, as Sartre claimed, a humanism. Heidegger explained that he was neither an existentialist nor a humanist. His *Letter* placed a definitive theoretical wedge between the ontological analysis he was promoting and Sartre's humanism.

In April 1951, Beaufret began an analysis with Lacan, his male lover being already on Lacan's couch. Beaufret soon noticed that if he wanted to pique Lacan's curiosity, he only had to mention Heidegger. He told Lacan once that Heideggr had asked about him, and Lacan jumped up, wanting to know more. After two years of analysis, in 1955, Beaufret and Lacan traveled to Freiburg to meet Heidegger. Lacan asked for permission to translate "Logos" and Heidegger agreed. When Lacan launched *La Psychanalyse*, the first issue contained his "Rome Discourse," "The Function and Field of Speech and Language in Psychoanalysis," the most programmatic of his *Écrits*, along with his translation of Heidegger's "Logos," a detailed commentary of Heraclitus' fragment 50. In fact, the journal was edited and masterminded by Lacan who saw an urgent need to educate the psychoanalysts of his school. He would force them to read contemporary philosophy, and also taught them about structural linguistics.

After the visit to Freiburg, it was Heidegger's turn to come to France as he had been invited to participate in a conference at Cerisy in August 1955. He spent a weekend at Lacan's country house at La Prévôté with his wife and friends. Roudinesco evokes Heidegger's supernatural calm next to his wife's barely concealed panic when they were driven at a manic speed by Lacan (Roudinesco:1997, p. 226). Her negative view of Heidegger's influence on Lacan gives birth to a political contextualization of Lacan's translation that derives from her sense that Heidegger's position was tainted. It is true that Heidegger never apologized for his endorsement of the Nazi regime in the 1930s. Roudinesco offers an ambivalent account of "Function and Field of Speech and language in psychoanalysis" from the same issue, as we saw. This extended manifesto ushered in Lacan's revolutionary conception of psychoanalysis, and Heidegger is a key influence in it, when Lacan promotes an original theory of language. In it, Heidegger is quoted twice, first p. 212, when the subject of memory is presented as "*gewesend*," that is "having been," and then p. 262, where death is mentioned as bringing an unsurpassable limit for all humans. Heidegger's imprint is unmistakable throughout the essay.

In Roudinesco's appraisal, the Rome speech would evince a disquieting compound of rational ideals coming from Freud, de Saussure, and Lévi-Strauss, and darker philosophical themes inspired by the anti-democratic, anti-progressive, and anti-humanist Heidegger. Hence a "mixture of darkness and light in the 'Rome Discourse'" (Roudinesco:1997, p. 225). A universalist psychoanalysis founded on the ideas of the Enlightenment would clash with Heidegger's thought of "human existence as a bottomless pit where truth is expressed amid error, deceit and ambiguity" (Roudinesco:1997, p. 225). For Roudinesco, the symptom of Lacan's hesitation is the fact that he translated the first version of the essay from 1951 but not the expanded version from 1954. Between 1951 and 1954, Heidegger had added three pages to his essay. This choice would betray Lacan's covert struggle against Heidegger and reveal a wish to redirect or skew the philosopher's theses. Roudinesco, influenced by the distinguished Hellenist Jean Bollack's reading, assumes that Lacan distinguished between the first version, a detailed commentary of one sentence by Heraclitus, and the second version that was rejected because the three added pages revealed Heidegger's ideas about the eminence of the German language. They provided a rationale for a wish to "germanize" the Greek text. Lacan would have pushed back and forced Heidegger to become more francophone thanks to his punning Mallarmean appropriation. This astute analysis leads to a strategic meditation on translation:

> ... where Heidegger played on the fact that the verbs *legen* (German) and *legein* (Greek) sounded alike, Lacan played on the similarity, in French, of the word *léguer* (to bequeath), *legs* (legacy) and *lais* (poetic lays). This Mallarméan transposition was clearly one way of nullifying Heidegger's claim that the German language was philosophically superior. He also denegativized the text: wherever Heidegger used the term *Unverborgenheit* (nonobscurity, unconcealment) to denote that which perceives being in Heraclitus, Lacan translated it as *dévoilement* (unveiling), giving more importance to the act of exposure itself than to the idea of a quest carried out via "nonoccultation" (de- or uneclipsing).
>
> (Roudinesco:1997, p. 228)

Roudinesco concludes that Lacan's decision to translate the 1951 version was a "sacrilege." Lacan would have avoided translating that passage because in it Heidegger stated "that a return to the West's great beginnings could save modern man from the domination of science and technology" (Roudinesco:1997, p. 228). Such a deletion of the "coda" could not be ascribed to oversight: Lacan quotes the 1954 version in his footnotes. Lacan would have amputated the text by rejecting pages in which Heidegger appeared as "the preacher of salvation and German superiority" (Roudinesco:1997, p. 228).

It is undeniable that Lacan's decision to translate "*logos*" as "*legs*" (legacy) and *lais* (poems) was the product of a pun in French: as he writes in a footnote to his translation in *La Psychanalyse*, it is a pure pun, a "*calembour*" (Lacan:1956, p. 61). However, the fact that the pun is trilingual, splicing Heraclitus's *logos*, Heidegger's *Lege*, and Lacan's own *legs*, is loaded with dramatic or agonistic overtones in Roudinesco's account. By reclaiming his inheritance from Heraclitus translated by Heidegger, Lacan would have accomplished a "murder-by-translation" and mixed "truth and untruth" confusingly:

"And it was just when he was departing the furthest from Heidegger's work that he paid emphatic tribute to the man himself. 'When I speak of Heidegger,' he wrote in 1957, 'or rather when I translate him, I do my best to let his own words retain their supreme significance.' A curious way of mixing truth and untruth in order to dismiss the person by whom you claim to be inspired!" (Roudinesco:1997, p. 230).

While I agree with Roudinesco's contextualization, in this case, despite our old friendship and my sincere admiration for her scholarship, I query the general argument. In my reading, the three pages added by Heidegger to "Logos" in 1954 do not extol German as a superior language. The new conclusion of the essay criticizes the inability of ancient Greek philosophy to problematize the link between man and language in a context marked by the dissemination of technology. The issue here is the technological arraignment of the world, which amounts to a negative version of globalization: "Through technology the entire globe is today embraced and held fast in a kind of Being experienced in Western fashion and represented on the epistemological models of European metaphysics and science" (Heidegger:1984, p. 76). In spite of this conservative tone, Heidegger never mentions the exceptional status of German as a privileged language that would be closer to Greek; there is no hint that Germany would be the predestined site for philosophy. Heidegger adds in the new conclusion a more critical appraisal of Heraclitus's fragment. Whereas the first version praised Heraclitus for his new insights, the three new pages deplore the inability of the most perceptive of the pre-Socratic philosophers to think Logos as language.

According to Heidegger, Heraclitus would have intuited that Logos might open up the essence of language but then failed to think through fully the consequences of his intuition. Here is why Heidegger calls "logos" a "laying that gathers" in an elaborate paraphrase whose oxymoronic tension suggests a missed opportunity (Heidegger:1984, p. 77). Heidegger describes the limitation of Heraclitus's vision in a beautiful metaphor: it is like an inaugural flash of lightning that lets for an instant Being appear as such: "But the lightning (*Blitz*) abruptly vanished. (...) We see this lightning only when we station ourselves in the storm of Being (*Gewitter des Seins*)" (Heidegger:1984, p. 78). Such an inability to be true to the essence of language because it is impossible to face Being as such became Lacan's main theme. We glimpse a "storm of Being" but the vision soon vanishes. The calm that follows is deceiving. Heidegger adds these ominous words: "But this calm is no tranquility. It is only anesthesia; more precisely, the narcotization of anxiety in the dace of thinking" (1984, p. 78).

Why would Lacan have omitted those pages deliberately when they brings so much psychoanalytic grist to his mill by calling up the theme of anxiety? Either Lacan did not realize that he left out the three pages, or he saw the first version as sufficient in itself. Heidegger's disquisition on logos was not the opposite of the philosophy of the Enlightenment: such a role would be left to

Marquis de Sade, as we will see. Heidegger was not Sade, even if the enlightenment he was searching for was marked by a tragic awareness that it could not survive. For Lacan as for Heidegger, thought is produced while a terrifying storm of Being rages outside, as we will see in his writings from the seventies like "Lituraterre." Here is the moment when language captures the *Angst* or anxiety generated. This led Lacan to assert that anxiety is the affect that never lies—we will return to this question in a later chapter.

Roudinesco was entirely right to call Lacan's translation "Mallarmean." Lacan's tendency to call up the French poet would be due to the answer to a problem: given Heidegger's idiosyncratic style, one has to invent French equivalents. Lacan's Mallarmean style looks like a privileged stylistic filter and not a partisan's wish to promote French culture over German obscurity. Here is an example of Heidegger's text followed by what Lacan makes of it:

So west der Λογοϳ als das reine versammelnde lesende Legen. Der Λογοϳ ist die ursrprüngliche Versammlung der anfängliche Lese aus der anfänglichen Lege. O Λογοϳ ist: die lessened Lege und nur dieses.

(Heidegger:2000, p. 221)

Tel est essentiellement le Logos comme le pur lit de ce qui se lit dans ce qu'il recueille. Le Logos est la recollection primordiale du choix fait au commencement dans le lais original. O Λογοϳ est: le lais où se lit ce qui s'élit, et ce n'est que cela.

(Lacan's translation in Lacan:1956, p. 68)

Lacan enriches the homophonic *"versammelnde lesende Legen"* (literally, "a laying down that is both a gathering and a reading") by rendering it as *"le pur lit de ce qui se lit dans ce qui se recueille"* (literally, the pure bed [*lit*] of what can be read [*lit*] in what is gathered). A footnote explains that *"lais"* translates *Lege*, but is then expanded as *"legs"* (legacy, inheritance). This proves first that Lacan not only was faithful to Heidegger's meaning, although he modifies slightly "reading" as "inheriting," but also imitated his translation method, with calculated displacements following the shifting logic of echoing signifiers in a given language.

If the strong idea of language speaking through subjects and providing a home for them belongs to Heidegger, it also irradiates Lacan's thought. Translating Heidegger and Heraclitus at once, Lacan proved that by this process he was inheriting Freud's *legacy*: his *legs*, his inheritance, cannot avoid being marked by a "dark enlightenment," a theme that includes Freud as Roudinesco herself has shown in her more recent biography of Freud (see Roudinesco:2016). By translating *logos* as *legacy*, Lacan stressed that he assumed the inheritance of Freud. Being an inheritor and not an author entailed not only distinguishing between cutting-edge analyses and the weaker passages in the works, but also, more fundamentally, seeing what was alive and what was ghostly.

Roudinesco's *Lacan* was published in 1993. Her critical survey of the links between Lacan and Heidegger had been preceded by an even more critical reading dating from 1973; this time it came from the camp of French Heideggerians. The first reception Lacan's translation of Heidegger was devastating. Philippe Lacoue-Labarthe's and Jean-Luc Nancy's *The Title of the Letter* exposed the theoretical incompatibility between a science of language and culture defined by Saussure, Lévi-Strauss, and Freud on the one hand, and what brought Heidegger on the other hand. The objection came from philosophers in the name of theoretical consistency. *The Title of the Letter*, a slim but dense book, faults Lacan for misguided attempts at blending structuralist linguistics and Heidegger's ontology of language. Lacoue-Labarthe and Nancy object to the irruption of the Heideggerian Truth as *aletheia* in the "The Instance of the Letter in the Unconscious, or Reason since Freud," an *écrit* glossed systematically and debunked mercilessly.

At the end of the "The Instance of the Letter in the Unconscious, or Reason since Freud," Lacan concluded with a facile pun linking the letter (*la lettre*) and Being (*l'Etre*) in the subtitle of *The Letter, being, and the other* (Lacan:2006, p. 435). In the "Instance of the Letter…," Lacan surveys his translation of Heidegger's *Logos* and rejects accusations that he would have suffered from "Heideggerianism" or "neo-Heideggerianism" (Lacan:2006, p. 438). In their commentary, Lacoue-Labarthe and Nancy wonder how Heidegger's Being can climb up the tree of Saussure's signifier without disrupting the circular logic of the letter. Above all, they accuse Heidegger's "Logos" of having turned into a "master word" (Nancy and Lacoue-Labarthe:1992, p. 134). To highlight the idea of mastery, Lacoue-Labarthe and Nancy quote a sentence that Roudinesco had quoted but translated differently: "When I speak of Heidegger, or rather when I translate him, I at least make an effort to leave the speech he proffers us its sovereign significance" (Nancy and Lacoue-Labarthe:1992, p. 134). The version given by Bruce Fink is: "When I speak of Heidegger, or rather when I translate him, I strive to preserve the sovereign signifierness of the speech he proffers" (Lacan:2006, p. 438). Lacoue-Labarthe and Nancy see in this sentence, with its ominous mention of "sovereignty," a sign of Lacan's arrogant assertion of a mastery over Truth. As they remind us, Heidegger's "Logos" is an essay about translation even if at the end Heidegger argues that "Logos" remains untranslatable (Nancy and Lacoue-Labarthe:1992, p. 135).

Heidegger presented Logos as a Greek word situating Being in Language, although it ended up confining it within Reason. Historically, Logos replaced Myth, as we know from genealogies of Greek philosophy in which myth is seen on the side of poetry and Logos on the side of abstract reasoning. However, logos can never fully rid itself of mythical overtones, as so many of Plato's dialogues show. If Lacoue-Labarthe and Nancy rightly read Heidegger's

"*Logos*" as an essay on translation, it is because it was not so much a translation of Greek into German, but a translation of Greek into Greek, and then of German into German, and finally of French into French. The sequence of these three operations is essential if one wants to grasp the modus operandi of "Logos": Logos is a myth-inflected language-legacy, a meaning conveyed by the French *legs* translated by Lacan. The effort to keep translating means that one is aware of language as a site for the birth of subjectivity. This insight kept guiding Lacan. He owed it to his reading of Freud via Heidegger.

Reading Logos as the Being-of-Language derives from Heidegger's interpretation of truth as *aletheia*. *A-letheia* is glossed as un-forgetting, moving away from the *Lethe*, the mythical river of forgetfulness. Such an interpretation rests on a conflict between hiding and unconcealment. Heidegger's *aletheia* will not lead to a revelation that brings objects into the light of Reason, a light thanks to which we can compare, produce equations and adequations, for in fact *aletheia* follows a movement that "withdraws itself from representation" (Nancy and Lacoue-Labarthe:1992, p. 142). However, Heidegger's insistence on reading the history of metaphysics in terms of its unthought thought does not usher in a history of repression that could be called Freudian. Heidegger is not looking for the repressed content that remains hidden under appearances.

According to the philosophers, Lacan replicated a pattern of concealment and unconcealment that underpins Heidegger's thought. Such a dialectical opposition sustains his effort at dismantling the relation between signifier and signified. By insisting on the excessive slippage of the signifier, by subverting the Cartesian cogito in the name of the Unconscious ("I think where I am not"), Lacan had attempted to escape from the discourse of metaphysics that reduces ontology to the adequation of thought to facts. Lacan privileged metaphor in so far as it indicates Being over metonymy, which in his system refers to a constitutive lack, or to desire. He preserved the opposition between an intersubjective adequation guaranteed by a pact passed with the Other of the Unconscious. Lacan's truth as *aletheia* would offer itself in present adequation of a speech functioning as a full utterance. Lacan would thus imitate Heidegger in his wish to remain faithful to an unconscious truth defined as unconcealement; however, this wish forces him to try and translate what remains de facto untranslatable. For Heidegger and Lacan, as long as translation relies on *homoiosis* (the likeness between signifieds), it misses the essential dimension of *aletheia*, the groundwork for the unfolding of philosophy. In their later seminars, Heidegger and Lacan meditate on cryptic and condensed sayings, for Heidegger a quote from the pre-Socratics, a line from a poem by Hölderlin, Rilke, or Trakl, and for Lacan, paradoxical mottoes like "there is no sexual rapport." They then translate themselves by moving upward in spiraling improvisations.

Heidegger's goal was to read the unthought thought of pre-Socratic Greek philosophers such as Heraclitus by reading Logos against itself. This gesture was meant to introduce a rupture within the register of meaning as defined by *homoiosis*, or the adequation between words and things. The destruction of metaphysics he wanted to bring about would lay bare the philosophical field before ushering in a new beginning by playing on poetic language creatively. Because we "dwell poetically in language," as Hölderlin suggested, we cannot reduce language to a positivist system of signs. What is more, Lacoue-Labarthe and Nancy locate the question of Lacan's relation to the unthought thought in a beyond the text, beyond that would always be forgotten or repressed. It calls upon an experience that withdraws from re-presentation, that presents itself only by withdrawing. However, psychoanalysis always finds a ready answer in desire. Hence the conclusion reached by Lacoue-Labarthe and Nancy: "(Freudian) desire occupies the *same* position as (Heidegger's) truth" (1992, p. 138).

To go beyond discourse in an experience of co-presence sends us back to the clinical moment in which an analysand and an analyst engage in dialogue, the clinical moment alluded to by Lacan's repeated phrase of "in our experience…" By such a revealing idiom, the psychoanalyst tends to parade a knowledge of the ineffable. The nest question is: what is it that can limit that experience? Is it buttressed on the disclosure of a text, a text refusing to be determined by the economy of truth as presence? On this point, Lacoue-Labarthe and Nancy hesitate. At times, they recognize that there is a poetic textuality at work in Lacan's writings; such a poetic textuality prevents Lacan's texts from closing themselves and offering a unified doctrine, especially when it claims that it is defined by its scientificity. However, Lacan's constant appeal to the truth allows him to assert mastery, a mastery over discourse but not over text: there is a structural tension between text and discourse. In so far as it is a discourse, Lacan's teaching denies its status as a text. In so far as it progresses via poetic metaphors, his discourse tends to undo itself and turn into a poetic text, as we see in the last decade of his teaching and writing.

I will summarize the sites of my disagreement with Lacoue-Labarthe's and Nancy's strictures in five points.

(1)   Lacan was aware that he translated a text by Heidegger as literally as possible, which does not mean that his practice was founded upon an ideology of "adaptation," a literalist correspondence defined as *homoioosis*. As we have seen, Lacan adapts, invents, and appropriates, a practice presupposing that there is no preordained Truth that would sway over the mechanisms of language(s). In other words, there is no metalanguage, even if, Lacan agree with Heidegger's saying of "language speaks" (*die Sprache spricht)*. No absolute truth is to be found in "Logos" or in the Freudian symptom.

(2)   Lacan never privileged metaphor over metonymy as *The Title of the Letters* assumes. Indeed, these two main tropes correspond to

different logics, like the name of the father and the desire of the hysteric. None has a more dignified ontological place in a hierarchy.

(3)   The reproach that the experience of psychoanalysis is predicated upon a mystified illusion of "presence" or "co-presence" looks like glib Derridianism. So is the objection that a metaphysics of presence would be founded upon a myth of desire. Neither Freud nor Lacan ever talk about the practice of the talking cure as a "two-body" situation around the couch. On the contrary, for both, the key is the detour via a third "instance," whether it be the "Other" or the Unconscious structured as a language.

(4)   Heidegger's truth as *aletheia* may have led Lacan to believe that he "owned" Freud's text, and such a reproach is more damning. There are passages in Lacan's texts and seminars in which he suggests that he has grasped the true meaning of Freud's writings. However, once more, one will not hit upon a master signifier for the metalanguage providing an absolute truth is lacking. Because "there is no meta-language" according to Lacan, we are brought back to Foucault's insights when discussing the "return to Freud." As have seen, the return entails re-reading and re-translating primary texts produced by the founders of discursivity, an effort at re-reading that brings about a perception of gaps and inconsistencies in texts, not the plenitude of full meaning.

(5)   Is there a beyond the text in Heidegger and in Lacan? I would argue that there is. Could this "beyond" be the locus of sexuality, in other words, would difference be moving from Heidegger's ontological difference to Freud's sexual difference? Can we introduce sexual difference when we speak of the disjunctive unity of being and Being, or *Dasein* and *Sein*? These issues will force us to investigate Lacan's ontology. It is a Being beyond language, or a Logos as language? I will return to these questions in a chapter dealing with Nancy's revision of his appraisal of Lacan.

I end this chapter by suggesting that readers tend to be more easily irritated by translations than by original texts. Roudinesco was irritated by the way Lacan imported features of Heidegger's philosophy that she did not appreciate. Bettelheim and Lacan were irritated by bad translations of Freud. Freud was irritated by the pseudo-scientific terms used to render his concepts in English. What remains clear behind these irritations is an insight shared by all: when the Unconscious speaks, it speaks like a foreign language begging to be translated. Such a practice of translation develops potentialities of language that exceed Reason, even the Greek *logos*, as Heidegger suggested when he would read Heraclitus's *logos* as language, thus paving the way to Lacan's practice.

Lacan kept exploring the autonomy of literary language and its "beyond," as we will see with "Lituraterre" in the last chapter. Like Heidegger, he translated freely and abundantly by letting the potentialities of language determine a progression in meaning from signifier to signifier: their chain proffers its own logic as we see with *Logos*, *Lege*, and *legs*. Similarly, Lacan's concept of the *Le Nom-du-Père* (the Name of the Father), which sounds almost religious when we think of "in the name of...," in fact conceals a *Non du père* (the Father's No): this negation derives from the Oedipal pattern in which a father forbids access to the mother's body. A decade later, the same syntagm is pluralized as *Les Noms du Père* but then it reveals another meaning if we hear in it the identically sounding *Les non-dupes errent* (those who believe they are not duped are in error). This echolalic double meaning calls up the pattern of deception that dominates in Edgar Alan Poe's tales of Dupin, a character with which Poe invented the detective novel, if not psychoanalysis itself.

Unhappily, it is almost impossible to render in English the polyphonic echoes of *Les non-dupes errent*. Here is another irritation: given the stubbornness or the opacity of the signifier, one loses all the time at the game of equivalences. Only in a felicitous moment of inspiration will one "gain" and compensate for the structural lack: for instance, it is only in English that one can familiarly call Lacan "Jack the lack..." This suggests the need for an ethics of translation: translation has to remain a heretic exercise, by which I mean that a translator must "choose" all the time, which means excluding other possibilities and also rejecting a previous orthodoxy (*hairesis*, or "choice," comes from *haireomai*, "to choose"). Thus, if each language irritates in a specific manner a given orthodoxy, each language will be irritated differently. However, Freud, fluent in several languages, happened to be irritated in German only, as we will see.

Notes

1 I owe this reference to Daniel Katz. One finds a good analysis of the translation process among the Bloomsbury group in Michaud:2022.
2 My subtitle distorts T. S. Eliot's original title for the *Waste Land*, a quote from *Our Mutual Friend* by Dickens. In the novel, a young boy is praised for his ability to read novels with mimetic gusto; he can "Do the Police in Different Voices." See Eliot: 1974.
3 I owe the point to Shirley Sharon-Ziser: 2020, p. 78, note 7. See also Shirley Sharon-Zisser: 2022.

Bibliography

Benjamin, Andrew (1992). "Translating Origins: Psychoanalysis and Philosophy" in *Rethinking Translation: Discourse, Subjectivity, Ideology*, Ed. Lawrence Venuti, London, Routledge, p. 18–41.

Basile, Elena (2005). "Responding to the Enigmatic Address of the Other: A Psychoanalytical Approach to the Translator's Labour," *New Voices in Translation Studies*, 1 (2005), p. 12–30.

Bettelheim, Bruno (1984). *Freud and Man's Soul*, New York, Vintage Books.

Bonaparte, Marie (1994). 1964 *Topsy, the story of a golden haired chow*, New Brunswick, Transaction Publishers.

Borges, Jorge Luis (1999). *Collected Fictions*, trans. Andrew Hurley, New York, Penguin.

Cassin, Barbara (2004). *"Das Unheimliche"* in *Dictionary of Untranslatables: A Philosophical Lexicon*, edited by Barbara Cassin, translated by Emily Apter, Jacques Lezra, and Michael Wood, Princeton, Princeton University Press, p. 432.

Collodi, Carlo (1949). *Le Avventure di Pinocchio: Storia di un burattino*, Milano, Einaudi.

Derrida, Jacques (1978). *Writing and Difference*, trans. Alan Bass, Chicago, The university of Chicago Press.

Dews, Peter (1995). "The crisis of Oedipal identity: The early Lacan and the Frankfurt School" in *Psychoanalysis in Context*, Ed. Anthony Elliott and Stephen Frosh, New York, Routledge, p. 215–235.

Eliot, T. S. (1974). *The Waste Land: A Facsimile and Transcript of the Original Drafts Including the Annotations of Ezra Pound*, Ed. Valerie Eliot, London, Faber.

Freud, Sigmund (1932). "De quelques mécanismes névrotiques dans la jalousie, la paranoia, et l'homosexualité," translated by Jacques Lacan, *Revue française de psychanalyse*, V, n° 3, p 391–401.

Freud, Sigmund (1933). Neue Folge der Vorlesungen zur Einführung in die ... - Psychanalyse.lu; https://www.psychanalyse.lu/Freud/FreudNeueVorlesungen.pdf, n.p.

Freud, Sigmund (1953–1974). *The Standard Edition of the Complete Psychological Works of Sigmund Freud*, V, trans. James Strachey, London, The Hogarth Press. Abbreviated as SE, the number of the volume, and the page.

Freud, Sigmund (1962). *Three Essays on the Theory of Sexuality*, trans. James Strachey, New York, Basic Books.

Freud, Sigmund (1965). *The Interpretation of Dreams*, trans. James Strachey, New York, Avon Books.

Freud, Sigmund (1973a). "Sur quelques mécanismes névrotiques" in *Névrose, Psychose et Perversion*, trans. D. Guérineau, Paris, Presses Universitaires de France.

Freud, Sigmund (1973b). "Über einige neurotische Mechanismen bei Eifersucht, Paranoia und Homosexualität" in *Studienausgabe*, VII, *Zwang, Paranoia und Perversion*, Frankfurt, Fischer, p. 219–228.

Freud, Sigmund (1985). *The Complete Letters of Sigmund Freud to Wilhelm Fliess, 1887–1904*, trans. Jeffrey Moussaieff Masson, Harvard, Harvard University Press.

Freud, Sigmund (1989a). *New Introductory Lectures on Psycho-Analsysis*, trans. James Strachey, New York, Norton, 1989.

Freud, Sigmund (1989b). *Jugendbriefe an Eduard Silberstein, 1871–1881*, ed. Walter Boehlich, Frankfurt, Fischer.

Freud, Sigmund (1990). *The Letters of Sigmund Freud to Eduard Silberstein, 1871–1881*, ed. Walter Boehlich, trans. Arnold J. Pomerans, Cambridge, Harvard University Press.

Freud, Sigmund (1999). *The Interpretation of Dreams*, trans. Joyce Crick, Oxford, Oxford University Press.

Freud, Sigmund (2003). *The Uncanny*, trans. David McLintock, New York, Penguin.

Freud, Sigmund Freud and Breuer, Joseph (2004). *Studies in Hysteria*, trans. Nicola Luckhurst, London, Penguin.

Freud, Sigmund (2013). *A Case of Hysteria (Dora)*, trans. Anthea Bell, Oxford, Oxford University Press.

Freud, Sigmund (2024). *The Revised Standard Edition of the Complete Psychological Works of Sigmund Freud*, James Strachey, translator, Revised edition by Mark Solms, translator, 24 volumes, Lanham, Rowman and Littlefield.

Heidegger, Martin (1956). "Logos" translated by Jacques Lacan, *La Psychanalyse*, n. 1, Paris, 1956, p. 59–79.

Heidegger, Martin (1984). *Early Greek Thinking: The dawn of Western philosophy*, trans. D. Krell and F. A. Capuzzi, San Francisco, Harper and Row.

Heidegger, Martin, (2000). *Vorträge und Aufsätze*, Frankfurt, V. Klostermann.

Hoffmann, E. T. A. (2006). *Fantasiestücke*, Frankfurt, Deutscher Klassiker Verlag.

Horkheimer, Max, editor (1936). *Studien über Autorität und Familie*, Paris, Felix Alcan.

Janicaud, Dominique (2015). *Heidegger in France*, trans. François Raffoul and David Pettigrew, Bloomington, Indiana University Press.

Kwon, Teckhyoung (2019). *Nabokov's Mimicry of Freud: Art as Science*, Lanham, Rowman & Littlefield, Lexington Books.

Lacan, Jacques (1956). "Logos" de Heidegger, *La Psychanalyse*, vol. 1, p. 59–79.

Lacan, Jacques (1966). *Ecrits*, Paris, Seuil.

Lacan, Jacques (1980). *De la psychose paranoïaque dans ses rapports avec la personnalité*, Paris, Seuil.

Lacan, Jacques (1993). *The Seminar, Book III, The Psychoses 1955–1956*, trans. Russell Grigg, New York, Norton.

Lacan, Jacques (2001). *Autres Ecrits*, Paris, Seuil.

Lacan, Jacques (2006). *Ecrits*, trans. Bruce Fink, New York, Norton.

Lacan, Jacques (2007). *Le Séminaire XVIII: D'un Discours qui ne serait pas du semblant*, ed. J-A Miller, Paris, Seuil.

Lacoue-Labarthe, Philippe, and Nancy, Jean-Luc (1988). *The Literary Absolute: The Theory of Literature in German Romanticism*, trans. Philip Barnard and Cheryl Lester, Albany, State University of New York Press.

Luchelli, Juan Pablo (2017). *Lacan: De Wallon à Kojève*, Paris, Editions Michèle.

Ornston, Darius Gray, editor (1992). *Translating Freud*, New Haven, Yale University Press.

Mahony, Patrick (1982). "Towards the Understanding of Translation in Psychoanalysis," *Meta*, 27. 1, pp. 63-71

Mahony, Patrick (2001). "Freud and Translation," *Imago*, 58.4, p. 837–840.

Marcuse, Herbert (1970). *Five Lectures*, trans. Jeremy J. Shapiro and Shierry M. Weber, Boston, Beacon Press.

Marini, Marcelle (1992). *Jacques Lacan: The French Context*, trans. Anne Tomiche, New Brunswick, Rutgers University Press.

Marx, Karl (1977). *Selected Writings*, ed. David McLellan, Oxford, Oxford University Press.

Michaud, Henriette (2022). *Freud à Bloomsbury*, Paris, Fayard.

Nancy, Jean-Luc and Lacoue-Labarthe, Philippe (1992). *The Title of the Letter: A Reading of Lacan*, trans. François Raffoul and David Pettigrew, Albany, SUNY Press.

No subject (2019). Wo Es war, soll Ich werden - No Subject - Encyclopedia of Psychoanalysis (2019). https://nosubject.com/Wo_Es_war,_soll_Ich_werden

Rabaté, Jean-Michel, editor (2001). *The Cambridge Companion to Lacan*, Cambridge, Cambridge University Press.

Rabaté, Jean-Michel (2014). *The Cambridge Introduction to Literature and Psychoanalysis*, Cambridge University Press.

Roudinesco, Elisabeth (1997). *Jacques Lacan*, trans. Barbara Bray, New York, Columbia University Press.

Roudinesco, Elisabeth (2016). *Freud: In his time and ours*, trans. Catherine Porter, Cambridge, Harvard University Press.

Sharon-Zisser, Shirley (2022). *Writing, Speech and Flesh in Lacanian psychoanalysis: Of unconscious grammatology*, New York, Routledge.

Sharon-Zisser, Shirley (2020). "Derrida after Shakespeare: A Lacanian Reading" in *The Undecideable Unconscious*, vol. 7.

Solms, Mark (2018). "Extracts from the Revised *Standard Edition* of Freud's complete psychological works," *International Journal of Psychoanalysis*, 99.1, p. 11–57.

Strachey, James and Strachey, Alix (1985). *Bloomsbury/Freud: the letters of James and Alix Strachey, 1924–1925*, ed. Perry Meisel and Walter Kendick, New York, Basic Books.

Withy, Katherine (2015). *Heidegger on Being Uncanny*, Cambridge, MA, Harvard University Press.

Chapter 2

Freud's irritations

I will highlight two moments in Freud's career that evinced encounters with figures of irritation. Both generated a dull and smoldering anger in him, and the annoyance was caused by the perception of forms of obsolescence that led to deliberate ignorance. One took place early in his career, the other toward the end. In both cases, the meetings caused Freud a lasting irritation.

2.1 Nordau: Civilization as irritation

The first meeting took place during Freud's stay in Paris in 1885–1886. He visited Max Nordau, a famous journalist known for his dispatches from the French capital to German periodicals such as the *Neue Freie Presse*. Nordau who was born in Budapest had been living in Paris since 1880. Friends of Freud's had advised him to see Nordau who had just published a very successful book on the "social lies" of modernity, and they saw parallels with the young Freud's rebellious spirit. This book, *Die konventionellen Lügen der Kulturmenschheit*, translated as *The Conventional Lies of Our Civilization*, was first published in 1883; the English version was published in 1895. Nordau was a renowned public intellectual at a time when Freud was an impoverished medical student who could only boast of a few articles in specialized journals. It turned out that Freud was disappointed by this encounter, at least according to Ernest Jones's biography: "He called on Max Nordau with a letter of introduction, but he found him vain and stupid and did not cultivate his acquaintance" (Jones:1953, p. 188). Obviously, there were too many parallels, too many overlapping themes in their works, and such proximity could not help. I want to explore what might have caused this missed encounter. Just a few years before Freud went to Paris to work with Jean-Martin Charcot on hysteria, Nordau did the same; he was already a physician and completed a second dissertation under Charcot's supervision. His French dissertation has a Freudian ring: *On the Castration of Women* (1882) expanded his research as a gynecologist in Pest, which not yet part of Budapest. The Hungarian dissertation was called *Sexual Maladies in Women*. The second academic work *On the Castration of Women* is a bold political intervention.

DOI: 10.4324/9781032715834-3

In it Nordau severely criticizes the practice, still common then, of removing ovaries in a misguided effort at curing hysterical women; these women had been diagnosed since Antiquity as suffering from their errant of wayward wombs, and the response was simply: remove them! Had Freud read that dissertation, he might have avoided a major conceptual blunder, the repeated confusion he made between castration and eviration. Unlike Nordau who knew the proper meaning of castration and was aware that it referred both to the excision of the clitoris and to the ablation of testicles, Freud talks of castration loosely, mostly to evoke fears about the severing the penis. As anybody who has worked in a farm with bulls and horses will know, castration is systematically employed to neuter animals; however, no one seriously imagines chopping off their penises. Gary Taylor has pointed out that Freud was quite ignorant of the basics of farm life and of the techniques of spaying and neutering (see Taylor:2002). For Freud, castration remained at the level of a fear, therefore, was more a fantasy or an unconscious complex than a fact or a concrete practice. For Nordau, already the reformer and social critic, it meant the terrible physical harm inflicted on women and followed procedures based on lack of scientific evidence. This difference illustrates their opposed conceptions of reality and of a medical cure.

Both men were proud of being Jewish while not being religious. Nordau's father, Rabbi Gabriel Südfeld, had educated his children in the liberal German tradition. His son took Heinrich Heine as a literary model. He followed Heine's example by moving to Paris. The French capital was his home, which later posed problems for him during the war. Nordau had to move to Madrid and his properties were confiscated. He had officially changed his name to sound like the opposite of his father's name: "Südfeld" meaning "South field," he became "Nord-au," or the "North meadow." Similarly, Freud changed his first name from Sigismund to Sigmund, perhaps to make clearer his wish to succeed, will, and triumph (*Sieg* means victory, *Mund* mouth). If one compares two photographs of 1886, one notes that, although Nordau was only seven years older, he looks like a mature man about town displaying a huge grey beard and a well-earned social gravitas. Freud still young and single was unsure of what he would do next. He was planning to marry his fiancée Martha Bernays and controlling his social awkwardness in Paris by taking huge doses of cocaine daily. Nordau must have wanted to take Freud under his wing; he could not have resisted an impulse to show him the "gay Paris." Nordau was a man about town and had published *Paris Sketches* in 1878, then *Paris under the Third Republic* in 1880 and "Paris letters" for varied German and Austrian periodicals. This would not have sat well with Freud who was abstemious, hard-working, on a shoe-string budget, hence extremely wary of French dissipation.

Nordau was feted all over Europe for his debunking of what he called the "conventional Lies of our civilization." Surprisingly, his analyses anticipate theses found in *The Future of an Illusion* and *Civilization and Its Discontents*.

The book, published when Nordau was thirty-four, making him a celebrity, was translated into twenty languages. Freud read it and appreciated it. He found a tone and modes of cultural critique that echoed with his earlier socialist leanings and his juvenile admiration for the philosopher Ludwig Feuerbach. In a later interview with Chaim Bloch, Freud admitted that he had not only read *The Conventional Lies of Our Civilization* but taken the book as a model. At that time, he had to explain why he had written his *Moses* book, a book that antagonized his Jewish friends. Freud famously claimed that Moses was an Egyptian and, therefore, that monotheism as such had not been a Jewish invention. Defending his motivations, Freud mentioned Nordau because both had been friends of Herzl, one of the best-known Zionists:

> I did not see the harm that Nordau caused when he clearly and simply stated that the Holy Scriptures are a heap of superstitious beliefs and Egyptian teachings and customs and traditions. I do not wish to conceal the fact that when I read his book, *The Conventional Lies of Our Civilization*, and his judgment on the Scriptures, I decided to examine this question myself.

> (Bloch:1951, pp. 101–108)

Nordau's fast and furious book combines essays that had been published as feuilletons, and the main butt of his social satire is religion. Right at the beginning, Nordau lashes at the "the lie of religion." In this chapter, Nordau exposes religion not just as an "illusion," as Freud later did, but as a systematic obfuscation, mere propaganda, a political manipulation of the masses. One passage attacks Schopenhauer as a thinker because he had reintroduced in a non-Christian sense the idea of a "will" in Nature, an attack quite in line with Nietzsche's rejection of his former mentor (Nordau:1895, pp. 41–42). In tones that announce the Freud of the 1920s, Nordau exposes human delusions, denounces the way we unconsciously cling to mystical and transcendental ideas that are relics of the child's awe facing the parents. Nordau often alludes to the sphere of the "unconscious" to account for the success of such a gross mystification. His view of civilization thus corresponds to what Freud later highlighted, for he foregrounds a sense of a *malaise*, an *Unbehagen*, a "discontent" that afflict modern men and women. Another name Nordau gives to that "discontent" is "irritation." From the start, Nordau takes on the role of a physician ready to treat symptoms of what is wrong in culture: the lack of harmony between classes, endless fighting between warring political enemies, nervous fatigue and wholesale depression emerging as "the universal disease of the age" (Nordau:1895, p. 6). Nordau includes nihilism, pessimism, and anti-Semitism under the heading of modern societal ills. A pervasive pessimism about all values would be the key feature of the disease:

Every man of culture feels this sense of irritating discomfort which he ascribes to some slight, casual cause, inevitably the wrong ones, unless he analyzes his feelings with unusual care—it leads him to criticize and harshly condemn the varying phases of our modern life.

(Nordau:1895, p. 6)

These negative influences exert an "exciting even exasperating effect" on all; then irritation will reach a climax expressed by one single term—*decadence*.

Nordau relies on the physiology of the nerves when sketching portraits of neurotics who flee into artificial paradises; self-delusion allows them to be blind to the distressing realities of life under a capitalistic regime. Thus, alcohol, narcotics, and fin-de-siècle culture have one single aim: to erase the unease generated by modern life:

A dull sensation of irritation, sometimes self-conscious, but more often only recognized as a vague, irresistible discontent, keeps the aspiring in a state of gloomy restlessness, so that the struggle for existence assumes brutal and desperate phases, never seen before.

(Nordau:1895, p. 16)

Such a dissatisfaction with social rules and cultural norms might lead to a wish for radical change, which can be dangerous. Nordau was not a socialist, and he criticized Communism (see Nordau:1895, pp. 253–255 and 264–268). Soon, he would find an outcome by becoming a devoted Zionist. The mental distress experienced by artists and neurotics is a new phenomenon that he associates with modernity, and he adds that this evolution finds no equivalent in the upheavals and revolutions of previous ages. Nordau asks again: "To what cause can we trace the developments of this unparalleled irritation and embittering which prevails with such alarming severity among all the thinkers of an age which seems to offer even to the poorest a wealth of material and intellectual pleasures...?" (1895, p. 25). The answer is simple: it is a form of ideology whereby modern society obliges all subjects to lie to themselves.

The success of the book on social lies was due to its mixture of banter and sarcasm leveled at the powerful, the aristocrats, royalty, the Pope, American bankers, the rich, the bourgeois, etc. Nordau had traveled extensively in Europe and knew enough to deride the foibles of the higher classes. His rationalist debunking religion then ushered in rants on the weakened and obtuse aristocrats. He touched on religion, politics, and economics before concluding with an astute analysis of what he called the worst lie of all: this was the lie of married life, the falsity of sexual hypocrisy underpinning bourgeois pretentions to fidelity and monogamy. Sexuality emerged as the domain in which such a deliberate deception generated endless neurosis, acute hysteria, and rampant depression.

Contrarily to what is suggested by Jones's biography, Freud did not break up with Nordau; indeed, we know that their interaction continued for a long time. A letter shows that Freud had remained in touch with Nordau more than fifteen years later. It was Nordau who advised him to send the *Interpretation of Dreams* to Theodor Herzl for a recension. On September 28, 1902, Freud sent an autographed copy of *The Interpretation of Dreams* to Herzl with this letter:

> Dear Dr. Herzl, at the suggestion of your colleague Mr. Max Nordau, I have taken the liberty of having the Detick bookshop send you a copy of my book on the interpretation of dreams, published in 1900 (...). I don't know whether you will find the book suitable for the idea Mr. Nordau has in mind, but I beg you to consider it as a token of the high esteem in which I and so many others have held the writer and fighter for the rights of our people for many years.
>
> (quoted in Pawel:1992, p. 430)

This letter illustrates Freud's ambiguous attitude toward Zionism, a movement jointly founded by Herzl and Nordau. In 1902, Freud was in solidarity with the movement that Herzl embodied. He knew Herzl personally; they had been neighbors: from 1896 to 1898, Herzl lived at 6, Berggasse, while Freud lived at number 19. In 1894, the Jewish communities of Vienna debated Herzl's shocking play *The New Ghetto*, in which a Jewish lawyer is killed by an Austrian officer. The dispute about anti-Semitism left its mark on Freud as we see in his dream "My son, the Myops..." (Freud:1965, p. 478). Soon, Freud took distances from the "muscular Judaism" advocated by Nordau who had coined the term *Muskeljudentum* in 1989 at a Zionist congress and then from the ideology Zionism. This distance is evident in a 1930 letter to Chaim Koffer in which Freud states that he "does not believe that Palestine should ever become a Jewish state" (Roudinesco:2004, pp. 5–17).

Nordau and Freud had first considered Palestine under the British Mandate as a shelter for persecuted Jew, until Freud began questioning the theocratic utopia of a sovereign state founded on a biblical map. Here lies the ultimate meaning of his last book *Moses and Monotheism*, in which he argues that Moses was an Egyptian. Attacking Judaism at its root had a political function: it would tell anti-Semites that they were wrong to focus on Jews who had been enslaved by the Egyptians and then freed by one of their high priests, one of those who had invented monotheism. Today, Freud's theory remains a powerful irritant to orthodox Jews—I am always careful when I announce its topic before teaching Freud's book in class, having been surprised more than once by the virulence of some students' reactions. Freud foresaw the inevitable violence and endless infighting that the creation of a Jewish state would entail. We will return to the figure of Moses in the next chapter.

This debate shows why it is crucial to probe the roots of Freud's disappointment when he met Nordau in Paris. When everything could have united them, both being engaged in a struggle to help hysterical patients against a male-dominated chauvinist society, a fundamental divergence separated them. The root of their disagreement did not lie in their Jewishness or in a Zionism still to come. Freud was irritated by the famous journalist, physician, and social critic above all because they did not share the same concept of sanity, hence of Reason. What was disappointing in the celebrated journalist, physician, and social critic was that he defended diametrically opposite ideas about rationality. The clash was captured by a supporter of Nordau who uncritically endorses the latter's optimism facing the "normal" values that an enlightened bourgeoisie should uphold:

> Nordau gave the bourgeoisie what Freud later denied them. Freud, so it seemed to the emerging middle class, showed them that everything they worked so hard to attain, their respectability, their embrace of education, and even the idea of acculturation itself, was suddenly dirty and suspect. (...) With Nordau, the nascent middle class could condemn the new and innovative literature that was threatening bourgeois order and culture by claiming that its own, hard-fought for position was the more modern. *Degeneration* further helped the bourgeoisie come to terms with its fear of anarchism, socialism, deviant sexuality, and low birth rates by explaining that these threats to bourgeois order (evident, according to Nordau, in the works of Wagner, Nietzsche, Ibsen and Zola) were serious and real.
>
> (Söder:2009, p. 71–72)

This assessment is correct, except that Söder fully agrees with Nordau against Freud's alleged pessimism. At the time, Freud had not yet begun the correspondence with Wilhelm Fliess that would lead him, some ten years later, to elaborate a theory of culture founded on sexual repression. Nordau glimpsed that factor, but harked back to an idea of Reason taken as an undisputable ground for "normalcy." This is why Nordau could explain and condemn the work of those he considered as neurotics, perverts, and madmen—by which he meant the most famous artists, poets, and philosophers of the second half of the nineteenth century.

This insight underpinned became the 1982 compendium of *Degeneration*, a book that lastingly shaped the popular perception of "decadence" in European culture while introducing new ideas in literature and the arts. The choice of the word *Entartung* (the book was translated as *Degeneration* in 1895) was logical given Nordau's wish to promote a medical view of culture as a symptom of a physical and moral disease. The term derives from "*entarten*" ("to degenerate") but also echoes with "art" as in "art for art's sake," one of the cultural heresies skewered by Nordau. The term was unfortunate in retrospect given its use by the Nazis in the 1930s: they too denounced "degenerate art" to attack the moderns. Nordau, a Jewish, rationalist, and pro-Dreyfusard writer, would have been shocked by this historical turn. Indeed, he made a belated alliance with Emile Zola, although he had denounced Naturalism in *Degeneration*.

In spite of its negative diagnosis, *Degeneration* provided a competent panorama of nineteenth-century literary avant-gardes from France, England, Germany, Russia, and the Nordic countries. William Greenslade has explained why this diagnosis had such a hold on the imagination of the Victorian public (Greenslade:1994, pp. 120–133). With an unerring good taste in his virulent denunciations, Nordau took to task Ibsen, Baudelaire, Nietzsche, the pre-Raphaelites, the French Symbolists, Tolstoy, Wagner, and Zola for displaying unwholesome symptoms of a regression betraying a degeneracy of the human race. The medical assessment was based on categories he borrowed from Cesare Lombroso to whom the book is dedicated and from Bénédict Augustin Morel. Lombroso, also a Jewish thinker, sketched a dire portrayal of dissolute women and male geniuses who happened to be insane. Morel's 1857 medical treatise, *Traité des dégénérescences physiques, intellectuelles et morales de l'espèce humaine et des causes qui produisent ces variétés maladives*, was a pre-Darwinian attempt at classifying forms of physical and mental retardation.

Among the symptoms of fin-de-siècle disease, Nordau lists enervated "mysticism" or "ego-mania," both of which always tend to descend into madness and criminality. Nordau adduces experimental psychology and scientific positivism; next to Lombroso and Morel, he quotes Taine, Ribot, Binet, and Krafft-Ebing. Specializing in "abnormal" psychology, he disqualifies and criminalizes whatever he deems not normal, or lacking healthy relationships. Everything that falls short of this norm is condemned. *Degeneration* places Ibsen next to Nietzsche to whom Nordau grants a measure of talent in his "rants" even if appears insane from birth, hysterical and imbecile (Nordau:1968, p. 453). In whatever direction he looks, he only sees perversion, anthropophobia, or criminality. This hymn to positivistic commonsense doubling as a stubborn refusal of modernity involuntarily echoes Gustave Flaubert's dictionary of "received ideas." The result is often hilarious or grotesque, as when Nordau asserts that Impressionist painters produced blurry works because their retinas had degenerated. However, when he discusses Symbolism, he evinces good taste in the choice of quotes. The chapter on "Decadents and Aesthetes" gives the full measure of his talent. Not only did he read Baudelaire closely, but he also explains how the schools that followed expanded Baudelaire's ideas from Satanism to the glorification of evil, from sexual explicitness to pietism or perverse Catholicism. Nordau also quotes in full Théophile Gautier's enthusiastic endorsement of decadence (Nordau:1968, pp. 299–300). Even when the medical language sounds demeaning, most analyses are solid, based on first-hand readings with original quotes. Thus, Nordau explains that decadent urge to express a new truth, even though it might come from a "mystically degenerate mind with its shifting nebulous ideas, its fleeting formless shadowy thought, its perversions and aberrations, its tribulations and impulsions" necessarily entails the creation of a new language: "To express this state of mind, a new and unheard of language must in fact be found, since there cannot be in any customary language designations corresponding to presentations which in reality do not exist" (Nordau:1968, p. 300). The tone has suddenly shifted, one senses a grudging approval of such a linguistic innovation.

In fact, Nordau's book had the reverse effect of his original thesis, for he did more than any other critic, thinker, or artist, to spread and promote the values of decadence. Single-handedly he appears as a link between Romanticism and the fin-de-siècle culture in which Freud thrived. Typically, the young Georg Lukacs would praise Nordau for his good taste in detestation. Lukacs read *Degeneration* in his father's copy and discovered new authors:

> I read the book and came to understand what real decadence meant in the work of Ibsen, Tolstoy, Baudelaire, Swinburne and others. Fortunately, Nordau provided literal quotations of the poems of Baudelaire, Swinburne, and so on. I was carried away completely and of course became a staunch supporter of Ibsen and Tolstoy who were despised by my family.
>
> (Lukacs:1983, p. 30)

Having devoured Nordau, Lukacs bought all the works of these poets and even tried to write a play in the style of Ibsen.

James Huneker, well-known in the United States as a cultural critic at the turn of century, followed suit by simply inverting Nordau's categories. In his 1909 *Egoists: A Book of Supermen* (1909), Hunecker established a counter-genealogy of anti-degeneration. Huneker praised Stendhal, Flaubert, Baudelaire, and Karl-Joris Huysmans in a reversal that throws light on the transition between decadence and modernism that has been studied by Vincent Sherry and Stanley Gontarski (see Sherry:2015 and Gontarski:2018). When Huneker rewrote positively Nordau's criticism, he was aware of the paradoxical effect of *Degeneration*. If Nordau disseminated the works and ideas of those he was quoting at length, by contrast, Freud looks timid in his endorsement of fin-de-siècle artists. What began with hysteria as the psychic condition of fin de siècle symptoms ended for Nordau in perversion: as he saw it, the sadism of a previous century would come back to haunt civilization like the return of the repressed. This insight would have to wait until Lacan took up the gauntlet of Marquis de Sade in his dialogue with Reason.

As for Freud, he had understood hysteria as a knot of symptoms devoid of organic roots and deriving from unconscious traumas translated into a bodily imaginary. Note the parallels: Freud published his first essays on hysteria in 1893, a year after the publication of *Entartung*. The book co-authored with Josef Breuer, *Studies on Hysteria*, dates from 1895. Freud owed to Nordau's book a first acquaintance with Nietzsche, a thinker analyzed and of course criticized in detail (see Gasser:1997). One can even say that it was partly to Nordau's book that one owes the popularity of Nietzsche in English-speaking circles. Nietzsche was then seen as a critical "physiologist" who dissected modern values with a scalpel. As we have seen, Barbara Stiegler (2005) has pointed out how much Nietzsche thought of the living body as the origin of all "transvaluations of values," an expression quoted by Freud in *The Interpretation of Dreams*. For Freud, the dream generates an "*Umwertung aller psychischen Werte*" (a transvaluation of all psychic values) (Freud:1965, p, 365). Stiegler has shown how much Nietzsche drew on the biology of his time; for these theories, the concept of irritability still provided a key. For Nietzsche's favorite authors, such as Ernst Haeckel and Rudolf Virchow, what mattered was the body's capacity to receive the other into itself, which was called "intussusception." Nietzsche's physiological dialectic aimed at combining excitation raised through irritability, and the assimilation of the foreign body through digestion. Nordau had given an example of a similarly embodied dialectic but made it rest on a naive concept of reason that, by contrast, proves Freud's innovative role. Freud would have to make other discoveries in order to progress. He would to this thanks to two important interlocutors, a woman psychoanalyst who gave him a first glimpse of the death drive, and a physician who helped him reject the distinction between health and disease by exploring their foundation in the Id. The first was Sabina Spielrein, the second Georg Groddeck.

2.2 Spielrein and the death drive

Sabina Spielrein was brought to the attention of a larger public by the success of the 2011 film *A Dangerous Method*, although it is marred by historical distortions and a Hollywoodian metamorphosis of the protagonist played by Keira Knightley. In real life Spielrein did not have an affair with Jung while she was being "psychoanalyzed" by him; however, it is true that she fell in love with him. Finally, she appealed to Freud when her situation became impossible in Zurich. Beyond the fact that she was the first person to become a psychoanalyst as a consequence of her psychoanalysis, it remains that Spielrein had disappeared from most chronicles of psychoanalysis until recently; now she is given her due (Plastow:2019, and Sells:2017). I focus on her main contribution, her ground-breaking 1912 essay "Destruction as the Cause of Coming into Being" (Spielrein:1995). Spielrein introduced Freud to the concept of the death drive ten years before he introduced it in *Beyond the Pleasure Principle*, in which he duly, if ambiguously, salutes Spielrein's innovation (Freud:1989, p. 66, footnote).

Spielrein left Zurich and moved to Vienna to work with Freud. In November 1911, she presented a lecture on "Transformation" that contained a draft of her essay published one year later. She had worked with schizophrenic patients in the Burghölzi clinic, presenting her medical thesis about them at the University of Zurich in 1911. The title of her essay *"Die Destruktion als Ursache des Werdens"* means "Destruction as the origin of becoming." This compelling of Freudian theory and metaphysical speculation takes Nietzsche as a point of reference. Spielrein began by pointing out that the sexual drive or "reproductive drive" includes negative features like anxiety and disgust, which are overcome when the drive reaches its aim. Sexuality is intimately linked with death—she quoted Wilhelm Stekel, Eugen Bleuler, Otto Gross, and Carl Jung on this topic. In *Metamorphoses and Symbols of the Libido*, Jung had insisted that the very fact of giving birth spells out the future death of the parents, adding that anxiety is a normal and frequent component of sexuality.

Spielrein moved boldly into an ontological investigation: in procreation, each cell is destroyed as autonomous unit; this is how life emerges from destruction. Any creation entails an *Untergang*, meaning "ruin, decline, decadence, downfall." Mutual destruction plays out first at the level of the individual:

> The male part dissolves itself into the female part; the female part becoming restive develops a new form through the foreign intruder. The transformation affects the entire organism; destruction and regeneration, which are always taking place under ordinary circumstances, take place abruptly. The organism discharges the sex product like any excretion.
>
> (Spielrein:1995, p. 88)

Even more boldly for the time, Spielrein questions one of the founding principles of Freudian theory. Freud began by positing that when the ego emerged, it was caught up between reality and pleasure as two opposite principles, but Spielrein insisted that one must go deeper when analyzing the Unconscious. A different principle seems to be at work if one witnesses that, at times, one wishes to inflict "self-damage" in such a way that this generates "joy in pain" (Spielrein:1995, p. 94). Paradoxical unconscious wishes of this type would remain incomprehensible if one remained fixated on the "I-life," as she calls it, which means ego-wishes dominated by the principle of pleasure. What is more, for Spielrein, one cannot speak of an individual as a single "I" because any subject is a "Dividuum" (Spielrein:1995, p. 94): she has intuited the division of the subject given the agency of desire, a desire that may not follow rational lines of self-interest. When one delves into the depths of the psyche, an "I" looks very much like a "We": subjects are definitively pluralized. To make this point, Spielrein adduces a case of dementia praecox, which was the topic of her dissertation; her main patient once declared: "I am a complete stranger to myself" (Spielrein:1995, p. 95).

From these clinical considerations, Spielrein turned to Nietzsche who found satisfaction in images of self-destruction. Under the mythical disguise of Zarathustra, Nietzsche expressed a wish to drown and be sucked in the depths of the sea like the sun at sunset. Such a regressive version of love would unite him with his mother, the sea. If the dissolution process could succeed, Nietzsche would become a generating Mother. He would be one with the principle of Becoming as such (Spielrein:1995, p. 107). Anticipating both Jacques Derrida's analysis of femininity in Nietzsche (Derrida:1979), and Gilles Deleuze's Nietzschean developments on the concept of becoming (Deleuze:1989), Spielrein connected Nietzsche and Wagner whom she tried to reconcile. She was obsessed with *Tristan and Isolde* and had projected on Jung and herself the image of the two lovers who must die. She often alluded to the extraordinary scene in which the lovers exchange their identities: Tristan becomes Isolde, Isolde becomes Tristan. Spielrein saw in this fusion a confirmation of her initial idea that any act of procreation entails self-destruction. Shakespeare knew it, she argues from *Romeo and Juliet*, a play in which the thwarted lovers face "more obstacles onto which they unload the destruction impulse, but no obstacle is great enough to pacify the passion, which only finds peace with complete destruction, with the death of the personality" (Spielrein:1995, p. 115). Wagner and Nietzsche avoid being classified as "decadent": meeting Shakespeare, they give voice to a universal myth.

Spielrein concludes her survey by moving on theoretically and postulates a need to expand Freudian metapsychology by taking into consideration the death drive hidden within the sexual drive. In fact, her essay ends on a note that sounds anarchist: "No transformation can proceed without destruction of the old state" (Spielrein:1995, p. 118). This last note betrays the influence of Otto Gross whom she quotes several times and who was the "bad boy" of wild psychoanalysis. Gross followed suit by quoting her in his 1914 essay on "On the symbolism of destruction" (Gross:1914, pp. 525–534). Spielrein tried hard, but ultimately failed, to reconcile the points of view of Jung and Freud. She was the first psychoanalyst able to move seamlessly between case studies, astute analyses of symbols, theoretical advances, and conversations with philosophers. She intuited before Freud the truth that Thomas Mann had discovered thanks to Nietzsche: disease is also an instrument of knowledge (Mann:1937, p. 10).

2.3 From Groddeck to Svevo: Irritation and regeneration

Another non-conformist psychoanalyst who brought new insights to Freud was Georg Groddeck. The only contemporary novel that Freud deemed worthy of being called a "psychoanalytic novel" was penned by this "wild" or "rogue" disciple. Surprisingly, it has not been translated into English yet, although there are French and Spanish translations by Roger Lewinter

(Gallimard, 1982) and José Aníbal Campos (Sexto Piso, 2014). This strange text stages a forceful link between the teachings of psychoanalysis about the body, health, and disease, and ideas of decadence and regeneration. Groddeck, a German physician, had published *Nasamecu* in 1913, meaning with this strange title to condense his theory of health and disease: *Natura sanat, medicus curat.* Nature heals, the task of the physician is only to "cure," which means understanding the workings of Nature and allowing affected subjects to become conscious of the Id working through their bodies and souls.

Groddeck would heal an amazing number of psychosomatic afflictions like skin diseases, bowel trouble (he wrote at some length on constipation), nose bleeding, asthma, allergies, and even cancer. *Nasamecu* barely alluded to Freudian psychoanalysis, for Groddeck kept his distance, believing that psychoanalysis was the "infection" or "symptom" of the disease it attempted to cure, as Karl Kraus famously quipped: "Psychoanalysis is that mental illness for which it regards itself as therapy." However, in 1917, Groddeck was converted to Freudian theories, and wrote to Freud to stating his new allegiance. Freud responded warmly and endorsed Groddeck as a legitimate fellow psychoanalyst. Soon after, Freud borrowed the concept of the "It" (*das Es*) from him, a notion developed in Groddeck's 1923 *The Book of the Id*.

Groddeck's novel *The Soulseeker* is set in a fictional German city in which one recognizes Baden-Baden, where he had a sanatorium. This picaresque tale is situated at the turn of the century. The wild satirical novel based on *Don Quixote* had been planned as early as 1906. Groddeck wanted to debunk social hypocrisy under all its forms. *The Soulseeker*, finally completed in 1919, makes fun of the royal family, the nobility, doctors, the police, the army, second-rate painters, and even hysterical feminists; at one point, the hero is seen enjoying in the company of gay men. The novel was too unconventional, It was rejected by all publishers until Groddeck sent it to Freud who helped with the publication. If the original title *"The bug killer, or the unveiled soul of Thomas Weltlein"* could not be accepted, Freud expressed his admiration for a powerful and original text. The novel had a surprising ending: the hero dies in a train accident and his headless and charred body is recognized from a scar on the thigh. This was a modern *Don Quixote*, Freud said, and there was no greater praise from him. Groddeck paid for the book's publication arranged by the Psychoanalytical Society Press. It was Otto Rank who found a suitable title, *Der Seelensucher, ein psychoanalytischer Roman* (see Groddeck:1998, pp. 269–276).

Sándor Ferenczi had spent some time in Groddeck's sanatorium where he was cured of various ailments including nephrosclerosis. This stay made him aware of Groddeck's acumen. Ferenczi wrote a glowing review in 1921, praising the display of bawdy humor in which serious psychoanalytical concepts are treated grotesquely. The main protagonist, August Müller, is an intellectual who welcomes in his house his widowed sister Agathe and her teenage daughter, Alwine. Alwine falls in love with her uncle, an affair develops, although we perceive this at the end only: only she can identify the body when she recognizes the hidden scar on his buttocks. Because of the sexual tension and the incestuous undertones, Alwine must have her own bedroom; Müller forces the old maid to vacate it, and she gets her revenge by infecting his bed with bed-bugs. Bitten repeatedly, Müller develops a fever that renders him all but psychotic. He experiences a skin irritation, the rash invades his entire body, and in that dismal state then he leaves his home to wander through the world and preach. He changes his name to Weltlein, which means "little world." Like a mad Zarathustra infected with bed-bugs bites, he rants endlessly about health and sickness, art and politics, sexuality, and symbolism. Each time, he encounters grotesque characters while he delivers absurdist speeches; each time, his adventures end in disaster. He is arrested as a vagrant, detained in jail and a hospital. What he teaches sounds like an over the top, a crazily exaggerated version of Freudianism explaining that absolutely everything in life hinges around the grossest mechanisms of sexuality and sexual organs, from symbols to numbers and human interactions.

The publication of the novel by the official press of the psychoanalytic movement infuriated the Swiss members of the association whose contingent was led by the very pious Oskar Pfister. Aware of the scandalous nature of the book, Ferenczi's review of the novel defused the bomb by writing: "The indignant bourgeois would immediately call for the straightjacket; but as the mocking author has already donned it himself, even the guardians of public morals have no choice but to put a good face on it and laugh" (Ferenczi:1957, p. 346). He condensed the book's philosophy as the deployment of a systematic symbolism rooted in organic and symptomatic bodily drives:

> Sexuality is the pivot round which the whole world of symbols revolves. All the work of man is only plastic representation of the genitals and of the genital act, of that archaic prototype of all longing and endeavour. (...) The whole body thinks; thoughts can find expression in the form of a moustache, a corn, even of excreta. The soul is "infected" by the body, the body by the contents of the soul; and in fact, it is not permissible to talk of an "ego." One does not live but one "is lived" by a "something."
>
> (Ferenczi:1957, p. 347)

Ferenczi sums up Groddeck's tenets by simply stating that we, as subjects, do not think or act: we are thought and acted upon by the cosmic and sexual *Es*, the Id that Freud borrowed. The *Seelensucher* adds to this inversion a modern concern for auto-immune diseases or auto-infection. Groddeck develops the trope of infestation by introducing the rather ludicrous presence of bed-bugs. Like the image of a vermin (*Ungeziefer*) used by Kafka's "Metamorphosis" for his character Gregor Samsa, in the novel, those pesky and proliferating bugs offer a metaphor of creative madness. At one point,

Müller, the hero, even believes that he can kill the bed-bugs that torment him by contaminating them with his infested blood. This error generates a sort of reverse metamorphosis, and he begins seeing bugs everywhere. The German word for bed-bug, *Wanze*, stands at the core of the delirium: close to *Wahn*, which means delirium and madness, it invades the center, and the generalized irritation brings both madness and wisdom; what had started as a skin disease caused by insect bites spreads through the blood and then corrupts everything from the hero's body to the body politic, while allowing Müller to open his eyes, see a new truth, and become able to denounce the ills of society.

The *Wanze/Wahn* echo reveals how astutely Groddeck plays with signifiers. When a Prussian royal prince saves Weltlein from humiliation, he is not spared. Weltlein, completely drunk, screams that the Prince is a bloodsucker. Calling him the "Red Prince," he accuses him of being a "mere insect pumping our blood" (Groddeck:1998, p. 262). The bed-bugs that bite him all over help him invent a theory of "inner contamination." There would be a parallel contamination going from body to soul and from soul to body. This theory of generalized irritation implies that the conceit of a reversible contamination is possible: because of those pesky bed-bugs that bite him all over that the hero turns into a Freudian Don Quixote. When the irritation spreads, Weltlein himself begins to "bug" all authorities and all orthodoxies. Indeed, some of his theories come across as ravings, as a passive-active irritation. Groddeck's worldview was similarly activist and left room for politics. He died in 1934 of a heart attack caused by the Gestapo who had roughed him up in spite of his age. Groddeck had tried but failed to meet Hitler in person: he imagined that if he could talk to him man to man, he would cure him and make him less irrational. In fact, he was considered as a dangerous agent provocateur by the Nazi police, and jailed for a while.

Groddeck was as provocative and rambunctious as his fictional hero. He shocked the Freudians during his first appearance at a psychoanalytic conference when he mentioned his bed-wetting as a child and the erotic associations triggered then, before concluding: "I am a wild psychoanalyst." He was too wild for most. His monism of the "It" provided an antidote to Freud's dualism. Groddeck would have agreed with Freud's later speculations, for he wrote in 1925: "Death is always voluntary: no one dies except he has desired death" (Groddeck:1951, p. 96). The "It" underpins all manifestations of love, desire, and transference; the blind causes health and sickness: "... no one is altogether ill, there is always some part which remains sound even in the worst illness; and no one is altogether well, there is always something wrong even in the perfectly healthy" (Groddeck:1951, p. 96).

Freud's admiration for Groddeck's novel confirms Adorno's offhand maxim that "In psycho-analysis, nothing is true except the exaggerations" (Adorno:1974, p. 49). Groddeck exaggerates all the time in his teachings as in his fiction. Like Weltlein, he saw everything in culture, from the cross of

Christianity to the mechanism of the steam engine, as representing images of copulation. He explains this theory to his readers via parody, satire, and exaggeration. The mock-heroic mode creates ironic distance and prevents any identification with Weltlein, a balding, stooping, hectoring hero who, moreover, displays a huge beer-belly, a sign of his desire for male pregnancy. His prominent red nose is dotted with pustules that he squeezes whenever he gets overexcited. No doubt, Weltlein had to die at the end when his "little world" is shattered by a locomotive accident.

The true heir of Thomas Weltlein is Zeno Cosini, Italo Svevo's fictional alter-ego. Aron Ettore Schmitz, Svevo's real name, spent a few weeks in Groddeck's sanatorium, to which he had brought his brother-in-law. During that time, Groddeck managed to cure the brother-in-law of his addiction, although this could never be Zeno's case. Zeno is a compulsive smoker. Whenever he tries to stop, he smokes another "last cigarette." In Groddeck's sanatorium, Svevo, whose first language was German, discovered the *Seelensucher* and appreciated its humor, its comedic gusto, and its insights on disease as moral and mental contamination. Above all, he understood that his addiction expressed the "It," which provided a point of departure for *La Coscienza di Zeno*. Smoking cigarettes was a vice that could be condoned, even indulged, once it was seen as a libidinal disposition linking him to his Mother via the oral drive, while calling up the figure of a dead Father who smoked too.

It was Groddeck who gave Svevo the courage to undertake a psychoanalytical novel. *Zeno's Conscience* begins with a statement by the hero's psychoanalyst who explains that he has asked Zeno Cosini to write everything he can remember about his past; the doctor hopes that the writing cure will "rejuvenate" Zeno: "But he was an old man, and I hoped that recalling his past would rejuvenate him, and that the autobiography would serve as a useful prelude to his psychoanalysis" (Svevo:2003, p. 3). The novel ends when the protagonist attempts to retrieve the written documents given to Doctor S. If the psychoanalyst concludes that Zeno is cured, Zeno must disagree; he launches into a severe critique of psychoanalysis; all the doctor has managed to make him confess sounds most banal—he only discovered that he was in love with his mother and wanted to kill his father. The trite diagnosis forces him to deny that he was ever sick:

> My therapy was supposedly finished because my sickness had been discovered. It was nothing but the one diagnosed, in his day, by the late Sophocles for poor Oedipus: I had loved my mother, and I would have liked to kill my father. (...) An illustrious sickness, whose ancestors dated back to the mythological era! And I'm not angry now, either, alone here with my pen in hand. I laugh at it wholeheartedly. The best proof that I never had that sickness is supplied by the fact that I am not cured of it.
>
> (Svevo:2003, p. 403)

I was not sick because I could never be cured: this superb double-bind encapsulates Svevo's ambivalence facing Freudian therapy. The diagnosis does not allow him to make sense of his father's last gesture, a death-bed acting out that still baffles Zeno afterward. His father was on the bed half-unconscious. Zeno approached to kiss him a last time, and at that instant the father slapped him with all the strength he could muster. He then fell back on the bed, dead. It did not help Zeno to know Freud's theory of the Oedipal drama. Svevo guessed that psychoanalysis had to be enacted differently, either via irritations or dramatizations—this idea gave him a solution to his psychic quandary, and he staged it in his later plays.

Zeno's Conscience was the first European novel framed as a psychoanalytic cure quite some time before *Portnoy's Complaint* and *Lolita*. The novel was written during World War I. At the end, the irruption of the war interrupts Zeno's introspective digressions. The end offers no real salvation. Zeno's psychoanalysis may have worked or not, but urgent problems are pressing, issues like pollution, the rise of technology and the specter of a bomb capable of annihilating the human race (Svevo was a perceptive prophet of doom, in advance of time). The novel concludes with images of death and desolation, which proves that redemption through art, as was the case with Proust and Joyce, will have to fail. In fact, Svevo's humor was more in tune with Kafka's despair than with his friend Joyce's paradoxical optimism displayed in his human comedy.

Svevo had two literary careers, the first one ending in failure. Two novels published in 1893 (*Una Vita*) and 1898 (*Senilità*) aroused absolutely no interest. When he met Joyce in Trieste by chance in 1907 (Svevo hired him to learn English), a second career began. It was crowned by international recognition due to the success of *Zeno's Conscience* (1923). The continuity between the three novels has been captured by P. N. Furbank who sees well Svevo's central obsession, his main worry that hinged around the idea of "senility," which meant obsolescence. Furbank explains that if Svevo's major novels are all "studies in weakness," "senility" is used as a mobile concept in order to explore and perhaps cure neurosis: "Senility, in this metaphorical sense, is an infection of the will, a withdrawal from reality into day-dreaming, an incapacity for taking real decisions combined with the constant illusion of doing so" (Furbank:1966, p. 158.)

From this angle, one can outline common themes in all three novels. In *A Life*, Alfonso, the protagonist, ends up committing suicide after he is rejected by the woman he has previously rejected. In *Senilità*, the protagonist's sister kills herself by absorbing ether when she realizes that her brother's friend, the swashbuckling sculptor who seduces all women, just pretended to be interested in her to humor the brother. *Zeno's Conscience* fleshes out a secondary character named Guido, at first the narrator's successful rival. Guido has married the woman Zeno was in love with. Zeno then marries her sister as a second-best option even though he finds her plain and unattractive.

However, Guido is pushed to suicide by bad debts and losses on the stock exchange. Furbank recognizes in Svevo echoes of Nordau's diagnosis: "In his analysis of the degenerate type, Nordau might be describing Svevo's Alfonso word for word" (Furbank:1966, p. 161). The disease is stated in *Una Vita*, a cure is attempted in *Senilità*, but it fails. *Zeno's Conscience* proposes a method that might help, psychoanalysis that too soon exhibits its limits. It would behoove *Regeneration*, Svevo's last play, which was completed it in 1928, just before he died, to present a solution (Svevo:1969, pp. 165–302).

A bawdy comedy, *Regeneration* is a fantastic extravaganza with three dream sequences. Once more, Svevo worries about old age and gives vent to his longing for rejuvenation. The modern Mephisto is another Guido, a rather unscrupulous young physician who incites his uncle, an older and tired businessman named Giovanni Chierici, to undergo the operation that will cure him both of his absent-mindedness and his sexual apathy. The operation was not exactly the Steinach type, the operation Freud underwent, but a similar technique invented by Serge Voronoff, a French surgeon of Russian origin. Both were founded on identical principles. In the 1920s, Voronoff began grafting tissue from monkey testicles into the scrotum of his patients. Svevo had read Voronoff's books with great interest. In the play, after some hesitation and a near-miss (Giovanni almost lets his grandson, whom he was taking for a walk, get hit by a car), the operation is performed. Alas, it turns Giovanni into a libidinous old man, an insatiable womanizer. In spite of his age and physical weakness, Giovanni repeatedly tries to kiss the attractive young maid who works in his house. The seduction turns into a farce: both fall asleep side by side, having drunk too much. Finally, realizing the absurdity of his attempts, Giovanni admits the inevitability of death. The newfound strength gained from the grafted gonads brings back obliterated memories of his youth; he recaptures a half-forgotten and submerged image of a young woman he had been in love with but had rejected because she came from a poor background. Giovanni succeeds in grafting her image onto that of his wife, who has remained tolerant and loving from beginning to end.

Svevo did not have time to undergo the operation; he died too soon. For him, writing had truly been the cure, following a tip given by the psychoanalyst, Doctor S., to Zeno at the end of *Confession*: writing should bring about the desired regeneration. The psychoanalyst had outlined a writing program that relied on the verb "rinverdire": "I hoped that recalling his past would rejuvenate him," is *"ed io speria che in tale rievocazione il suo passato si rinverdisse"* (Svevo:1985, p. 3). The verb, which is not "regenerate" exactly, suggests rather "making green again," or "rekindling," "reawakening..." The term sums up Svevo's itinerary from a sense of "senility" experienced at the age of thirty to a regenerated and hard-won "youth" felt at the age of seventy-four, which is Giovanni's age in the play. The real-life model for Guido in the play was Aurelio Finzi, Svevo's actual nephew, who, like Guido, was a medical student. It was with Finzi that in 1918, Svevo translated

Freud's short book *Über den Traum* (*On the dream*), as confirmed by Livia Svevo (see Svevo:1951, p. LXXXIX). Freud's 1901 book summarized the main theses of the *Interpretation of Dreams* and added a few dream analyses. Not only had Svevo read Freud closely but because he translated him, he could be impatient and creative. His self-knowledge was ironical and critical; it relied on a tension between "senility," the sense that a past with ancient roots in Oedipal conflict weighs heavily on the subject, and "regeneration," the utopian striving for rebirth. In the end, he reached a truce between impossible desires and a deeper insight into the libidinal structures any subject is caught.

Can the paradigm of degeneration/obsolescence followed by regeneration apply to psychoanalysis itself, or to the career of his founder? Many critics have evoked the "death" of psychoanalysis, which is regularly announced in reviews and conferences. What is at stake is a certain obsolescence, or more precisely, a conceptual "decadence" that has taken various forms. "Decadence" calls up images of degradation, decay, increasing technical malfunction. Adorno objected to what he called the "californization" of psychoanalysis, having witnessed its ravages first-hand during his American stay (1938–1949). In a lecture given in English in 1946 at the psychoanalytic society of San Francisco (Adorno:2014, pp. 326–338), Adorno attacked Freudian revisionism, singling out Erich Fromm and Karen Horney as psychoanalysts eager to erase what they deemed to be Freud's innate pessimism. Indeed, Horney and Fromm had replaced Freud's metapsychology of the drives with a weak culturalism. In "Revised Psychoanalysis," Adorno denounces Karen Horney who had changed Freudianism into a theory of social adaptation. Culturalism clashed with the darker side of Freud, whose philosophy was closer to that of Marquis de Sade. Freud's grandeur, for Adorno, was his ambivalence facing culture and civilization, his insistence that social harmony could not be taken as a norm and had to be questioned. Adorno's solution was to traverse death facing the obsolescence of psychoanalysis. That robust positioning of death found its forerunner in Hegel whose *Phenomenology of Spirit* begins with a Preface foregrounding a decision to look at death squarely in its face (Hegel:1977, p. 19), that movement should not be reduced to mythical Wagnerism but provide a more solid foundation. Only thus can psychoanalysis keep its critical edge, resist the dangerous drift into meliorism, social adaptation, all the attendant religious and humanistic pieties.

For Freud, the confrontation with death took place with *Beyond the Pleasure Principle*, in which Spielrein was duly credited for her input. The theme of death was ushered in via the concept of repetition facing pleasure and reality. Freud deduced from the compulsion to repeat a tendency to return to previous states of matter. Life would be a detour, a "circuitous path" before a return to inorganic matter, conforming to the motto: "The aim of all life is death" (Freud, 1989, p. 46). This idea was deployed in the surprising image of "guardians of life" helping the organism to strive for survival, who then turn into "myrmidons of death"; however, once Freud made this point, he turned around to exclaim: "It cannot be so" (Freud:1989, p. 47).

This reversal crowns the complex, tortuous even, movement leading from chapter V to chapter VI. Freud multiplies detours, aporias, and counter-examples before introducing the death drive surreptitiously, in a parenthesis of the original text: "The opposition between the ego or death instincts and the sexual or life instincts would then cease to hold..." ("*Der Gegensatz von Ich(Todes-)trieben und Sexual(Lebens)trieben würde dann entfallen...*") (Freud:1989, p. 53). Hence, the striking about-face: "Let us turn back, then, to one of the assumptions that we have already made, with the exception that we shall be able to give it a categorical denial" (Freud:1989, p. 53). The assumption attacked here is that any conception of life moving inexorably to death, when we think that we are destined to die from internal causes, is debunked by Freud. The very idea is a way of providing comfort: "If we are to die ourselves, and first to lose in death those who are dearest to us, it is easier to submit to a remorseless law of nature..." (Freud:1989, p. 53). If death is construed as the "law of Nature," there is no reason to believe that we have voted it.

Testing the validity of this widespread belief about the inescapability of death, Freud goes into another direction. He reopens the biological debate by opposing dying cells to an undying germ-plasm. Death becomes less "natural" when it appears as a late acquisition of organisms. Woodruff had shown that infusorians can, if placed in a refreshed and nourishing environment, reproduce themselves by fission for more than 30,000 generations (Freud:1989, p. 57). The focus of the discussion becomes that of "senescence" or "degenerescence" versus "rejuvenation." In cases when the solution has not been renewed and degeneration is observed, the process can be reversed when animalculae blend together. They achieve an instant regeneration, avoid the degeneration leading to death. In the heady context of such speculations, Freud asserts that he believes in a dualism of the drives: there is a constructive principle and a destructive principle (Freud:1989, p. 59). Freud insists on the idea that death is not as natural as we think, but that there is in each of us an enjoyment of death caused by the death drive.

Freud's dialectical thinking forces him to speculate always further in an anticipation of Adorno's negative dialectics. First, Freud finds a theoretical support in Schopenhauer. For Schopenhauer, death is the purpose of human life, but the unconscious "will" embodying sexual instinct remains on the side of life (Freud:1989, pp. 59–60). Freud refuses to be stuck in an idealistic dualism and makes the even "bolder" step of assuming that libido can "rejuvenate" cells. Egoistic narcissism leads to death via the uncontrolled reduplication of cells, as in cancer. If the ego-drive can be equated with death, the sexual drive with a life-giving force (Freud:1989, p. 63). Freud almost hints that love could cure cancer. Freud's dialectical tension between "obsoles-cence" or "degenerescence" and a term like "regeneration" can be under-stood via the idea of "juvenescence," or to quote Eliot's term, "*juvescence.*" Eliot coined that strange word in his poem "Gerontion": "In the juvescence of the year/ Came Christ the tiger" (Eliot:2004). No regeneration, hence without a previous death. All agree on this point from Nordau to Svevo and Eliot, from Spielrein to Freud and Adorno.

This consensus should help us understand Freud's decision to undergo a "Steinach operation" meant to rejuvenate him, exactly as Giovanni Chierici imagined. In November 1924, Freud had a vasectomy because he trusted the idea of male enhancement surgery promoted by Eugen Steinach. What would "rejuvenate" older males, according to Steinach, was an infusion of home-grown male hormones spreading through the entire body, with the aim of revitalizing its main functions. The vasectomy would prevent sperm from getting into the testicles; such a male castration would, it was hoped, benefit the patient's general health and increase his sexual activity. The same vasoli-gation was performed on William Butler Yeats in April 1934. It worked won-ders, according to the poet who announced that he felt an increased vitality. Indeed, Yeats could testify to regained powers in his sexual life and creativity. If Freud was less enthusiastic, he thought that the operation had brought a temporary respite in his struggle with his jaw cancer. Trusting the budding science of endocrinology, Freud applied to himself the central principle of castration. The desired "operation" offered less a path toward desire, as Lacan often puts it, than a hope of reversing the aging process.

2.4 Freud's irritant: Cornering Viereck

It was the issue of the Steinach operation that brought together Freud and George Sylvester Viereck, an American writer of German origins. After they had exchanged a few letters, Viereck attracted Freud's attention with a little book on Steinach that he published in 1923. This was quite a popular book, *Rejuvenation: How Steinach Makes People Young*, signed by "Corners," as a way of translating Viereck's name, which means literally "four corners." Freud was so impressed that he decided to undergo a Steinach operation himself, which he did, as we saw, on November 17, 1923. He hoped that the operation would block the progression of the jaw cancer for which he had just undergone surgery. In 1923, Freud was interviewed a first time by Viereck. Freud had high expectations, for he imagined that he could explain psychoanalysis in the same way he had presented Steinach to a broad American audience. A second interview with Viereck was later reprinted in *Glimpses of the Great* (Viereck:1930, pp. 28–40) under the title "Sigmund Freud confronts the Sphinx." Typically, *Glimpses of the Great* has a chapter on Steinach as "Steinach discovers the secret of life" (Viereck:1930, pp. 212–225), and a chapter on Voronoff who is presented as a bad disciple of Steinach in "Voronoff: from Super-sheep to Super-human" (Viereck:1930, pp. 226–234).

During the second interview, one catches signs that Freud grew increasingly disappointed and irritated. Freud did his best to hide his anger until it flared. It slowly dawned on Freud that Viereck would not be instrumental in helping him bring a better version of psychoanalysis to the United States, as he had first surmised. Viereck would not write the book explaining Freud's conceptions first because he misunderstood Freud's ideas but also because there was a deeper reason for the chasm opening between them: Viereck was a Nazi fellow-traveler.

In 1910, at the age of twenty-five, Viereck had begun his literary career with the publication of *Confessions of a Barbarian*, an engaging memoir recounting his itinerary from New York to Hamburg, Berlin, and Copenhagen. The style is sprightly, the tone alert. He does not shy from inserting poems about Berlin prostitutes in the vein of Swinburne. However, the book ends ominously with the peroration of an unnamed character who considers the American melting pot to be the cause of its decline. The voice declares ominously: "We Aryans have been appointed masters of the world" (Viereck:1910, p. 191). Indeed, during World War I, Viereck had championed Germany's cause, which made him unpopular with Americans. Soon after, he became interested in psychoanalysis and decided to befriend Freud. As Jones's biography reports, Viereck called a "prominent American journalist," first sent Freud newspapers cuttings from New York in an effort to prove that psychoanalysis was recognized there; soon Freud let him know that he preferred receiving food, given the dire shortage of goods in Vienna at the time (Jones, 1957, p. 11). This led to a 1923 interview with the new "Oedipus." Viereck proudly announced that he was given the first interview that explained psychoanalysis to a broad public (Freud:2020, p. 59). Three years later, Viereck visited Freud at his country house in Semmering to interview him a second time. Just after completing the interview, he went to Germany and met Hitler and Goering, whom he also interviewed. Finally, in 1934, Viereck gave a public speech in New York's Madison Square Garden in which he compared Hitler and Roosevelt. Repression and imprisonment followed. In 1942, he was jailed and accused of being a Nazi agent. He remained in an American prison until 1947. Already in 1926, Viereck evinced deep misunderstandings about Freud's ideas. Their tense conversation gives us an intimation of Freud's growing irritation when he saw the source of Viereck's resistance to his theses. Even when he knew he faced a popularizer and a journalist who would simplify his ideas, Freud made efforts to avoid falling into clichés. In the end, he decided that they had to part. To understand this disappointment, we need to read Viereck's account between the lines.

Already presented in bombastic and hyperbolic manner as the great Austrian explorer of the inner world of the soul, Freud is compared to Oedipus, Galileo, and Christopher Columbus by Viereck. Typically, he uses the term *subconscious* instead of Unconscious when he writes: "Freud is to psychology, what Galileo was to astronomy. He is the Columbus of the subconscious" (Viereck, n.d., p. 1). Soon enough, the conversation goes the wrong way. Viereck notes how aged Freud looks to him after three years. He is aware of his pallor, of the speech impediment caused by the prosthesis in his jaw that Freud calls a "mechanical jaw" (Viereck, n.d., p. 2). Because of his knowledge of the influence of Steinach's theories and of the recent operation, Viereck tries to elicit from Freud a confession that he desires immortality. Freud, who was seventy then, resists the insinuation. His words display a staunch stoicism in the face of the inconveniences of old age, drawing the bitter lesson that the gods deliberately make life unpleasant in old age: "Perhaps the gods are kind to us (…) by making life more disagreeable as we grow older. In the end, death seems less intolerable than the manifold burdens we carry" (Viereck, n.d., p. 2). However, Freud concedes that his life has been satisfying, that he has received enough honors for his tireless work. Viereck, who seems to be on a different wavelength, insists on a fin-de-siècle pessimism that he takes as the key to Freud's doctrine. But he also quotes G. Bernard Shaw, one of his mentors, who imagined that the duration of human life would be lengthened by science. Viereck asks whether Freud believes in an afterlife, and he replies that since everything that lives perishes, he should not entertain illusions about survival. Freud evokes Nietzsche's idea of the eternal return but criticizes the conceit: there is no sense to "return" without memory. Freud, urged on by Viereck, explains that Steinach's operation does not aim at prolonging life but simply fighting old age. For instance, he thinks that Steinach by "tapping the reservoir of strength within our own bodies… helps the tissue to resist disease" (Viereck, n.d., p. 3). The main outcome would be the possibility to block biological accidents like cancer taken in its early stages. Freud concludes wryly: "It makes life more livable. It does not make it worth living" (Viereck, n.d., p. 3). Thus, there is no reason why we should want to live longer, but it is understandable that we should want to live with as little discomfort as possible. Freud adamantly rejects the idea that he would be possessed by a desire for immortality. In contradistinction, Freud then exposes the thesis that, we saw, he had reached at the end of *Beyond the Pleasure Principle*. He explains to Viereck that "It is possible (…) that death itself may not be a biological necessity. Perhaps we die because we want to die" (Viereck, n.d., p. 3). Freud insinuates that we contain side by side the death wish and the life wish; Death accompanies Love, and they rule together. Seeing that Viereck does not understand, Freud insists: "We may entertain the fanciful suggestion that Death comes to us by our own volition. It is possible that we could vanquish Death, except for his ally in our bosom" (Viereck, n.d., p. 3) and adds with a smile that "we may be justified in saying that all Death is suicide in disguise" (Viereck, n.d., p. 3).

At this point, Viereck expresses an almost total incomprehension; he even thinks that Freud's philosophy justifies suicide: "It should lead logically to the world suicide envisaged by Eduard von Hartmann" (Viereck, n.d., p. 3). Of course, Viereck would have taken to von Hartmann's philosophy of the Unconscious that derived from Schopenhauer's metaphysics. Viereck, who claims to have grasped Freud's concept of the unconscious, was in fact much closer to von Hartmann and Schopenhauer. Freud disagrees, saying that in every normal person, there should be a desire for life strong enough to counterbalance the desire for death. Freud's ideas about the death drive disconcert Viereck who keeps silent for a while. A chill sets in as the night falls. The two men walk in silence and go back to the house. Then they exchange banalities. Anna Freud passes by with a young patient.

Viereck chooses a new tack; he suggests that Freud not only gives tools allowing one to understand everything in human personality but that this reveals his desire to pardon everything in a spirit of Christian charity. This misunderstanding exasperates Freud. Freud cannot hide his anger any longer. He literally "thunders" to refute this idea:

"On the contrary," thundered Freud, his features assuming the fierce severity of a Hebrew prophet. "To understand all, is not to forgive all. Psychoanalysis teaches us not only what we may endure, it also teaches us what we must avoid. It tells us what must be exterminated. Tolerance of evil is by no means a corollary of knowledge" (Viereck, n.d., p. 4).

Viereck, taken aback by this vehemence, deduces that Freud reveals a typical feature of his "Jewish race," thus naively betraying his prejudice. Freud's Jewishness would explain his irascibility and intolerance. Viereck blithely generalizes:

I suddenly understood why Freud had quarreled so bitterly with those of his followers who had deserted him, why he cannot forgive their departure from the straight path of orthodox psychoanalysis. His sense of righteousness is the heritage of his ancestors. It is a heritage of which he is proud, as he is proud of his race.

(n.d., p. 4)

The interlocutors are now on the slippery slope of racism. Freud goes further, claiming to be a member of a persecuted minority in Germany:

My language is German. My culture, my attainments are German. I considered myself a German intellectually, until I noticed the growth of anti-Semitic prejudice in Germany and in German Austria. Since that time, I consider myself no longer a German. I prefer to call myself a Jew.

(Viereck, n.d., p. 4)

At this point, Viereck expresses his disappointment, because, as he says, for the first time he discovers that Freud is not superhuman. This pride in being Jewish would be his "Achilles heel." Viereck glosses this naively: "It seemed to me that Freud's spirit should dwell on heights, beyond any prejudice of race, that he should be untouched by any personal rancor" (n.d., p. 4). Taking refuge in the heights of pure thought would allow him to avoid seeing the anti-Semitism of his German friends. Viereck's deliberate blindness turns into naivety; he explains how delighted he is to realize that Freud is a mere mortal and that he is a man who has "complexes" like all the others: "I am glad... Herr Professor, that you, too, have your complexes, that you, too, betray your mortality." To this Freud replies suavely: "Our complexes (...) are the source of our weakness; they are also often the source of our strength" (Viereck, n.d., p. 4), a paradox that again escapes Viereck's comprehension.

Inevitably the interview takes a turn for the worse. Freud, increasingly irritated, begins questioning Viereck's hidden motives. Viereck appears to him as a star-struck journalist always looking for strong personalities that he interviews as a series of father-substitutes. Indeed, Freud captures the most unpleasant side of Viereck. Already in 1910, when he visited Copenhagen, he narrates how he forced his way into the home of the old critic Georg Brandes. He did this violently and never respected the wish for privacy clearly expressed by the famous Jewish scholar. Viereck stops following what Freud is saying and wonders what his own complex might be. Freud offers a dry diagnosis:

> You are devoting many years of your life to lion-hunting. You have sought, year after year, the outstanding figures of your generation, invariably men older than yourself. There was Roosevelt, the Kaiser, Hindenburg, Briand, Foch, Joffre, George Brandes, Gerhart Hauptmann, and George Bernard Shaw...

Hearing this, Viereck defends himself lamely: "It's part of my work," he says, but Freud remains unfazed: "You are seeking the great man to take the place of the father. It is part of your father complex" (Viereck, n.d., p. 5). Viereck first rejected this vehemently, although later he confesses that he had to recognize the validity of Freud's observation.

Freud did not know that he should have added Goering and Hitler to the list of those father figures but takes a step back, avoids Viereck's biased questions to launch into a development on animals. Rejecting his interlocutor's insinuation that there are forms of human life that are closer to animality, which confirmed Viereck incipient racism, he quips that he prefers the company of dogs to that of humans. At least they're not divided and neurotic; their love for their master remains undiminished. Seizing a classical parallel related to his interviewer, Freud adds that a dog's emotions remind him of the heroes of Antiquity. That's why we unconsciously name them after heroes like Achilles or Hector. Viereck then replies that he owns a small Doberman named Ajax! Freud relaxes a little and adds in a mocking tone: "I am glad," I added, "that he cannot read. It would certainly make him a less desirable member of the household if he could yelp his opinion on psychic traumas and Edipus (*sic*) complexes!" (Viereck, n.d., p. 5). Touched by this irony, Viereck counters by accusing Freud of having made life more difficult because he "complicated" it: "Before you invented psychoanalysis, we did not know that our personality is dominated by a belligerent host of highly objectionable complexes. Psychoanalysis has made life a complicated puzzle" (p. 5). At this point, it looks as if Freud is restraining a burst of laughter or stifling a scream. He replies cuttingly: "By no means," Freud replied. "Psychoanalysis simplifies life. We achieve a new synthesis after analysis. Psychoanalysis reassorts the maze of stray impulses and tries to wind them around the spool to which they belong" (Viereck, n.d., p. 5). This image leads Viereck to raise the question of sexuality—on this topic, both agree on the centrality of sexuality in human life. Interestingly, Freud quotes Whitman on the topic: "I reply with the words of your own poet, Walt Whitman: 'Yet all were lacking, if sex were lacking'" (Viereck, n.d., p. 6). He mentions that he stresses what lies "beyond" the pleasure principle, that is, death, pain, and the negation of life. Viereck thinks that he can counter the allusion to Whitman by adducing ideas developed by Bernard Shaw, of whom he was a great admirer. Freud gruffly objects that Shaw had nothing to say about sexuality, and blurts out that Shaw "does not understand sex. He has not the remotest conception of love. There is no real love affair in any of his plays" (Viereck, n.d., p. 5).

For Freud, there was only one English-language writer who understood and expressed sexuality: it was Walt Whitman. Freud quotes from memory the poem "A Woman Waits for Me": "A woman waits for me, she contains all, nothing is lacking, // Yet all were lacking if sex were lacking, or if the moisture of the right man were lacking..." This sensual poem ends up praising a bisexual body for Whitman presents himself as re-enacting the "maternal mystery" when he imagines that he is filled with "seminal milk." Freud does not insist on these aspects, but when the 1856 poem, originally entitled "Poem of Procreation," was published it shocked American readers who had never encountered such an outspoken hymn to sexuality. Whitman sees himself both as a male lover who impregnates his partners and as a woman who enjoys a sexual embrace. His idea of sexuality is linked with an epicene fertilization. Maternity and paternity blend in a capacious hymn praising bisexual regeneration.

Viereck who does not sound convinced by Whitman's poem uses the opportunity to emphasize the literary side of psychoanalysis. Freud agrees, only to refer once more to Nietzsche, of whom he says forcibly that he was one of the first psychoanalysts:

It is surprising to see the extent to which his intuition prefigures our discoveries. He adds: "No one else so profoundly foresaw the duality of the motivations of human conduct and the insistence of the pleasure principle to predominate indefinitely", then quotes Zarathustra as saying:

"Pain says: Pass on and be done with it! But all joy wants eternity. Wants
deep eternity!"

(Viereck, n.d., p. 6)

Freud has quoted the last hymn of *Zarathustra*, a song of intoxication or the
midnight hymn. This is a sublime poem that Freud knew well, and it is sung
in the fourth movement of Mahler's Third Symphony: *Doch alle Lust will
Ewigkeit! Will tiefe, tiefe Ewigkeit!* (But all pleasure craves eternity!/Craves
deep, deep eternity). Freud had treated Mahler in 1910 and knew this sublime symphony quite well.

Then Freud began to realize that none of his efforts would succeed. If
Viereck could not be his spokesman, his disciple, his explainer to the
Americans, at least he hoped that he would not distort his views too severely.
At the end of their interview, a visibly weary Freud pleads: "Don't make me
appear a pessimist," he says, as he shakes Viereck's hand. For someone who
was about to meet the future *Führer* of the German people in Munich, Freud's
thought was too complex, too paradoxical in its mixture of resignation to
bodily ills and a demanding quest for truth.

2.5 A death drive that resists death

There was one point about which Freud was wrong in 1926: it would not be
difficult for the Americans to accept his so-called pansexualism. However, it
would be impossible to get them to accept the death drive. The rapid evolution of popular culture in films, advertising, videos, and literature after World
War II proves that sexualization was acceptable if not inevitable in the United
States. However, resistance to the idea of the death drive was tenacious and
still endures. Unable to attack Viereck for his regrettable political drift toward
with Nazism, Freud pretended to see him as an American only, that is, as a
mystified journalist incapable of going beyond religious or moralistic slo-
gans. Freud, who remained critical of American culture throughout his life,
expresses the same reservations to Viereck:

> American interest in psychoanalysis does not go very deep. Extensive pop-
> ularization leads to superficial acceptance without serious research. People
> merely repeat the phrases they learn in the theater, or in the press. They
> imagine they understand psychoanalysis, because they can parrot its pat-
> ter! I prefer the more intense study of psychoanalysis in European centers.
>
> (Viereck:n.d., p. 7)

Even if he admits that America was the first country that recognizes the worth
of his work, it has not continued the research and made "few original contributions to the study of psychoanalysis" (Viereck:n.d., p. 7). What is to blame
is the American idea of imposing a medical curriculum to the training of

psychoanalysts. At the time, Freud was launching his campaign against the medicalization of psychoanalysis. His idea of "lay analysis" was anathema for his Anglo-Saxon colleagues. Freud meant to drive the point home: "To leave psychoanalysis solely in the hands of doctors would be fatal to its development" (Viereck:n.d., p. 7). Freud had a point, for the recuperation of psychoanalysis by medical science had severe ideological effects in the United States.

The exchange of views with Viereck in 1926 demonstrates the extent of the misunderstandings that would follow. Freud would be branded as an incurable pessimist, a sex-obsessed clinician eager to achieve immortality, a stern Jewish father who wants to control the organization he has founded by stifling dissenting voices mercilessly, an inflexible Moses who lays down the tables of the psychoanalytic law once and for all. These clichés pave the way for the debate that began after World War II, a debate in which Lacan took part. Freud had understood from his second conversation with Viereck that the key issue was that of his alleged pessimism. As Walter A. Weisskopf observed in 1957 in a collection that included Viereck's interview, Freudian psychoanalysis had become Americanized and, above all, thoroughly desexualized: "A shift took place, away from the emphasis on individual biological drives, to socially-acquired traits as prime movers of human behavior" (Weisskopf:1957, p. 53). Weisskopf deplores this transformation and thinks that too many useful concepts and intuitions have been lost in the process. The reason of this is, as he puts it, that "Freudian irrationalism, dualism and pessimism are incompatible with the American optimistic belief in the rational, progressive perfectibility of man and society" (Ibid.). Therefore, a return to Freud's earlier concepts and analyses was a logical step for whoever denounced the obsolescence of psychoanalysis. Social values had replaced the complex combination of the drives, libido, and the rather negative presentation of the super-ego. Adorno, Marcuse, and Lacan all agreed on that point, but Lacan went further, as can be seen in a passage from the seminar on identification in which he quotes Bausset, the moralist preacher. Bausset, who had written a biography of Bossuet, insisted on the scandal caused by death: death, in one fell swoop, strips us of everything. But this is only the death of the body, or to quote the great physiologist Xavier Bichat, "animal death," the death of the brain or of the heart as opposed to "organic death," the death of organs like the stomach, the intestine, etc. Lacan continues by evoking the notion of the "second death," the theological concept of a death of the soul after the death of the body. This allows him to usher in the death drive conceived as the keystone of Freudian metapsychology. Lacan quotes Bichat's famous opening in his 1805 *Physiological Researches upon Life and Death*, the statement that "Life is the set of functions that resist death" (Bichat:1805, p. 1). Lacan modifies Bichat's sentence slightly:

... the physiologist who was the greatest genius, one might say, of all those who have the sense of this angle of the biological approach, Bichat, said:

"Life is the totality of the forces which resist death." If something of our experience can be reflected, may one day take on a stable meaning in this very difficult plane, it is this precession produced by Freud of this formula of the whirlwind of death to the flanks of which life clings in order to avoid falling into it.

(Lacan:1962, p. 276)

Lacan had read *Beyond the Pleasure Principle* correctly. Death must not be confused with the inanimate. Death considered in its connection with other drives or natural forces cannot be the equivalent of a simple absence of life; on the contrary, the death drive can be construed as a force that pushes life forward: a life that never ceases throwing itself against death. In that endless whirlpool of death, one grasps an intimation of a non-religious infinity. Finite life propels itself against infinity because it attempts to perpetuate itself. Lacan reiterates this idea in a more condensed form in "Position of the Unconscious": "The letter kills, but we learn this from the letter itself. This is why every drive is virtually a death drive" (Lacan:2006, p. 719). Whoever learns from the letter uses a certain type of writing, a point to which I will return. Writing is in league with the death drive. When we invoke the death drive, we imply cruelty, blood, and aggressive affects, which will provide the themes of the next two chapters.

Bibliography

Adorno, Theodor W. (1974). *Minima Moralia*, trans. by E. F. N. Jephcott, London, Verso.

Adorno, Theodor W. (2014). Adorno's *"Die revidierte Psychoanalyse"* (1946) had been read in an English version that exists as an unpublished manuscript, retranslated by Nan-Nan Lee as "Revisionist Psychoanalysis," in *Philosophy and Social Criticism* 40, no. 3, 2014, p. 326–338.

Bichat, Xavier (1805). *Recherches physiologiques sur la vie et la mort*, Paris, Brosson.

Bloch, Chaim (1951). "Pegishathi Im Freud Vehitvakhuti Itho Al Moshe Rabbenu," *Bitzaron*, 23, Nov. 1950/51, p. 101–108.

Deleuze, Gilles (1989). *The Logic of Sense*, trans. Mark Lester and Charles Stivale, New York, Columbia University Press.

Derrida, Jacques (1979). *Spurs: Nietzsche's Styles*, trans. Barbara Harlow, Chicago, University of Chicago Press.

Eliot, T. S. (2004). "Gerontion," Poetry Foundation: Gerontion by T. S. Eliot.

Ferenczi, Sándor (1957). *Final Contributions to the Problems and Methods of Psycho-Analysis*, vol. III, trans. by Eric Mosbacher, New York, Basic Books.

Freud, Sigmund (1965). *The Interpretation of Dreams*, trans. James Strachey, New York, Harper and Collins.

Freud, Sigmund (1989). *Beyond the Pleasure Principle*, trans. J. Strachey, New York, Norton.

Freud, Sigmund (2020). "Georg Sylvester Viereck: Mean Men Explained by Freud / Surveying Life at Seventy," in *Gesamtausgabe*, vol. 21, edited by Christfried Tögel and Urban Zerfaß, Gießen, Psychosozial-Verlag, p. 103–124.

Furbank, P. N. (1966). *Italo Svevo, The Man and the Writer*, London, Secker and Warburg.

Gasser, Reinhard (1997). *Nietzsche und Freud*, Berlin, Walter de Gruyter.

Gontarski, Stanley (2018). *Revisioning Beckett: Samuel Beckett's Decadent Turn*, New York, Bloomsbury.

Greenslade, William (1994). *Degeneration, Culture and the Novel 1880-1940*, Cambridge, Cambridge University Press.

Groddeck, Georg (1951). *The Unknown Self*, trans. by V. M. E. Collins, London, Vision.

Groddeck, Georg (1982). *Le Chercheur d'âme, un roman psychanalytique*, trans. Roger Lewinter, Paris, Gallimard.

Groddeck, Georg (1998). *Der Seelensucher*, Frankfurt, Stroemfeld/Roter Stern.

Groddeck, Georg (2014). *El buscador de almas*, trans. José Aníbal Campos, Mexico, Sextopiso.

Gross, Otto (1914). « Über Destruktionssymbolik», *Zentralblatt für Psychoanalyse und Psychotherapie*, Vol. 4., 1914, p. 525–534.

Hegel, G. W. (1977). *The Phenomenology of Spirit*, translated by A. V. Miller, Oxford, Oxford University Press.

Huneker, James (1909). *Egoists: A Book of Supermen*, New York, Charles Scribner's Sons.

Jay, Martin (1973). *The Dialectical Imagination*, Boston, Little, Brown.

Jones, Ernest (1953). *The Life and Work of Sigmund Freud*, vol. I, New York, Basic Books.

Jones, Ernest (1957). *The Life and Work of Sigmund Freud*, vol. III, New York, Basic Books.

Lacan, Jacques (1962). *Seminar IX: Identification*, unpublished version translated by Cormac Gallagher from unedited manuscripts. https://www.valas.fr/IMG/pdf/THE-SEMINAR-OF-JACQUES-LACAN-IX_identification.pdf

Lacan, Jacques (2006). *Ecrits*, trans. Bruce Fink, New York, Norton.

Lukacs, Georg (1983). *Record of a Life: An Autobiography*, trans. Rodney Livingston, London, Verso.

Mann, Thomas (1937). *Freud, Goethe, Wagner*, trans. H. T. Lowe-Porter, New York, Knopf.

Nelson, Benjamin, editor (1957). *Psychoanalysis and the Future*, New York, National Psychological Association.

Nordau, Max Simon (1895). *The conventional lies of our civilization*, Chicago, Laird and Lee.

Nordau, Max (1968). *Degeneration*, New York, Howard Fertig.

Pawel, Ernst (1992). *Theodor Herzl ou le Labyrinthe de l'exil*, Paris, Le Seuil.

Plastow, Michael Gerard (2019). *Sabina Spielrein and the Poetry of Psychoanalysis: Writing and the end of analysis*, New York, Routledge.

Elisabeth, Roudinesco (2004). "A propos d'une lettre inédite de Freud," *Cliniques Méditerranéennes*, 2, n. 70, p. 5–17.

Sells, Angela M. (2017). *Sabina Spielrein, the woman and the myth*, Albany, SUNY Press.

Sherry, Vincent (2015). *Modernism and the Reinvention of Decadence*, Cambridge, Cambridge University Press.

Söder, Hans-Peter (2009). *That Way Madness Lies: Max Nordau on fin-de-siècle genius*, High Wycombe, Rivendale Press.

Spielrein, Sabina (1995). "Destruction as Cause of Becoming," trans. Stuart K. Witt, *Psychoanalysis and contemporary thought*, 18, 1995, p. 85–118.

Stiegler, Barbara (2005). *Nietzsche et la critique de la chair: Dionysios, Ariane, le Christ*, Paris, Presses Universitaires de France.

Svevo, Italo (1969). trans. P. N. Furbank, in *Further Confessions of Zeno*, trans. P. N. Furbank, Berkeley, University of California Press.

Svevo, Italo (1985). *La Coscienza di Zeno*, Milan, Mondadori.

Svevo, Italo (2003). *Zeno's Conscience*, trans. William Weaver, New York, Random House, Vintage.

Svevo, Livia Veneziani (1951). *Vita di mio marito*, Trieste, Edizioni dello Zibaldone.

Taylor, Gary (2002). *Castration: An Abbreviated History of Western Manhood*, New York, Routledge.

Vierek, George Sylvester (1910). *Confessions of A Barbarian*, New York, Moffat, Yard and Company.

Viereck, G. S. as G. F. Corners (1923). *Rejuvenation: How Steinach Makes People Young*, New York, Thomas Seltzer.

Viereck, George Sylvester (1923). "Freud's first interview on Psychoanalysis," *New York American*, August 19, 1923, collected in Sigmund Freud, *Gesamtausgabe*, *Gesamtausgabe*, vol. 21, edited by Christfried Tögel and Urban Zerfaß, Gießen, Psychosozial-Verlag, 2020, p. 103–124 as "Georg Sylvester Viereck: Mean Men Explained by Freud / Surveying Life at Seventy."

Viereck, George Sylvester (1927). "Interview: Mean Men Explained by Freud, Interview with George Sylvester Viereck", *London Weekly Dispatch*, July 28, 1927. Also in *Psychoanalysis and the Future*, edited by Benjamin Nelson, New York, National Psychological Association, p. 1–11.

Viereck, George Sylvester, (1910). Interview with Freud. Online Psychanalyse-lu An Interview with Freud.

Viereck, George Sylvester (1928). "Professor Freud über den Wert des Lebens. Ein Gespräch mit dem großen Gelehrten," *Neue Freie Presse*, August 28, 1928, Morgenblatt, p. 4.

Viereck, George Sylvester (1930). *Glimpses of the Great*, New York, Macaulay.

Weisskopf, Walter A. (1957). "The "Socialization" of Psychoanalysis in contemporary America," in (Nelson:1957, p. 51–56).

Chapter 3

Affects and their vicissitudes

Despite his failings, Viereck had a point when he presented Freud as display-ing the "severity of a Hebrew prophet" (Viereck:n.d., p. 4). He had guessed Freud's life-long identification with Moses, a passion to understand the prophet that led him to write his last book on the founder of Israel. Freud's fascination began early and found a perfect visual expression when he visited Rome, which he did regularly. He had discovered Michelangelo's famous statue of Moses in 1901; thereafter, each time he visited Rome, he would pay a visit to that monumental display of power and control staged in the church of San Pietro in Vincoli. Facing the statue, Freud would replay in his mind the drama condensed in stone. Moses was about to throw the tables of the law then checked his impulse and decided to keep the tables offering them to the rebellious Hebrews. Freud's elegant essay on the statue, first published anon-ymously in 1914, begins by stating his own strong affects facing Moses:

> How often have I mounted the steep steps from the unlovely Corso Cavour to the lonely piazza where the deserted church stands and have essayed to support the angry scorn of the hero's glance (*den verächtlich-zürnenden Blick des Heros*)! Sometimes I have crept cautiously out of the half-gloom of the interior as though I myself belonged to the mob upon whom his eye is turned—the mob which can hold fast no conviction, which has neither faith nor patience, and which rejoices when it has regained its illusory idols.
>
> (Freud:1997b, p. 124)

Freud's critical gaze emerges slowly from his fascination; he needs to think, interpret, and understand in order to overcome his paralysis. Focusing on the movement of the fingers on the beard, Freud reconstruct the trajectory of the hand. What Michelangelo made us witness is how Moses, first caught resting on his throne with the tables of the law, was startled by the unruly crowd carrying the Golden Calf, and seized by wrath and indignation, his reaction was to punish, destroy, annihilate the wrongdoers, but then he checked him-self, clutching the left side of his beard with his right hand as he overcame his

DOI: 10.4324/9781032715834-4

indignation, and in the end decided not to destroy the fickle Jews or the tables. All this in one monumental stone statue.

Freud reconstructs the prophet's movements thanks to four drawings that follow the trajectory of the hand and finger because he supposes that the moment depicted by Michelangelo collapses different scenes in the Bible: the destruction of the original tables written by God, and the moment of reconciliation when Moses brings the new set of tables written by himself under God's dictation. In the third part of the essay, the reconstitution is accompanied by a reading of Moses' affects in so far as they are discernible in his facial expression and the remarkable tension of his muscles: "The lines of the face reflect the feelings (*Affekte*) which have won the ascendancy" (Freud:1997b, p. 142). Freud summarizes his analysis in these terms:

> He remembered his mission and for its sake renounced an indulgence of his feelings (*die Befriedigung seines Affekts*). His hand returned and saved the unsupported tables before they had actually fallen to the ground. In this attitude he remained immobilized, and in this attitude Michelangelo has portrayed him as the guardian of the tomb.
>
> (Freud:1997b, p. 142)

Among the strong affects displayed, Freud lists fury, wrath, pain, rage, contempt, passion, and revenge. Such a dramatic condensation is paralleled with from the sculptor's complex relationship with Pope Julius II whose tomb the statue was to adorn. The artist had a fiery temperament, which was comparable to the Pope's own violence, arrogance, and truculence. Michelangelo carved his Moses "as a warning to himself, thus, in self-criticism, rising superior to his own nature (*mit dieser Kritik über die eigene Natur erhebend*)" (Freud:1997b, p. 146). When Harold Bloom interpreted this moment as Freud's return to the Romantic sublime, he highlighted the important links between the sublime and Freudian sublimation (see Bloom:1978). Indeed, the movement of "rising above" (*erhebend*) one's affects and one's nature calls up the German word for the sublime (*das Erhabene*).

In 2007, I chose the opposite way because I had been inspired by the spirited if somewhat perverse interpretation of Alain Roger who tempted me to notions of profanation and radical desublimation (Rabaté:2007, pp. 13–32). In *Hérésies du Désir: Freud, Dracula, Dalí* (Roger:1985, pp. 24 and 46), Roger proposes a paranoid-critical approach akin to Dalí's own images. He takes his point of departure in the descriptive passages Freud devotes to the prophet's beard. Roger argues that Freud's essay sexualizes the beard which is pictured as a soft feminine mass into which the "despotic finger" of the prophet plunges with sensual abandon. Moreover, if one looks carefully, the shape of the beard looks very much like a four-legged animal—why not a calf, possibly the golden calf exhibited by the mob of Hebrews triggering Moses' wrath? Freud's solution to the riddle of the statue would have enacted a return of the repressed by making the garlands of the beard speak. The beard's convoluted coils offer as little resistance to the palpation of Moses' index as to Freud's sharp gaze. At the time he was writing his essay on Michelangelo, Freud was writing a preface to a translation of Bourke's *Scatological Rites of All Nations* (1913) in which he outlined many examples of infantile connections between scatology and sexuality. His excremental interpretation of Michelangelo's statue might have been inspired by the visual suggestion of an anal penetration of the Golden Calf by Moses' finger. If we accept the concept of such a sublimated sodomy, Moses' "despotic" finger would have enacted a mimetic revenge—the rebellious heretics regressing into animal cults and orgiastic rituals just get what they deserve—while regaining his own self-mastery.

I am not sure that I would repeat the same analysis today; nevertheless, the skeptical probing of Moses' gesture has left me with an unresolved question: what to do with these unruly affects? Is their fate to be sublimated? Is there no other way out than the sublime? This was one of the issues treated by Sianne Ngai's excellent *Ugly Feelings*, a book in which she discussed envy, irritation, anxiety, paranoia, and what she called "stuplimity." Presenting that compound affect made up of stupidity and sublimity, Ngai quotes Lacan's theory of the "Thing" because it offered a better version of sublimation (Ngai:2005, pp. 279–281). Indeed, Lacan had proposed to replace Freud's model of a displacement of drive-dominated urges toward the higher regions of culture with a statement he found in artists like Picasso who were able to "raise an object (...) to the dignity of the Thing" (Lacan:1992, p. 112). This line of research has been well exemplified by Slavoj Žižek in numerous books; it finds a perfect domain of application in horror movies (see Trigg:2014). Lacan discovered the concept of the Thing in a dense passage of Freud's *Project for a Scientific Psychology* and deployed it in Seminar VII (1959–1960). Whereas the *Project for a Scientific Psychology* pointed to the remainder of exteriority in objects that could not be processed by consciousness, the concept of the "Thing" gave Lacan a tool with which he could upgrade the Freudian process of sublimation.

However, the movement from the object to the Thing, well observed as it is, cannot give use access to a new interpretation of the role of affects in psychoanalytic theory. Thus, when Ngai discusses irritation, she focuses one single literary example, Nella Larsen's 1928 novel *Quicksand* (Ngai:2005, pp. 175–208), and does not try to link her reading with the rest of her theoretical elaborations. We need to return to more foundational definitions; we know Freud uses the term *affect* to cover the whole range of psychoanalytical descriptions of emotions. Since Aristotle, we know about the power of terror, pity, or anger and their social uses via catharsis or purgation. Freud's method was first called a "cathartic method." Starting from the basic opposition between pleasure and displeasure, Freud studies both negative affects, such as anxiety, fear, disgust, and positive affects, such as love, joy, compassion, up to the "oceanic feeling" mentioned in *Beyond the Pleasure Principle*, a sense of a dissolution of the self in the world. "Catharsis" was the term used by Aristotle to describe the therapeutic function of tragedy, which works by the purgation (*catharsis*) of passions. It had been extensively discussed by Jacob Bernays, the uncle of Freud's wife, in 1857. Bernays presented Aristotle as a physician of man's soul, and in his carefully argued work, distinguished between "affect" (the general function of passions on humans) and "affection" (the way one person will experience the same affect in the singular): "In brief, παθοσ is the affect and παθημα is the affection" (Bernays:1857, p. 149). Freud's colleague Breuer used the term for the first time and was followed by Freud as we see in their jointly written *Studies on Hysteria*, in which language was proposed as a tool for the possible "abreaction" of affects. The most concise and systematic discussion of this operation is provided by Freud at the beginning of his essay on "Psychopathic characters on stage" that goes back to Aristotle's *Poetics*, its true foundational statement. Whenever Freud uses *Affekt*, I translate by "affect" to point out how often the term is repeated:

> If, as has been assumed since the time of Aristotle, the purpose of drama is to arouse "terror and pity" and so "to purge the affects," we can describe that purpose in rather more detail by saying that it is a question of opening up sources of pleasure or enjoyment (*Lust- oder Genußquellen*) in our affective life (*Affektleben*), just as, in the case of intellectual activity, joking or fun (*wie beim Komischen, Witz, usw.*) open up similar sources, many of which that activity had made inaccessible. In this connection the prime factor is unquestionably the process of *unleashing* one's own affects (*Austoben*, the word is underlined), and the consequent enjoyment (*Genuß*) corresponds on the one hand to the relief produced by a thorough discharge, and on the other hand, no doubt, to an accompanying sexual excitation that, as we may suppose, appears as an additional gain (*Nebengewinn*) whenever an affect is aroused (*Affekterweckung*), which gives people the sense they so much desire of raising the level of intensity in their psychical state."
>
> (Freud:1997a, p. 87, trans. modified)

The passing reference to jokes and the comic signals that Freud is still thinking in terms outlined in his book on jokes in which he analyzes both the process leading the condensation of a *Witz* (witticism) as deriving from a relief, a discharge, but also an intensification of pleasure. What happens when the affect is a negative one, as Moses' shifting from rage to self-control and moderate irritation? Is his fury affected by his own "critique," a true "self-critique," and is this comparable to the process of sublimation? If we try to explore more deeply the function of affects in Freudian theory, we should know what we mean when we talk about affects, and also whether there is an agreement between Freud and Lacanian. This was the question that launched Colette Soler's survey of *Lacanian Affects: The Function of Affect in Lacan's Work* (Soler:2016).

Providing a solid overview of Lacan's theses on affects, Soler details affects like "anguish" (Fink prefers that word to the more common "anxiety" to translate *angoisse*), sadness, joy, guilt, boredom, moroseness, anger, shame, love, hatred, and enthusiasm. Soler insists on Lacan's Freudian point of departure and highlights his distinctive contribution, even though she acknowledges that his concept of affect is fraught with tensions, false starts, or even contradictions. Lacan, as usual, offers brilliant insights couched in impenetrable and punning prose.

Soler follows the evolution of Lacan's thought and distinguishes several moments in his elaboration on affects that culminated in the seminar on Anxiety (Lacan:2014). When Adam Phillips had to praise it, his blurb asserted that this was one of the "most remarkable psychoanalytic and philosophical works of our time" (Lacan:2014, back cover). Lacan opened vistas on "this fundamental experience that paralyzes speech and so immobilizes people's lives" (Lacan:2014, back cover). However, what struck Phillips as a novelty also points to the concern that many other therapists voice facing Lacan: it seems that Lacan tackles the manifestations of anxiety in our lives by granting a central role to speech and language, and they tend to see in affects a non-verbal manifestation, a bodily production that remains below the level of verbalization. For Lacan's critics, the major objection is that he reduced affects to language, and language to signifiers.

3.1 Affects or language?

This criticism was made repeatedly by André Green, who had attended Lacan's seminar even though he was a member of the Paris Psychoanalytic Society affiliated with the International Psychoanalytic Association. However, he soon became a relentless critic of Lacan on the issue of affects. According to Green's *The Fabric of Affects* (Green:1999), Lacan's mistake was to downplay the role of the body in psychoanalysis because of his unwholesome obsession with language, or more precisely, with the signifier.

Green's book contains a spirited and systematic attack on Lacan's linguistic turn. To avoid the reference to structural linguistics, Green goes back to Freud, in a solid effort to conceptualize rigorously Freud's theory of affects. Thinking that Lacan had been guilty of neglecting affects, Green argues that this omission would reveal Lacan's blindness. A passage from "Subversion of the Subject and the Dialectics of Desire" seems to him to be symptomatic of this avoidance:

In the Freudian field, the words notwithstanding, consciousness is a characteristic that is as obsolete to us in grounding the unconscious (…) as affect is unsuited to play the role of the protopathic subject, since it is a function without a functionary.

(Lacan:2006, p. 692)

Querying the expression of *"protopathic subject,"* a term that suggests an immediate physiological response to basic stimuli, Green opposes that dismissive rejection of a phenomenology founded on consciousness and the psychology of affects that he sees inseparable from the constitution of a Freudian subject. Indeed, for Freud, the Id manifests itself mostly through the subject's affects. Green compares this reduction of affects to psychology with Lacan's concepts of the drive and jouissance, concepts that are more distant from the subject's position. Lacan had begun well when describing language as a "subtle body." However, that was in 1953, and after that, he went astray when he reduced everything to signifiers. The Unconscious was equated with a linguistic structure following Lacan's famous motto, reiterated everywhere, that "The Unconscious is structured like a language" (Lacan:1979, p. 203).

What to do with the drives in such a critical appraisal of Lacan's system? Quite obviously, the drives cannot be reducible to language. This is acknowledged by Lacan in "Subversion of the Subject and the Dialectic of Desire" in which Lacan mentions the drive as "a pinpointing that is organic, oral, anal, and so on, which satisfies the requirement that the more he speaks, the further he is from speaking" (Lacan:2006, p. 692). In fact, that very formulation could look more evasive than an admission that here is a body outside language. This crux has been pointed out by Green and Jean Laplanche: both object to Lacan's notorious slant, finding in affects a lever proving that there must be a limit to the power of language (Laplanche:1981, p. 27–29). Laplanche considers that Lacan's omnipresent signifier translates Freud's representation theory. Even if we agree that the Unconscious is "structured like a language," such a thesis is not sufficient to turn affects into a linguistic manifestation of the Unconscious. The same issue recurs: how to tackle affects in Lacanian psychoanalysis, if Lacan thinks that affects can only be approached psychoanalytically when mediated by signifiers? For Green and Laplanche, on the other hand, the concept of affect must be understood as conveyed by nonverbal behavior. It is this assumption that Soler's book wants to dispel. Indeed, Lacan tried hard to distinguish between affects whose essence is not to be repressed and unconscious signifiers that were repressed, a distinction presented in the seminar on Anxiety. Lacan brushes away objections:

> What is anxiety? ... it's an affect. Those who follow the movements of affinity or aversion in my disquisition... think that I'm less interested in affects than anything else. That's absurd ...What I said about affect is that it isn't repressed. Freud says it just as I do. It's unfastened, it drifts about. It can be found displaced, maddened, inverted, or metabolized, but it isn't repressed. What are repressed are the signifiers that moor it.
>
> (Lacan:2014, p. 14)

The consequences of this distinction are important and require elaboration: "The relationship between affect and the signifier would necessitate a whole year on the theory of affects" (Lacan:2014, p. 14). However, Lacan never spent one year on such a project. In the same session, he hints that he has worked on anger, an affect best treated by Aristotle in his *Rhetoric*. This seems to be a useful suggestion: affects should be understood from the angle of political or rhetorical language. For Aristotle, anger is a political passion, not an individual symptom. Lacan discussed anger in the January 1960 seminar on the *Ethics of Psychoanalysis*. Here, the allusion to anger simply ensures that the domain of affect is not conscious but unconscious.

Lacan reiterates the position that he never abandoned: the danger lies in dealing exclusively with affects, a recurrent temptation for psychoanalysts, that is the danger of falling into mere psychology, or into the mute intuition of the other's emotions and feelings. The psychology of human passions is no doubt interesting, but this is not the locus of psychoanalysis. Here is why Lacan refuses to produce a comprehensive theory of affects:

> I haven't taken the dogmatic path of prefacing what I have to say to you about anxiety with a comprehensive theory of affects. Why not? Because we aren't psychologists here, we're psychoanalysts. I'm not developing a *psychology* for you, a disquisition on the unreal reality that is called the psyche...
> (Lacan:2014, pp. 14–15)

If anxiety is a key concept in psychoanalysis, it must be understood from the point of view of unconscious desire, not as one of the many-sided human emotions. We recognize Lacan's main tenet, his rejection of an American ego-psychology that made a travesty of Freudian psychoanalysis by stressing the subject's self-esteem.

Lacan's starting point is strictly Freudian. Freud maintained that affects were not repressed, which occurs by definition: "It is surely of the essence of an emotion that we should feel it, i.e. that it should enter consciousness. So for emotions, feelings and affects to be unconscious would be quite out of the question" (Freud:1963, p. 126). Freud adds an important qualification when he explains that in psychoanalysis one can speak of "unconscious love, hate or anger." Moreover, paradoxical phrases like "unconscious anxiety" (*unbewußte Angst*) are current (Freud:1982, p. 136). This way of speaking is justified because it condenses two factors: an affect will be perceived by consciousness, therefore be conscious, but misconstrued as such because of the work of unconscious repression.

Freud's analysis of affects in this essay distinguishes degrees in the repression of affects; he concludes that the aim of repression is to get rid of affect entirely, which leads him to distinguish repressed affects and repressed ideas:

> So that, strictly speaking (...) there are no unconscious affects in the sense in which there are unconscious ideas. But there may very well be in the system Uncs. affect-formations which, like others, come into consciousness. The whole difference arises from the fact that ideas are cathexes

(*Vorstellungen Besetzungen*)—ultimately of memory-traces—whilst affects (*Affekte*) and emotions (*Gefühle*) correspond with processes of discharge, the final expression of which is perceived as feelings (*Empfindungen*).

(Freud:1963, p. 127, trans. modified)

This passage exhibits three different levels that are often confused: affects, emotions, and feelings. Their order is not random: affects resemble unconscious ideas, feelings are conscious, and emotions remain in the space in between. It would be sufficient to rewrite Freud's "ideas" as Lacan's "signifiers" to get a faithful reconstruction of Lacan's mode of thinking in 1962.

How to distinguish further between affects, emotions, and feelings? Freud's footnote makes it clear: "affect" keeps the mechanical aspect of a forceful discharge, thus is more quantitative than qualitative. Emotions and feelings introduce qualitative factors:

Affectivity (*Affektivität*) manifests itself essentially in motor (i.e. secretory and circulatory) discharge (*Abfuhr*) resulting in an (internal) alteration of the subject's own body without reference to the outer world, the motility (*Motilität*) in actions that are designed to effect changes in the outer world.

(Freud:1963, p. 128, footnote, trans. Modified)

The original English translation was misleading; it introduced a semi-colon after "outer world," as if the definition of "motility" was a gloss on the previous sentence. Freud opposes clearly "affectivity" and "motility." Whereas "affectivity" remains an inner process, "motility" causes subjective behavior, which results in actions in the world. This dichotomy is important: Freud's "affectivity" presupposes a chain of actions and reactions working thanks to a process of "discharge."

Freud has not changed one iota the theory he had launched in his juvenile "Project for a Scientific Psychology," a chapter which sketches the problem of the disturbance of thought because of affect. Freud illustrated this disturbance with a simple example. Being in an "agitation caused by great anxiety," he simply forgot to use the telephone that had recently been introduced in his house. He concludes:

The recently established path succumbed to the state of affect. The facilitation—that is to say, what was established of old—won the day. Such forgetting involves the *loss* of the power of selection, of efficiency and of logic, just as happens in dreams.

(1977, p. 414, trans. modified)

The affect is always too close to the drives, to what Freud calls "primary processes." But can it avoid repression? Freud states that "the affective process approximates to the uninhibited primary process," which means that "it is the business of the ego to permit no release of affect, since this would at the same time permit a primary process" (Freud:1977, p. 415). This mechanism can be explained with the analysis the "*proton pseudos*," the first lie and also the first logical mistake of hysteria: an original trauma has been forgotten but then is reactivated when a second shock, apparently banal and innocuous, has been triggered (see Freud:1977, pp. 410–414).

We gauge how complex, subtle, and ramified Freud's theory of affects can be; it is also rich in new insights. Examples of this startling freshness appear in the analysis of affects in dreams from *The Interpretation of Dreams*. As Freud assures, the agency of repression is felt when one notices a sudden transformation of affect, be it from pleasure to unpleasure, from enjoyment to disgust, or from laughter to tears (Freud:1965, p. 643). In the last case, it happens that primary modes of reasoning are inhibited; this produces a comic relief as a main effect, for there is "a surplus of energy which has to be discharged in *laughter, if we allow these modes of thinking to force their way into consciousness*" (Freud:1965, p. 644). An example of this reversibility, a process that underpins the entire "joke-work," is provided by a dream Freud borrows from his friend Sandor Ferenczi.

Here is the dream. An elderly man woke up his wife at night: he was laughing profusely in his sleep. He explained that, in his dream, an unknown guest had entered the bedroom. The dreamer could not help laughing because he could see that his wife was still in a transparent nightshift in front of a total stranger. The dreamer, actually Ferenczi himself, surmised that the stranger represented Death. He, as an elderly man, was laughing in view of his imminent demise. What looked like bad tidings announcing his death was the fact that he had been impotent with his wife an hour before. The dream had transformed the terror of death into its exact opposite, sheer laughter (Freud:1965, p. 510). In half a page, Freud and Ferenczi treat us to a scene of slapstick shifting into existential angst as in a Beckett play.

A survey of Freudian metapsychology shows the complexity and refinement of his insights on affect. However, against Green's relentless critique, the same survey proves that Lacan was not wrong when he stated that he was a Freudian from beginning to end. Green contents himself with stating that the analysis of affect in the case of Emma, the young hysteric who had provided Freud with the theory of the *proton pseudos* just mentioned "would merit a whole study to herself"(Green:1999, p. 27). If we accept the reproach that Lacan replaced the process leading from "repressed ideas" to "repressed affects" with linguistic manifestations inscribed in key signifiers, we have to make sense of how Lacan posits the concept of the signifier in his general theory, and how he discovered its role in another theoretician's work on affects.

3.2 Sartre's signifier and signified

It may come as a surprise that the author who paved the way for Lacan's concept of the signifier, a term that offered him a privileged mode of access to affects, was not Ferdinand de Saussure but Jean-Paul Sartre. Sartre's early *Sketch of a Theory of Emotions* stages a confrontation between existential phenomenology and psychoanalysis. Sartre begins by explaining that his idea runs parallel to the program developed by Ludwig Binswanger, a thinker who later interested Michel Foucault. Foucault's first published work, "Dream, Imagination and Existence" (1954) was an introduction to Binswanger's existential psychiatry. Binswanger published his essay in 1930, just a few years before Sartre and Lacan came upon the scene. Here, one sees how Sartre discloses the origin of his rejection of the Freudian Unconscious, a recurring theme of *Being and Nothingness* (1943). Already then, Sartre deemed the Unconscious to be incompatible with a philosophy founded upon consciousness, even as he planned to launch an "existential psychoanalysis."

Sartre treats emotions as bodily affections that come to us from the outside. He quotes Charcot's disciple Pierre Janet and psychoanalysts like Wilhelm Stekel and Alfred Adler, and mentions Henri Wallon, the child psychologist who analyzed the "mirror stage" in 1931, providing Lacan with his first major handle on psychoanalysis. Lacan made a lot of the "mirror stage" in 1936, two years before Sartre wrote about emotions. Lacan found in this psychological moment determining for a child's identity the roots of his critique of the ego considered as a stable entity: the ego is only a visual projection, a mirage, a construction—"psychology" cannot provide a philosophical foundation.

Sartre examines cases of paradoxical behavior like the clumsy book thief who wanted to be caught in order to be punished (this was a symptom displayed by Jean Genet, thief and writer, who became a friend of Sartre). Sartre also discusses phobias. What is key is that in his investigation of affects, Sartre hits upon a loaded couple of terms, the binary of signifier and signified. This occurs in a discussion of psychoanalysis whose main position is rejected. Sartre identifies the dominant feature of psychoanalysis as providing interpretations of conscious phenomena all read as symbolic realizations of an unconscious desire, a desire that has been repressed by censorship. Such a desire only exists in our consciousness as an emotion, whether it manifests itself as a conscious wish or as a more obscure phobia. Psychoanalysis cannot but see things in this way, otherwise it would have to admit of the concept of "bad faith," a notion that psychoanalysis cannot allow. Sartre develops this:

> If it was otherwise and if we had some consciousness, *even implicit*, of our true desire, we would be in *bad faith*, and the psychoanalyst will not accept this. The consequence is that the signification of our conscious behaviour is entirely exterior to this very behaviour, or, if one prefers, that the *signified* is entirely cut off from the *signifier*.
>
> (Sartre:2010, p. 35)

Sartre means that only the psychoanalyst knows what truly motivates the subject. The behavior being totally unconscious, no subjective consciousness can relate the signifier (for instance, a symptom like sudden and inexplicable clumsiness in the moment one steals) to the signified (the wish to be punished stemming from the Oedipal root hidden from sight). Sartre expands the analysis in *Being and Nothingness* when he discusses "bad faith," a phrase in which he describes subjects as half-conscious of their lies and essential duplicity. Fundamentally, Sartre rejects the idea of the Unconscious as a "knowledge that is ignorant of itself" (Sartre:1993, p. 53). But then *Being and Nothingness* refers several times to the Stoician theory of language: it holds that language provides a *lekton*, which means a "sayable" sentence; the *lekton* will be split between a material side, the signifier, and the content or signified. Sartre knew Emile Bréhier's *La théorie des incorporels dans l'ancien Stoïcisme* in which the philosopher had several chapters on the "theory of the expressible" explained via the contrast between a *lekton*, the signifier and the signified (Bréhier:1908, pp. 14–33). The binary signifier/signified had been at the same time by Ferdinand de Saussure from whom Lacan borrowed it. De Saussure's famous *Course in General Linguistics* had been published posthumously by his students and foregrounded the double concept of signifier and signified to define the sign in general, thus launching semiotics (see Saussure:1959, pp. 68–69). Nevertheless, before he encountered structuralism in linguistics, Lacan had read Sartre's little book, which made him aware of the signifier/signified binary, even if Sartre mentions just to refute the binary in the name of an undivided act of signification.

In his summary of psychoanalytic technique, Sartre highlights the practice of deciphering: "The behavior of the subject is in itself what it is (if we call 'in itself' what it is *for itself*), but it is possible to decipher it by appropriate techniques, as one deciphers a written language" (Sartre:2010, p. 35). The Hegelian language used here generates a theory of signs that owes more to the Stoicians or Augustine's disquisitions than to the 1916 publication of de Saussure's notes on general linguistic, as the next sentence proves: "In a word, the conscious fact is for the signified as a thing is to some event, provided the thing be the *effect* of this event; for instance as traces of a fire lit in a mountain for those who have made the fire" (Sartre:2010, p. 35). The link is in both cases an external or causal link; the traces are passive remainders, and a consciousness deprived of the basic techniques needed to make a fire would not perceive these traces as signs.

Sartre understands that the exteriority of the signifier can be compared to a "thing" whose effect is understood through its production. His logic follows a circular pattern: consciousness cannot constitute itself as signification without being conscious of the signification it constitutes (ETE, p. 36).

In fact, Sartre was entirely correct in thinking that psychoanalysis splits the subject at the level of the sign, and that censorship or repression render the whole signification unavailable for the subject. This same split will be enhanced when Lacan decides to materialize it in the bar that separates signifier from signified, as we see in "The Instance of the Letter in the Unconscious" when Lacan rewrites Saussure's algorithm as

$$\frac{S}{s}$$

with the uppercase S above as the signifier, and the lowercase s underneath as the signified. The placing is revealing: the signifier dominates, and the bar allows for a constant sliding both of significations and of shifting signifiers caught in their very opacity or ambiguity. Lacan elaborates by describing the impact of the signifier on the signified as divided by the central bar, glossing the formulae in those terms: "The sign – placed in () manifests here the maintenance of the bar – which, in the first algorithm, denotes the irreducible nature of the resistance of signification as constituted in the relation between signifier and signified" (Lacan:2006, p. 428). For Lacan, the discovery of the signifier/signified binary ushered in an awareness of a double split: a split in the sign, whose signification was never conveyed whole, and a split in the subject, a concept he would often credit to the later Freud whose unfinished paper on the "Splitting of the Ego" became a recurrent reference (see Miller in Lacan:2006, p. 855).

Sartre was the first to point the complex nature of psychoanalytic signification, a deciphering entailing that the signs contained in psychoanalytical affects, split between signifier and signified, will never be available to the subject's consciousness. They require another person, an Other as he puts it, to read them. This leads to Sartre's main objection: the contradiction between the "in itself" and the "for itself" in the subject's *cogito* can never be solved, for whenever one finds a *cogito*, consciousness is forced to create all the signification. Sartre glimpses the problem of psychoanalytic doctrine, formalizes it, and rejects it all at once. Indeed, if one accepts the dichotomy between external signifier and internal signifiers, the affects that then appear determined from the outside are mere "things."

Lacan read these pages, we can imagine, with a mixture of interest and distaste. The hinge between signifier and signified, a conceptual couple that he deployed in the 1950s also points to a residual thingness of affects. Of course, for Sartre, the notion of "thingness" was entirely negative: the term conveyed passivity, opacity, alienation, a nausea generated by the sense of being glued to objects, an abandonment of the dynamics of the signifying activity of consciousness. In 1938, Sartre believed in a Cartesian cogito, and chose Husserl's reactivation of Cartesian intentionality over Heidegger's more suggestive examination of the affects spelling out fundamental modalities of the *Dasein*'s presence in the world. For Sartre's voluntarist drift, consciousness decides to make itself "moved" by the agency of purely internal significations. Only a phenomenological description will overcome the apparent contradiction between activity and passivity, a recurrent theme in theories of affects. Any emotion will be thus understood as a "transformation of the world" even if this generates a behavior that implies a loss of consciousness, as when I faint (Sartre:1993, pp. 45–46).

The theme of emotions allows Sartre to link his fundamental Cartesian rationalism with Heidegger's analysis of "Being-in-the-World," a term mentioned on the very last page of the book. Heidegger analyzed the mode of existence of consciousness and saw "care" (*Sorge*) as an opening to the truth that we are all destined to die. Emotion is thus a "structure of consciousness" that signifies something for my psychic life but cannot be understood in a deterministic system like that of psychoanalysis. For Sartre, human reality entails the power to make a world: one makes emotions that shape the whole universe, in a facticity that dispels any passivity. As Lacan quipped, what distinguishes Sartre in his brilliant, suggestive, but misleading descriptions, is his "wonderful talent for sidetracking" (Lacan:2014, p. 184).

Like Sartre, Lacan has read Heidegger closely, as we have seen. It is, therefore, surprising to see the Seminar on Anxiety pay little homage to Heidegger. Lacan barely mentions *Angst* (anxiety) and *Sorge* (care). As Soler notes, it is to Kierkegaard that he looks to develop a philosophical analysis of anxiety. However, anxiety provides a key symptom. As Lacan repeats, it is the only affect that does not lie. Anxiety is accompanied by recognizable bodily manifestations, it can be measured by heartbeats, blood pressure, sweats, etc. Freud opposed anxiety to fear because he believed that fear had an object, whereas anxiety appeared deprived of objects and was triggered by vague, diffuse, or abstract sources of worry like the fear of dying. Lacan inverted this idea when he argued that anxiety was the affect that "never deceives." Anxiety has an object: this object is lack, the paradigm of all a-symbolizable objects. "Affect" subsumes all emotions and passions; it relates them to the Other, to the Unconscious structured like a language, and remains caught up between the body, the signifiers and the drives.

3.3 From anxiety to Spinoza's affectus

In fact, the reference to Heidegger in Lacan's seminar on Anxiety tends to be replaced by a meditation on the poetry of T. S. Eliot. Lacan quotes twice *The Waste Land*, a poem that he had begun to translate into French during the World War II. The insight that Lacan finds deployed in the poem is the suggestion of an excessive female jouissance that triggers a discrepancy between desire and enjoyment. Tiresias, called "the patron saint of psychoanalysis" (Lacan:2014, p. 183), had been struck blind by the gods for having revealed that women know a higher degree of *voluptas* than men. Tiresias knew this because he had been changed into a woman, and then back into a man, which gave him an awareness of the superiority of feminine orgasms.

Eliot famously attributed to Tiresias the ability, despite his blindness, of seeing what constitutes "the substance of the poem." It is clear that this substance refers to sexual jouissance insofar as it is unevenly distributed between men and women. If there is an excess on the side of women, it is because there is a limitation put to male jouissance by castration. Here lies the ultimate cause of anxiety both for Freud and Lacan, but with a different twist in Lacan's elaboration. Freud assumed that anxiety was mostly male and derived from fears that the penis might be cut or maimed; such a fear is repressed and returns without having specific objects, which sketches a genesis for the phenomenon of anxiety. On the contrary, Lacan asserts that anxiety has an object: it is caused by being too close to the main object, which is the phallus, or the symbol of castration.

This would remain very abstract without illustrations. Lacan provides one by revisiting *The Waste Land*. He focuses on the "young man carbuncular" who has sex with a consenting but bored typist while Tiresias watches the scene. Lacan comments on the debasement of love-making that stains the whole of sexuality; sex is here reduced to an automatic and unsatisfactory action. This leads to formulations that anticipate the later maxim that "There is no sexual rapport": "Man's jouissance and woman's jouissance will never conjoin organically. (…) It is because the phallus doesn't achieve any matching of the desires, save in its evanescence, that it becomes the common-place of anxiety" (Lacan:2014, p. 265).

The Waste Land formalizes a sexual paradox: on the one hand, women enjoy sex much more than men; on the other hand, the lack of complementarity forces them to offer their partners an object hidden behind the phallic claim. This is the non-detumescent object capable of sustaining desire—a purely imaginary phallus. In Eliot's poem, the young woman is glad that the abortive sexual romp is over; music from a record helps her recover from a sexual fiasco. Meanwhile, the young man carbuncular slips away, having kept his illusion of a sexual triumph. The meaning of this scene is left for Tiresias to ponder, that is, to the psychoanalyst who meditates on all that one has had to endure or "foresuffer" in the pornographic dramas enacted by the others. Suffice it to say at this point that when affects are debased in such sordid travesties, love appears as a cheap poultice thrown on an open wound. This can be taken to characterize the dominant mood of modern times— times more illustrated by affects such as boredom and moroseness than by existential angst. By contrast, anxiety keeps a positive function. It even has a decisive role to play facing cheap farces of contemporary sexuality reduced to tendering mutual services with or without payment; only anxiety can open up the hole of truth. Anxiety subverts the weak consensus through which partners attempt to breach the gap in sexuality, and it is thus the indispensable counterpart of love.

Soler's book surveys other Lacanian affects like shame, moroseness, and boredom; pride of place is given to the couple love/hate deemed to express a complementarity. To this old couple, Lacan adds the passion for ignorance—our repeated attempt to deny the workings of the Unconscious, a passion that no doubt animated Sartre in his proliferating writings. One affect that is introduced rather weirdly by Lacan is shame that is introduced at the end of the Seminar *The Other Side of Psychoanalysis* in June 1970. Starting with the idea that some people can die of shame, Lacan linked that affect with the master signifier, death. Reversing Heidegger's notion that considerations of death should make us more authentic, Lacan argues that shame can be triggered if we perceive our lives as deprived of any cause for which it is worth to die (Lacan:2006, pp. 180–183). The context was political: Lacan addressed leftist students marked by the "events" of May 1968, who, after having overcome their revolutionary shock, returned to cynical modes of enjoyment, avoided taking risks, and renounced aiming at higher stakes. A revolt against their masters had just led them to wish to have new masters. Punning on the word *"honte"* (shame), Lacan tells the Vincennes students that they are stuck in their "shameontology" (*hontologie*). Already, Darwin had tried to pinpoint the uniquely human affect, the expression of shame. Darwin's book on the expression of emotions in humans and animals showed that there were parallels in expressions of affects such as anxiety, dejection, despair, anger, disgust, surprise, horror, and shame, with emotional expression in human and animals. Only one of these affects presents an exception: Darwin concludes that blushing is a uniquely human affect. His chapter on blushing, an affective or pathetic manifestation apparent even among blind people or subjects who cannot perceive the others' gaze, brings grist to Lacan's mill (Darwin:1965, pp. 309–346).

This moment corresponds to the increasingly ethical turn in Lacan's thought. It was exemplified pointedly in his television interview from 1973. Lacan responded to the usual objection that he had privileged the signifier and forgotten the body. As he responds pointedly, going back to a long tradition beginning with Aristotle and moving to Aquinas, Dante, and Spinoza, ending with Freud. Affects are generated by specific interactions between the body and the mind. The discharge of adrenaline generating unbearable anxiety is produced more by thought than by the functions of the body. However, thought is not just language, it includes what used to be called the "soul," or more precisely "the passions of the soul," as Aquinas thought (Lacan:1990, p. 21). The "passions of the soul" inherited their nomenclature from the hierarchy of human activities as Plato had shown in the *Republic* when he divided the soul according to three main functions, *nous* (the mind), *thumos* (spiritedness, or the wish to make oneself glorious), and *epithumia* (appetite, all the bodily desires for food, drink, or sex). Lacan calls *epithumia* the "overheart" (Lacan:1990, p. 22). Plato knew that such a body was already caught up in a structure of language in which the body had been metaphorized.

Symptomatically, Lacan's performance on television was the occasion for a display of aggressive wit with repeated attacks against the International

Psychoanalytic Association ("Damned PIPAAD!" Lacan:1990, p. 15). In fact, this volley of insults, denunciations, and invectives undercuts the flow of each demonstration, rendering them tortuous and funny at once; entertaining as they are, these interspersed attacks against psychoanalytic institutions, also side-by-side with digs against well-meaning humanism ("the empty forms of humanhysterianism," see Lacan:1990, p. 33) and the discourse of capitalism (Lacan:1990, p. 16) result in the creation of an even more opaque prose. The teaching itself almost disappears, but an irritated levity dominates. Having proposed the saint as a role model for the psychoanalyst (and a saint is defined as being "abject," as embodying the refuse of jouissance, Lacan concludes: "The more saints, the more laughter; that's my principle, to wit, the way out of capitalist discourse—which will not constitute progress, if it happens only for some" (Lacan:1990, p. 16).

In *Television*, Lacan confesses that he has followed the lead of Aquinas who distinguished between irascible and concupiscent appetites in his nomenclature of the passions of the soul. What seems obvious is the relish with which Lacan displays his irascible appetite, which corresponds to Aquinas's original development from the analysis of justified and ethical anger in Aristotle's ethics. What are these irascible passions for Aquinas? Above all, they are ethical, thus generate change, which ensures that their dynamism will *affect* a given discourse, which is irascible passions work only on "difficult" objects. Here is how Aquinas defines them:

> ... all irascible passions imply movement towards something. Now this movement of the irascible faculty towards something may be due to two causes: one is the mere aptitude or proportion to the end; and this pertains to love or hatred, those whose object is good, or evil; and this belongs to sadness or joy. As a matter of fact, the presence of good produces no passion in the irascible, as stated above, but the presence of evil gives rise to the passion of anger.
>
> (Aquinas:2017)

Lacan's irascibility would be one manifestation of a general irritability, which entails a whole rhetoric of opprobrium, with in-jokes and political asides. Lacan's ethics includes irritability in the positive sense. What he attacks is a "sin" manifested in language first. Thus, he can distinguish between anxiety, a true affect, as we have seen, and mere sadness, also called "depression," adding that sadness should not be construed as "a state of the soul": sadness is rather a "moral failing" as Dante and Spinoza thought (Lacan:1990, p. 22). Lacan develops his analysis in those terms: sadness is "a sin, which means a moral weakness, which is, ultimately, located in relation to thought, that is, in the duty to be Well-spoken, to find one's way in dealing with the unconscious, with the structure" (Lacan:1990, p. 22) There is a Kantian tone here, as if there would be a *"devoir de bien dire,"* this "duty to be

Well-spoken," which suggests an imperative, a law of discourse, the effort to say things well—after all, this is often the result of a successful psychoanalysis. Without feeling that one can say everything, one is ready to tackle all subjects, even those that appear as the most unpleasant or annoying. Lacan refers to the Roman rhetorician Quintilian who extolled the ability to "speak well," an ability that defined a perfect gentleman. Book 12 of his *Institutio Oratoria* gave specific instruction to develop and facilitate the idea launched by Cato that a good man is a *"vir bonus, dicendi peritus"*: a "good man is man speaking well." This *bien dire* suggests the possibility of stating what is truly good. One ought to express oneself as best as one can, whether facing the most horrible or the most trivial incidents in one's life. At the end of the televised interview, Lacan replies to Jacques-Alain Miller who was mocking his convoluted style by recalling the motto of French classicism as voiced by the poet Boileau, "What is well conceived can be clearly stated." Lacan replies by inverting the formula: "What is well spoken, one conceives clearly," he states (Lacan:1990, p. 45).

Does this mean that the imperative of *bien dire* is sufficient to ward off depression and sadness? Echoing Dante's condemnation of the Sullen in Canto 7, Lacan then focuses on the "sin" of sadness. The sadness that Spinoza characterized as a diminution of our being is here equated with a despair facing language, or rather a lack of courage in applying language to what eludes us for being unconscious. Sadness would be the sin of human speakers who fail to use language to battle with their unconscious. It is not simply what a psychoanalytic cure entails; indeed, the whole effort of literature in its straining toward expression comes under this double injunction: to have the courage to say, and to obey the duty to say things as well as possible, even if everything appears as ill-seen and ill-said, as Beckett thought.

This analysis sends us back to the Spinozist beginnings of Lacan. Lacan's doctoral dissertation had as its epigraph a Latin quote from *Ethics*, book III, proposition 57: *"Quilibet uniuscuiusque individui affectus ab affectu alterius tantum discrepat, quantum essentia unius ab essentia alterius differt."* Only at the end of the dissertation did Lacan provide the expected translation or paraphrase: "Let us say, in order to express the very inspiration of our research, that 'any affect of any given individual differs from the affects of another as much as the essence of the one differs from the essence of the other'" (*Ethics*, III-57). He adds:

> By this we mean that the *determining conflicts, the intentional symptoms and the instinctual* (pulsionnelles) *reactions* of a psychosis differ from the *relations of comprehension* defining the development, the conceptual structures and the social tensions of the normal personality according to a measure determined by the *history* of the subject's affections.
>
> (Lacan:1975, pp. 342–343)

Roudinesco has highlighted the fact that Lacan did not translate the Latin *affectus* as *affect* in French, which would have been closer to Freud's *Affekt*, but chose *affection* instead (Roudinesco:1997, pp. 54–55). Lacan was using the 1906 French translation by Charles Appuhn. At the time, Appuhn believed that "affect" was a Germanism and not really a French word. It is true that a classical dictionary like the Littré, whose last version dates from 1877, does not have an entry for "*affect*," whereas one finds "*affecter*" and "*affection*." "*Affection*" is glossed as the manner in which the soul has been touched by an object. Should one conclude that Lacan was not truly Freudian in his dissertation? I have tried to argue that the dissertation evinces the influence of Freud, as we have seen in the chapter on his translation of Freud's essay. However, it is undeniable that Lacan's main philosophical reference is Spinoza, and one can state that Lacan's theory of affects is predicated on Spinoza's *Ethics*, even though we have seen him rely on Aristotle and Aquinas as well.

In *Ethics*, Spinoza adds the concept of desire to his analysis of affects. If all affects are related to desire, joy, or sadness, it is desire that spells out the specific essence of individuals: "[T]he desire of each individual differs from the desire of another as much as the nature, or essence, of the one differs from the essence of the other" (Spinoza:1966, p. 101). Desire, affect, and differential personal genealogies converge. Gilles Deleuze analyzed the logic of expression in Spinoza's *Ethics* and began by distinguishing between suffering, passion, feelings, affection, and affect (Deleuze:1990, pp. 218–221). Thus, the expression of affect is not just a Romantic privilege granted to any creator, whether divine or artistic.

Spinoza's concept of expression dovetails with his concept of infinity. It is from this exalted point of view of infinity that the two main affects in Spinoza's philosophy are named: joy, which occurs when our being is augmented, sadness, when our being is diminished. Spinoza's *Ethics* relies on the notion of infinity, which is ultimately predicated on the unity between Nature and the human soul. All in all, the references to Spinoza's *Ethics* throw a bridge between Lacan and Deleuze, too often seen as theoretical enemies. Perhaps because *Ethics* provides such a systematic theory of affects, Lacan does not try to do the same. There is no system of Lacanian affects, and when he quotes Dante, Augustine, Spinoza, Freud, Sartre, Heidegger, no principle of economy or exhaustivity dominates in his proliferating nomenclature. Lacan's point is not interested in creating a philosophical system, nor is he an "anti-philosopher." He would agree with Ralph Waldo Emerson and Nietzsche that the point of philosophy is to startle people and make them think. As Nietzsche wrote, quoting Emerson: "Diogenes said when someone praised a philosopher in his presence: How can he be considered great, since he has been a philosopher for so long and has never yet *disturbed* anybody? That could be the epitaph of university philosophy: it disturbed nobody" (Nietzsche:1983, p. 194). Lacan too fought against weak consensus and misleading equanimity. He meant to disturb and irritate, if only to try and lift repression, or at least feel that he could die without shame.

3.4 No psychology of irritation!

Freud gave us a precious hint when he stated that the key issue is to be able to understand the connection between affects and repression; here is the point overlooked by Sartre's theory of consciousness. For Freud, repression is the key to social interactions; affects are hard to pin down because they testify to our "*Unbehagen*" or our "malaise" in culture. Here is why a psychology of irritation always tricky. One of the writers who attempted to explore this blurry domain is Katherine Mansfield. We see this in a short story from 1919 appositely titled "Psychology" published in *Bliss and Other Stories*. In the tale, an omniscient narrator is privy to the thoughts of a young woman who is about thirty, has written plays, and is happily surprised by the unexpected visit of a male friend. He is a close friend, also a novelist. Although she is delighted to see him, she does not want to betray her sexual excitement and gains time by preparing tea fussily and elaborately. In fact, he too looks ready for something like sex. The narrator glosses their intimacy in these terms:

> For the special thrilling quality of their friendship was in their complete surrender. Like two open cities in the midst of some vast plain their two minds lay open to each other. (...) And the best of it was they were both of them old enough to enjoy their adventure to the full without any stupid emotional complication. Passion would have ruined everything; they quite saw that.

> (Mansfield:1919)

While they may have been lovers in the past, what stands out is that their intimacy is fragile because founded upon a rejection of affects, a downplaying of tender emotions. They feel "modern" and have overcome bourgeois sentimentality. They allow intimacy to grow but are uncertain of how far to go. The man praises the lovely cakes and tea, adding that he always remembers her studio's most minute details whenever he leaves her and returns home. Her studio makes him feel at home, and he has never experienced this elsewhere. In spite of these engaging remarks, their conversation lapses into silences that are broken when both start speaking at the same time, so they move on to safer topics and engage in a glib literary conversation: "Weren't they just a little too quick, too prompt with their replies, too ready to take each other up? Was this really anything more than a wonderfully good imitation of other occasions?" (Mansfield:1919)

Mansfield excels at evoking the growing disconnect between a slowly surging sexual tension, with echoes of primitivism, and the inane polite chatter that covers it over with pure social pretense:

His heart beat; her cheek burned and the stupid thing was she could not discover where exactly they were or what exactly was happening. She hadn't time to glance back. And just as she had got so far it happened again. They faltered, wavered, broke down, were silent. Again they were conscious of the boundless, questioning dark. Again, there they were— two hunters, bending over their fire, but hearing suddenly from the jungle beyond a shake of wind and a loud, questioning cry...

The narrator harps on the dichotomy between an immediate response to sexuality and the civilized repression predicated on genteel notions of propriety:

Why didn't they just give way to it—yield—and see what will happen then? But no. Vague and troubled though they were, they knew enough to realize their precious friendship was in danger. She was the one who would be destroyed—not they—and they'd be no party to that.

(Mansfield:1919)

Then the idle conversation surveys the current popularity of psychological novels, by which they actually mean recent novels that have been impacted by psychoanalysis. This is seen as a fad, and the woman objects to it while the man approves enthusiastically. The woman jests: "Do you mean you feel there's quite a chance that the mysterious non-existent creatures—the young writers of to-day—are trying simply to jump the psycho-analyst's claim?" He replies seriously:

Yes, I do. And I think it's because this generation is just wise enough to know that it is sick and to realize that its only chance of recovery is by going into its symptoms—making an exhaustive study of them—tracking them down—trying to get at the root of the trouble.

(Mansfield:1919)

She then complains that this fad is going to produce a "dismal" perspective on life. Moreover, she is aware that by becoming engrossed in a theoretical discussion of psychological novels, they move further away from the possibility of sexual intimacy. And if the man feels he has made his point, he appears bored by his own theories. She deplores the direction their conversation has taken: "... she saw him laboriously—oh, laboriously—laying out the grounds and herself running after, puffing here a tree and there a flowery shrub and here a handful of glittering fish in a pool. They were silent this time from sheer dismay" (Mansfield:1919).

Given the silence that engulfs them, the man tries to stop their spiraling social embarrassment, but cannot decide whether he should speak or stay silent. How to avoid reducing speech to an "ordinary maddening chatter"?

Eager to break away from this morass, the man blurts out that he must leave: he has forgotten an appointment, a lame and belated excuse. However, instead of insisting that he stay, the woman pushes him out even faster, although she resents his glad acquiescence. She is hurt by his aloofness, yet does not allow her heart to speak out. Her ambivalence is rendered by a series of contradictions: "'You've hurt me—hurt me,' said her heart. 'Why don't you go? No, don't go. Stay. No—go!' And she looked out upon the night" (Mansfield:1919).

Once she is alone, she curses herself and him. She feels stupid not to have managed to retain him. In a rage, she decides that all is over between them; she swears that she will never see him again. At this point, the doorbell rings. She opens the door, thinking her male friend has changed his mind and come back, but it is only a bothersome older woman who has a crush on her and whom she usually dismisses. This time, her arrival entails a remarkable change in her feelings. The friend brings a miserable bunch of wilted flowers; to thank her, the woman embraces the visitor. This sudden show of friendliness renders the visitor wild with joy. Finally, they part and say good night to each other. Her mood has now changed, and she writes a letter to the male visitor offering another opportunity and send him an invitation to visit again.

This story falls in line with explorations of female ambivalence by Mansfield, and can be compared with the title story, "Bliss." Inexplicable moments of bliss are experienced by a young woman even after she discovers that her husband is having an affair with a woman friend she has invited to her dinner because she herself felt an inclination to her. Mansfield was known for her bisexual affairs and her volcanic temper; however, this plot goes beyond the impact of psychoanalysis on literary "psychology" often considered as a hallmark of the Bloomsbury group (see Pero:2016, pp. 100–112).

What Mansfield explores with amazing skill is the link between mobile affects that change so often that they are hard to name, and repression, especially sexual repression, but all this happens under the cover of meaningless social chatter. They are in language and in the symbolic, but the symbolic functions like a machine producing endless chains of empty signifiers, even if the fashionable discourse hinges upon an acceptance or rejection of the then new vogue for psychoanalysis in London. Their quandary corresponds to a sense that it is impossible to name affects adequately, especially when they deal with sexuality and its inevitable social sublimation. Hence hate and love are not opposites but keep blending and recombining themselves.

In "Psychology," it is the arrival of a silly friend who "idolizes" the main character that provides an unexpected solution. The introduction of a third person who is not invested libidinally breaks the spell; the woman renounces her hasty decision to break up with the frustrating male friend. Then social and sexual games can be restarted, and the next visit might see a better outcome. The irony is contained in the title: after psychoanalysis, especially after a psychoanalysis of affect, no "psychology" is available. This suggests that there is no "science of psychology," only textual explorations of its uncertain and shifting domain. Mansfield has thus illustrated the relation between language and affects. Her characters say things that do not correspond to what they feel, and even when the narrator renders their thoughts, we verify that they do not express the truth of affects like sexual desire, boredom, irritation, anger, spite, and mutual recognition. Mansfield does not for all that renounce rendering affects in language: what she explores is the irritating resistance of signifiers that are never adequate either to corresponding chains of "signifieds" or to bodily desires that do not allow themselves to be fully named. The object of desire has little to do with the deployment of an affect for affects are released unconsciously, half-way between a desiring body and the chains of signifiers that may or may not signify much. A gap opens here, which points to the site of affects, especially when they are unleashed or excessively "irritated" because of frustration.

Psychology thrives when it exhibits a taxonomy of emotions, feelings, and passions but quickly meets its limits with affects because of their curious reversibility, which has to do with the omnipresence of repression. The very idea of irritation suggests that we need to move from the active sense (something irritates me) to a passive sense (I am irritated by something, but don't know why or even what). The object can be reduced to little, almost nothing—often I do not know why I am irritated, which renders naming the experience difficult. This insight was shared by Mansfield and Marcel Proust. Proust's early story, "Madame de Breyves's Melancholy Summer Vacation," originally published in 1893 in *La Revue Blanche*, will provide an example. The plot can be summed up quickly. Madame de Breyves, a beautiful widow who is still young because she lost her husband when she was twenty, goes to a party at the Princess of A. There, she catches sight of a man who interests her although she finds him neither attractive nor intelligent. They don't exchange a word. As she is about to leave, they meet in the hall for a few seconds. He whispers into her ear: "Come tonight to my place," slips a card with his address and leaves. She is offended and considers that abrupt invitation as ill-mannered and preposterous. Nevertheless, because this is so far from her usual behavior, she keeps thinking about the possibility and imagines what might have happened had she accepted. She gathers information about the young man, a musician called Jacques de Lalande. She cautiously invites him to play the cello for her, but he has left Paris. She multiplies attempts with intermediaries, all in vain. Because of its repeated failure, the quest becomes an obsession. What makes her investigation even more desperate is that she knows that de Lalande has no inkling that she is looking for him. This ends up generating a full-fledged passion founded on nothing, a "passion of the soul" that takes the form of an addiction. The last pages delve on the young woman's self-torture; she curses her mental faculties, her will, her imagination, her ingenuity. She blames her body and her libido, her absurdly irrepressible desires, everything that brought about an absurd passion. Here is the last long sentence:

> Lastly she cursed her mind in its godliest forms, the supreme gift that she had received and to which people, without finding its true name, have given all sorts of names—poet's intuition, believer's ecstasy, profound feelings of nature and music—which had placed infinite summits and horizons before her love, had let them bask in the supernatural light of her love's enchantment, and had, in exchange, lent her love a bit of its own enchantment, and which had won over to this love all its most sublime and most private inner life, bonding and blending with it, consecrating to it—as a church's collection of relics and ornaments is dedicated to the Madonna—all the most precious jewels of her heart and her mind, her heart whose sighs she heard in the evening or on the sea, and whose melancholy was now the sister of the pain inflicted on her by his total absence: she cursed that inexpressible sense of the mystery of things, which absorbs our minds in a radiance of beauty, the way the ocean engulfs the setting sun—for deepening her love, dematerializing it, broadening it, making it infinite without reducing its torture, "for" (as Baudelaire said when speaking about late afternoons in autumn) "there are sensations whose vagueness does not exclude intensity, and there is no sharper point than that of infinity."
>
> (Proust:2003, p. 78, and Proust:1971, p. 75)

This suggests that an affect like love for nothing can be generated by repressed desire, heightened by frustration, which then turn it into a "Thing." Frustrated desire becomes an infinite irritation; it festers like an uncured wound by exacerbating its negativity. Proust's long and winding sentence sends us toward another root for affects, especially negative affects like hate and jealousy, which signals that we must investigate the tortures of cruelty.

Bibliography

Aquinas, Thomas (2017) *The Summa Theologiæ of St. Thomas Aquinas.* Second and Revised Edition, 1920, Literally translated by Fathers of the English Dominican Province, Online Edition Copyright © 2017 by Kevin Knight, Question 25, Article 3, Objection 3. Home > Summa Theologiae > First Part of the Second Part

Bernays, Jacob (1857). *Grundzüge der verlorenen Abhandlung des Aristoteles über Wirkung der Tragödie,* Breslau, E. Trewendt, p. 135–200.

Bloom, Harold (1978). "Freud and the poetic sublime: a catastrophe theory of creativity," *Antaeus,* 30.3, p. 355–377.

Bréhier, Émile (1908). *La théorie des incorporels dans l'ancien Stoïcisme,* Paris, Vrin.

Darwin, Charles (1965). *The Expression of the Emotions in Man and Animals,* Chicago, The University of Chicago Press.

Deleuze, Gilles (1990). *Expressionism in Philosophy: Spinoza*, trans. Martin Joughin, New York, Zone.

Freud, Sigmund (1963). "The Unconscious," in *General Psychological Theory, Papers on Metapsychology*, ed. Philip Rieff, New York, Collier books, p. 116–150.

Freud, Sigmund (1965). *The Interpretation of Dreams*, trans. James Strachey, New York, Avon Books.

Freud, Sigmund (1977). *The Origins of Psychoanalysis*, trans. Eric Mosbacher and James Strachey, New York, Basic Books.

Freud, Sigmund (1982). "Das Unbewußte," *Psychologie des Unbewußten, Studienausgabe III*, Frankfurt, Fischer, p. 119–173.

Freud, Sigmund (1997a). "Psychopathic characters on the Stage," in *Writings on Art and Literature*, trans. James Strachey, Stanford, Stanford University Press, pp. 87–93.

Freud, Sigmund (1997b). "The Moses of Michelangelo," in *Writings on Art and Literature*, trans. James Strachey, Stanford, Stanford University Press, pp. 123–150.

Green, André (1999). *The Fabric of Affects in the Psychoanalytic Discourse*, trans. Alan Sheridan, New York, Routledge.

Lacan, Jacques (1975). *De la psychose paranoïaque dans ses rapports avec la personnalité*, Paris, Seuil.

Lacan, Jacques (1979). *The Four Fundamental Concepts of Psychoanalysis*, trans. Aslan Sheridan, London, Penguin.

Lacan, Jacques (1990). *Television*, trans. Denis Hollier, Rosalind Krauss, and Annette Michelson, New York, Norton.

Lacan, Jacques (1992). *The Seminar Book VII, The Ethics of Psychoanalysis*, trans. Dennis Porter, New York, Norton.

Lacan, Jacques (2006). *Ecrits*, trans. Bruce Fink, New York, Norton.

Lacan, Jacques (2014). *Anxiety, The Seminar Book X*, ed. Jacques-Alain Miller, trans. A. R. Price, Cambridge, Polity.

Laplanche, Jean (1981). *Problématiques IV, L'inconscient et le ça*, Paris, Presses Universitaires de France.

Mansfield, Kate (1919). *Bliss and other stories*. Unpaginated online version at www.katherinemansfieldsociety.org/assets/KM-Stories/PSYCHOLOGY1919.pdf

Miller, Jacques-Alain (2006). "Division, splitting and fading of the subject," *Index of Lacan*: 2006, p. 855.

Ngai, Sianne (2005). *Ugly Feelings*. Cambridge, Harvard University Press.

Nietzsche, Friedrich (1983). *Untimely Meditations*, trans. R. J. Hollingdale, Cambridge, Cambridge University Press.

Pero, Alan, (2016) "'Jigging away into nothingness': Knowledge, Language and Feminine *Jouissance* in "Bliss" and "Psychology," in *Katherine Mansfield and Psychology*, ed. Clare Hanson, Gerri Kimber and Todd Martin, Edinburgh, Edinburgh University Press, 2016, p. 100–112.

Proust, Marcel (1971). *Jean Santeuil, précédé de Les Plaisirs et les Jours*, ed. Pierre Clarac and Yves Sandre, Paris, Gallimard, Pléiade.

Proust, Marcel (2003). *Pleasures and Days*, trans. Joachim Neugroschel, New York, Cooper Square Press.

Rabaté, Jean-Michel (2007). *Given 1° Art 2° Crime: Modernity, Murder and Mass Culture*, Brighton, Sussex Academic Press.

Roger, Alain (1985). *Hérésies du Désir: Freud, Dracula, Dali*, Seyssel, Champ Vallon.

Roudinesco, Elisabeth (1997). *Jacques Lacan*, trans. Barbara Bray, New York, Columbia University Press.

Sartre, Jean-Paul (1993). *Being and Nothingness*, trans. Hazel E. Barnes, New York, Washington Square Press.

Sartre, Jean-Paul (2010). *Esquisse d'une théorie des émotions*, Paris, Hermann.

Saussure, Ferdinand de (1959). *Course in General Linguistics*, trans. Wade Baskin, New York, McGraw-Hill.

Soler, Colette (2016). *Lacanian Affects: The Function of affect in Lacan's work*, trans. Bruce Fink, New York, Routledge.

Spinoza, Benedict de (1966). *Ethics*, trans. Edwin Curely, London, Penguin.

Trigg, Dylan (2014). *The Thing: A phenomenology of Horror*, Winchester, Zero Books.

Viereck, Georg, n.d. Interview with Freud. Online Psychanalyse-lu An Interview with Freud

Chapter 4

Cruor, or the cruel fiction of psychoanalysis

In a searching essay on psychoanalysis, Derrida asserts that the most important problem psychoanalysis has encountered as a discourse and a clinical praxis but failed to comprehend, rationalize, or treat is the persistence of cruelty in human being (Derrida:2002, pp. 238–240). It is true that, alas, cruelty exists, insists, and resists, which presents unsurmountable problems for Freud, and beyond, to Lacan. Cruelty evokes the idea of aggression along with the pleasure some find in pain. I will address Derrida's question by combining the insights of Jean-Luc Nancy, whose book *Cruor* (Nancy:2021) he completed just before he died in 2021, and of a psychoanalyst, Touria Mignotte, who tackles the complex concept of cruelty in *Cruelty, Sexuality, and the Unconscious in Psychoanalysis* (Mignotte:2020). Both deploy a notion of cruelty that is not cultural but psychoanalytical. By cultural cruelty, I refer to current worries about violence, horror, and mass murders. This is the domain explored by Maggie Nelson in her 2011 bestseller *The Art of Cruelty* (Nelson:2011). Nelson eloquently surveys the proliferating manifestations of cruelty, highlights the wanton displays of violence in media, literature, and the arts. Among these, Marquis de Sade's *120 Days of Sodom* and *Salò,* the filmic equivalent produced by Pier Paolo Pasolini in 1975, have kept their power to shock us. They repulse and fascinate.

More recently, the radical Swiss artist Thomas Hirschhorn has critiqued the display of perverse attitude in "De-Pixelation," a show exhibited at New York Gladstone Gallery from October 2017 to January 2018. He covers the walls with huge billboards showing montages of bloody images taken from recent conflicts, but here the dead bodies ripped apart are spliced with publicity images, which has a startling effect on the viewer. Both Maggie Nelson and Thomas Hirschhorn force readers, viewers, consumers to adopt a critical position, discovering ethical stakes facing the society of cruel spectacles in which we live. Mignotte has decided not to tackle these issues directly although she was aware of what has been invested in them, because she situates her approach at a foundational level within the discourse of psychoanalysis. I will sketch the theoretical context of her approach by comparing it

DOI: 10.4324/9781032715834-5

with Derrida's argument about psychoanalysis. Some points of convergence in their approaches include readings of Freud, Nietzsche, and Hegel. I will mention them before returning to the myth of Prometheus with which I had started; this time the tragic plot will be revisited by Freud and Kafka.

4.1 Cruelty and *Grausamkeit*

In July 2000, Derrida gave the opening lecture for the Paris *Etats généraux de la psychanalyse*. René Major, the main convener, had invited psychoanalysts and intellectuals from all parts of the world to assess the situation of psychoanalysis and offer predictions for the future by outlining new orientations. Speaking in the main amphitheater of the Sorbonne to some 1,200 psychoanalysts and academics, Derrida took stock of a particular political situation but also began by stating a personal complaint: he himself was in pain and suffering from cancer. Major had planned a conference that would call up the historical moment when the "estates-general" were convoked by Louis XVI, which led to the French Revolution. In June 1789, there was a split between the third estate made up of bourgeois and commoners and the representatives of the clergy and nobility. The third estate refused to associate with them and created a National Assembly. If this ushered in the French Revolution, no revolution was generated by the discussions held from July 8 to July 11, 2000. No common resolution led to a common program viable for a new century for division reigned. Tensions cropped up between various groups, nationalities, and specialties. It was in this fractious and contentious context that Derrida decided to focus on two terms that he linked, *sovereignty* and *cruelty*. He alluded to the French Revolution, wondering who could play the role of the king in such an assembly (Derrida:2002, pp. 246 and 248). Would that be Freud, or perhaps Lacan? Who would want to be the new Freud? Derrida went back to the etymology of cruelty, which derives from blood, and tried to engage with a broader psychic cruelty, asking: "Would such cruelty, if there is any and if it is properly psychical, be one of the horizons most proper to psychoanalysis?" (Derrida:2002, p. 239). Derrida then quoted the old Jewish joke: in order to become a psychoanalyst, one has to be a Jewish surgeon who cannot stand the sight of blood (Derrida:2002, p. 239).

At the time, Derrida was giving seminars on the death penalty, taking his point of departure in the Eighth Amendment to the United States Constitution that prohibits the infliction of "cruel and unusual punishments." That prevents the government from imposing penalties deemed either barbaric or too severe for the crimes committed. It has been operative in cases when the method used, like the electric chair, seemed to torture the sentenced person rather than kill efficiently. Derrida asks pointedly: have we avoided cruelty by choosing faster and more efficient ways of killing? He considers at some length the rhetoric of the "painless" severing of the neck that accompanied the invention and use of the guillotine. At a theoretical level, Derrida noted that by shifting from the Latin *cruor* to Freud's *Grausamkeit*, we move from a bloody cruelty to a bloodless cruelty, an echolalic *"sans sang"* in French. Pushing on, he asserted that it is not by replacing the bloody decapitation of the guillotine by a jolt from the electric chair, a lethal injection, or the gas chamber, that one abolishes cruelty. Derrida insists in "Psychoanalysis Searches the States of Its Soul" that the end of bloody cruelty is not a sign of the end of cruelty but merely corresponds to a social modification of the codes and norms that affect the visibility of cruelty. An invisible cruelty can be as ethically reprehensible. In German, *grausam* keeps no association with blood, its etymology being closer to that of "gruesome" in English, namely whatever can create horror, fear, shudder.

Indeed, Freud's "Three Essays" unfolds a theory of cruelty that he states quite clearly:

> the history of human civilization shows beyond any doubt that there is an intimate connection between cruelty (*Grausamkeit*) and the sexual drive (*Sexualtrieb*); but nothing has been done towards explaining the connection, apart from laying emphasis on the aggressive factor in the libido.
>
> (3 VII, p. 159, modified)

Freud mentions authors who see relics of cannibalism in sexuality and those who stress the link between pain and pleasure, for "every pain contains in itself the possibility of a feeling of pleasure." Freud lists neurotic symptoms that include the active and passive forms of the drive to cruelty (*Trieb zur Grausamkeit*) (Freud:1953, SE/VII, p. 166, modified), adding that this would be the root of the transformation of love into hate that is so common in paranoia.

Cruelty appears early in children:

> the cruel component of the sexual drive develops in childhood even more independently of the sexual activities that are attached to erotogenic zones. Cruelty in general comes easily to the childish nature, since the obstacles that bring the drive to mastery (*Bemächtigungstrieb*) to a halt at another person's pain—namely a capacity for pity—is developed rather late.
>
> (Freud:1953 VII, pp. 192–93)

Freud links the drive to cruelty with a more intense erotogenic activity. He cautions educators against using corporal punishments that will be experienced as sources of perverse pleasure by the child. "Three Essays" provides Freud's foundation for his later insights, even if he introduced nuances in his analyses. In *Beyond the Pleasure Principle*, the main philosophical statement of his maturity, Freud still insists on the links between sadism and the death drive.

Gilles Deleuze has attempted to deconstruct the idea that sadism and masochism should be linked or appear as the two sides of one single coin. Deleuze questioned the reversibility posited by Freud between activity (sadism) and passivity (masochism) in "Coldness and Cruelty," his preface to Sacher-Masoch's *Venus in Furs* (Deleuze:1991). Deleuze reminds us of the key fact that for Freud, the main site of cruelty is not the drive but the super-ego. The main difference between Deleuze and Freud is that the former looks at the texts written by Sade and Sacher-Masoch, whereas the latter attempts to understand sadism and masochism as two forms of perversions. Hence, for Deleuze, there is no sado-masochism as an entity, although there is, of course, cruelty: it reigns half-way between the "apathy" that the Sadean libertines want to conquer through a multiplication of crimes, and the "coldness" that the Masochist hero will gain after his many humiliations.

Like Deleuze, Mignotte appeals to a principle of monism, pushing the issue in the direction of a conceptual unity that she calls "destruction." She alludes to Freud's treatment of the young Lanzer, nicknamed the "Ratman" because his main symptom was an obsession with a horrible torture of pushing a rat into a victim's anus. The "Ratman" was fascinated by the punishment that already appeared at the end of Sade's *120 Days of Sodom*. The young man had heard it during his military service, when a "cruel" officer narrated it and "obviously took pleasure in cruelty" (Freud:2002, p. 134). Freud tries to make the young man speak about the torture that horrifies him. Lanzer confesses that the torture entails rats boring their way into the victim's insides via the anus; then he almost faints. Freud notes: "At all the more significant moments of his narration a very strange compound expression is visible on his face, which I can only interpret as *horror at the pleasure he does not even know he feels*" (2002, p. 134). Freud witnesses here the excessive affect combining pain and pleasure that Lacan later called "jouissance." The excessive and unspeakable combination blends suffering and ecstasy in an unconscious manner, which creates the apparent paradox of a feeling one is not aware of. However, the real or metaphorical pain inflicted by the rat in the anus is less destructive than the cruelty of the super-ego, which is why poor Lanzer feels obliged to keep on paying for a debt that he already paid.

What Lanzer brought to Freud was a notion that exceeded the economic logic that he had been relying on. It is the curious logic of jouissance, an excess that suddenly shifts from the plus to the minus, and as we have seen intuited earlier by Sabina Spielrein. Lacan reminds us that it was only later that Freud understood this. In *Civilization and Its Discontents*, jouissance appeared in all its dimensions of negativity and evil. There is an enjoyment making others suffer; this brings back the issue of cruelty, or "man's innate tendencies to 'evil, aggression, destruction, and thus also to cruelty'" (Freud quoted by Lacan:1992, p. 185). In a famous passage of *Civilization and Its Discontents*, Freud mentions that there are many human beings who will take pleasure in humiliating, torturing, or killing other people. Lacan quips that this passage seems to come from Marquis de Sade's writings. Jouissance is closer to evil than to good, which will lead to a well-known parallel between Kant and Sade that I will explore in a later chapter.

Cruelty would be the stumbling stone for all ethics, Lacan argues by reading Sade and Kant side by side: the very existence of an innate cruelty in humans destroys the belief in reciprocity which is the foundation of humanitarian rules of non-aggression. If we discard both the pleasure principle and the morality principle, then we will need to appeal to a more archaic and foundational substance. Mignotte's and Nancy's suggestion is that we dig deeper and tackle the issue of the substance before examining its containers. As Lacan repeated in the 1970s, the only substance known to psychoanalysis is jouissance, but I would like to suggest that it has to confront itself to another physiological substance, namely blood.

4.2 Is there a future for blood?

Here is the question posed by Derrida (Derrida:2017, p. 219). To examine the substance bequeathed to us by the etymology of the word "cruelty," which means looking at the meaning of blood, which goes from representations of the friend and the enemy to images of racist discrimination. The Latin language introduces an important distinction between *sanguis* and *cruor*. *Cruor*, closer to "gore," signifies blood seen flowing from a wound, and thus one can distinguish the "crude" (the Latin *crudus* comes from *crūrus* in Indo-European, linked with kruhrós, from krewth, meaning "raw meat, fresh blood") from the "raw" and the "cruel." Freud understood the mechanism of psychical cruelty, the pleasure taken in making someone else or oneself suffer, or otherwise by watching suffering, as a pleasure born from our bodies and their cycles. Nancy insists on a third term, *menstruum*, which is neither *sanguis* nor *cruor*, and refers to menstrual blood. In alchemy, it was reputed to have dissolving properties. As Nancy puts it: "There is the blood that nourishes life, the blood that leaves it, and the blood that gives it or retains and holds it back" (Nancy:2023, p. 9). Fundamentally, blood is linked with the drives and with the rhythm of Nature.

How to make *sense* of blood as such? We can begin by looking at Hegel's *Philosophy of Nature*, the most systematic attempt at providing a philosophical theory of blood that links elements of natural life and the concept or "Spirit." Hegel sees Nature as a huge body in which dissolution is never negative; it is more a relay leading to further productions and reproductions. In a ground-breaking book on Hegel (Semm:1994), Markus Semm has observed that the deployment of the Spirit in Nature adopts a general rhythm and follows the tempo of a vital pulse. Rhythmic exchanges are underpinned by a pulsation that runs through all phenomena. The pulsating beat enacting regenerative negativity finds a double exemplification in breathing and in the circuit of blood:

This dissolution of this persistence is the pulmonary system, the true, ideal process with the outer world of inorganic Nature, with the element of air; it is the organism's own self-movement which, as elasticity, draws air and expels it. The blood is the result, the organism which through its own interior process returns into itself, the living individuality which makes members (*Glieder*) into viscera.

(Hegel:1970, p. 366)

This vision leads Hegel to describe blood as an "axially rotating, self-pursuing movement," an "absolute interior vibration" before sketching its formation:

The blood elaborates itself from the air, the lymph, and the digestion, and is the transformation of these three moments. From the air, it takes pure dissolution, the light of the air, oxygen; from the lymph, the neutral fluid; from digestion, the moments of singularity, the substantial moment. And as thus the whole individuality, the blood opposes itself to itself afresh and generates shape.

(Hegel:1970, p. 367)

Blood combines dissolution, neutrality, and singularity, all three tied together in a unique substance. We follow successive transformations by which this substance ends up characterizing the individuality of the living subject. It is marked by a pulsation obeying a universal law. Blood thus allegorizes the logical progression of the Concept or Notion (*Begriff*): "The endless process of division and this suppression of division which leads to another division, all this is the immediate expression of the Notion which is, so to speak, here visible to the eye" (Hegel:1970, p. 368). The main factor that accounts for the rhythm of these successive negations is the essential "irritability" evinced by blood:

Blood in general, as the universal substance of every part, is the irritable (*irritable*) concentration of everything into the interior unity: it is heat, this transformation of cohesion and specific gravity—but not merely the dissolution produced by heat but the real, animal dissolution of everything. Just as all food is converted into blood, so, too, blood is dispensed as the source from which everything takes its nutriment. That is what pulsation (*Pulsieren*) is in complete reality.

(Hegel:1970, p. 368)

The picture of blood drawn by Hegel, a life cycle repeating itself to constitute a *perpetuum mobile*, entails that blood, not the heart pumping it, is the agent of the dynamic process. The heart is just a muscle that pumps, thus a material cause, whereas blood allegorizes the dynamism of life itself: "This is the blood, the subject, which no less than the will initiates a movement. As the whole movement, the blood is the ground and the movement itself" (Hegel:1970, p. 369). Hegel notes that if an invalid remains immobile for too long, he develops ankylosis; this banal example leads to a discussion of the difference between arterial blood, redder because it contains more oxygen, and venous blood, bluish because it contains carbon. A section devoted to breathing discovers the rationale for the endless movement: it deploys the term that Hegel had found in Albrecht von Haller, this same "irritability." Blood is "irritable" in itself, there is no other cause for its dialectical mobility. Hegel rejects theories that reduced the workings of the heart to a mechanical force:

> From whence comes this elastic pressure of the walls and the heart? "From the irritation (*Reiz*) of the blood" they reply. According to this, therefore, the heart moves the blood, and the movement of the blood is, in turn, what moves the heart. But this is a circle, a *perpetuum mobile*, which would necessarily at once come to standstill because the forces are in equilibrium. But, on the contrary, this is precisely why the blood must be regarded as itself the principle of the movement; it is the "leaping point" (*punctum saliens*), in virtue of which the contraction of the arteries coincides with the relaxation of the ventricles of the heart.
>
> (Hegel:1970, p. 369)

In 1628 Harvey discovered the mechanism of the circulation of the blood in animal bodies. In *De motu Cordis et Sanguinis in Animalibus (Of the movement of the heart and blood of animals)*, Harvey described the heart of an embryo as a *"punctum sanguinem saliens,"* a tiny pulsating point, the first spot in which can one recognize that a heart begins to beat. It is also a point of fire, a notion that was important for Freud as we will see, an *ignis scintillula*. Refusing to ascribe the cause of blood circulation to a reflex action, which would lead to an endless hen-and-egg exploration (the heart cannot beat without blood but blood needs the heart to circulate: here would be an argument *ad infinitum*), Hegel concluded that the "self-movement of blood" was the cause of the organic life cycle, which makes blood literally turn into the "subject": blood has a will of its own, a will that initiates and regulates the movement of the whole, as Semm has shown so well (Semm:1994, pp. 17–47).

Following Harvey, Francis Glisson introduced the concept of "irritability" in 1650 when analyzing psychosomatic diseases. His *De Natura Substantiae Energetica* (1672) describes a natural energy going through the body. This blind energy called "irritability" differentiates itself into sensations. "Irritable" reactions of organs like the intestines or the heart derive from their ability to be excited, which then causes bodily actions. Glisson general-ized the idea and included the whole living dynamism in a *"biousia"* that would explain why substance of bodies react to stimuli without requiring any mind, consciousness, or sensation. This notion reappears today when we speak of "irritable bowel syndromes" or when we go back to manifestations of classical hysteria.

One century later, the Swiss physician Albrecht von Haller took up the concept in his 1752 "Dissertation on the sensible and irritable parts of Animals." Trying to refute the materialist suggestion of a blind force animat-ing all living substances, Haller distinguished sensation and irritability. Sensation belonged to the nerves, irritability to the muscles. When he observed links between blood and the heart, Haller restricted the idea of irritability to the muscle of the heart; for him, the heart was first "irritated" by an influx of blood, and then responded with its systolic contractions. In his *Philosophy of Nature*, Hegel criticizes Haller: Haller fell into the trap of an *ad infinitum* causal reasoning. If irritability is *"Reiz,"* it is a stimulus that aims at evoking a response. Indeed, Haller had mentioned that there was a *Reitzleitung*, the "conduction of impulses" but Hegel pays attention to the fact that the word *Reiz* in German suggested the meanings of "appeal," "charm," "attraction," "excitement," and "stimulation." Thanks to that long semantic series, irrita-bility served to usher in the principle of subjectivity: for Hegel, it is the sub-ject who will display the same endless negativity that was seen working through blood. Let us follow this ground-breaking analysis in more details.

According to Hegel's reconstruction of biological cycles, in the human body one can say that the negativity of a blood that is like a fire will turn into thirst, hunger, and desire. Indeed, the same principle applies to the process of breath-ing: "The respiratory process is a spontaneously interrupted continuity. Exhalation and inhalation are a volatization (*Verdunsten*) of the blood, a vol-atizing irritability (*verdunste Irritabilität*)" (Hegel:1970, p. 392). The opera-tion of the lungs resembles the spontaneous mechanism of the heart and one can link this movement with the circulation of the blood. Hegel writes:

> Now why is the blood connected with this ideal assimilation of the abstract Element? The blood is this absolute thirst (*absolute Durst*), its unrest (*Unruhe*) within itself and against itself; the blood craves to be ignited (*hat Hunger nach Befeurung*), to be differentiated. More exactly, this assimila-tion is at the same time a mediated process with air, namely a conversion of air into carbon dioxide and venous (dark, carbonated) blood, and into arterial, oxygenated blood.
>
> (Hegel:1970, p. 392)

Like fire, blood is a living element perpetually consuming itself in its essential irritability:

Air is in itself the fiery and negative element; the blood is the same thing, but as a developed unrest—the burning fire of the animal's organism which not only consumes itself but also preserves itself as fluid and finds in air its *pabulum vitae*.

(Hegel:1970, pp. 392–93)

At work here is that "restlessness of the negative" that Jean-Luc Nancy has identified as Hegel's main discovery (see Nancy:2002). Blood would allegorize that subjective negativity in the most concrete terms. Therefore, one can say that blood is inherently and essentially "cruel." This restless "cruelty" derives from the law of all life: regeneration presupposes destruction, division, negation; then, even if there is a recombination, the cruelty will not have been evacuated.

To these insights, Mignotte adds the concept of the void. In the void, she claims, one finds a site preceding division similar to the empty space that appears in Plato's *khora* launched in *Timaeus*. The concept was taken over and developed by Derrida and Kristeva. For Plato, Derrida, and Kristeva, *khora* refers to a receptacle, an unnamable material substratum. *Khora* would call up a pure dehiscence ready to accept any "fulfilment," comparable to the empty grail ready to capture bitter drippings of blood from the sacred wound in medieval legends. The void is not a wound but a vacant place ready for further oozings and drippings.

Mignotte sends us back to Freud's unflinching analysis of the origins of human societies founded on collective murder. The murder was as soon forgotten as committed. It would return in the collective unconscious as guilt leading to the subsequent deification of the father killed by the sons. In "thoughts for the times on war and death," Freud contends that not only is "the primaeval history of mankind filled with murder" but that "if we are to be judged by our unconscious wishful impulses, we ourselves are a gang of murderers" (Freud: 1953, XIV, pp. 292 and 298), we can be comforted by recent Darwinian theory teaching us that this evolution was not so bad.

In *The Paradox of Goodness*, Richard Wrangham argues that Homo Sapiens evolved by a practice of social cooperation required for the preemptive killings of the dominant males of each group. In such a process, the need for communication, planning, and strategy implied a need for language, sociability, and tools. The worst and the best would thus have been entangled since the origins of human culture, language, and religion (Wrangham:2019). Even if Freud is not quoted in Wrangham's solidly documented book, he would have approved this sweeping Darwinian thesis about our constitutive "paradox." This is where the paradox of cruelty lies: our most esteemed foundations, those archaic impulses slowly leading to useful inventions like the institutions of democracy and tolerance are founded on cunningly planned collective murder.

4.3 The myth of cruelty: Prometheus revisited

Freud had found similar ideas in the works of Nietzsche, who more than any philosopher made "cruelty" a key value in his deconstruction of morality. Indeed, Maggie Nelson begins her book on cruelty with a quote by Nietzsche: "One should open one's eyes and take a new look at cruelty" (Nelson:2011, p. 3). Nietzsche knew the classical myth displaying cruelty as such: it was the cruel punishment of a Titan like Prometheus; here was and a first step in the rebellion of humanity against the power of the gods. Nietzsche discussed Prometheus in one early fragment from 1874, when he imagines that the ancient struggle will be forgotten after the ancient gods have faded out:

> Prometheus and his vulture were *forgotten* when the old world of the Olympians and their power were destroyed.
> Prometheus expects his redemption to come from human beings.
> He did not betray his secret to Zeus, Zeus perished because of his son.
> (Nietzsche:1995, p. 387)

Divine obsolescence derives from our lack of belief in the divinity of the gods, which is why Nietzsche can suggest that Prometheus created more than the human race: in fact, Prometheus was such a powerful demiurge that he would have created all the gods as well:

> Did Prometheus have to *fancy* first that he had *stolen* the light and then pay for that—before he finally discovered that he had created the light *by coveting the light* and that not only man but also the *god* was the work of his own hands and had been mere clay in his hands? All mere images of the maker—no less than the fancy, the theft, the Caucasus, the vulture, and the whole tragic *Prometheia* of all the seekers after knowledge?
> (Nietzsche:1974, pp. 240–241)

Prometheus, the Titan, started the transformation of humanity into Overhumanity. Prometheus was not totally helpless; as in all the myths concerning him aver, he had a weapon, knowledge. Prometheus knew Zeus' secret, the oracle announcing that Zeus will be dethroned or killed by a son, as he had done to his father. As Nietzsche would conclude, Prometheus is tortured so cruelly just because he knows the secret of the gods: the secret is that the gods are mortal too; they die of their own immortality.

Mignotte similarly posits the need for an intermediary between the gods and humans like Prometheus. We have seen earlier that Aeschylus ushered in a political drama by showing Zeus as excessively cruel, bent on making the Titan suffer. As he is being chained to the rock and pierced through with an iron stake, Prometheus gets this explanation from Hephaistos, who seems reluctant to accomplish his grim task. Hephaistos calls Prometheus a "god" who has no fear of angering the gods. However, Prometheus will spend the rest of his life screaming in pain because of the tortures inflicted on him by a jealous, pitiless, harsh, and cruel Zeus. This cruelty is blamed on the fact that Zeus is a new god, who only recently took over from his father. Aeschylus uses the word τραχύς, meaning *rough, hard, inflexible, cruel*. Zeus, a new-comer on the throne, has just dispatched his own father; like an African dic-tator, he begins his reign by dispatching and torturing anyone who shows the least sign of resistance. His cruelty marks him off as petty, vain, full of envy, and fury.

We have seen how Prometheus was to encounter Io who suffers as much as he does because of Zeus: she is constantly stung by the gadfly sent by a jealous Hera. A similarly relentless display of cruelty is exhibited by the two main gods of the Greek pantheon. Zeus is jealous of Prometheus, Hera is jealous of Io whom Zeus tried to seduce. Such political considerations bring us back to a more archaic substratum. Freud sees the myth of Prometheus as an intermediary between the humans and the gods when he meditates on the power of fire. Mignotte condenses this analysis in those terms:

> … in this external conflict between men and Zeus, Prometheus is the inter-mediary who closes the gaping hole of the devouring fire of the angry Zeus: he nourishes it with his own materialized fire by consuming his own body, reducing the latter to a substance of purified fire, the liver. I would say that Prometheus nourishes the gaping hole of Zeus with his own "deep blood" which passes through, without abolishing it, the gap that he has created and that he wants to maintain between the two parts of his being: the divine part and the human part.
>
> (Mignotte:2020, p. 78)

When the scholar Salomon Reinach discussed the "Resurrection of Gods and Heroes," he took Prometheus as his model, arguing that Greeks stories of metamorphosis were in fact earlier resurrection myths:

> Prometheus was a cunning Titan who stole fire from heaven and presented it to man. Zeus punished the thief by nailing him to a rock where an eagle devoured his liver, which was perpetually renewed. But in primitive mythologies, the eagle was the bird who mounted to the sun and took fire from it to give to man; on the other hand, the eagle was immune from thunderbolts, and was nailed to the summits of buildings to serve as a lighting conductor. Hence the name of eagles (*actoi*) given to the pedi-ments of Greek temples; hence also the legend of Prometheus, which cor-responds to the following ingenuous dialogue: 'Why was this eagle crucified?'—'To punish him for stealing fire from heaven.' Originally, the legend was that of the eagle's chastisement. When for the eagle, *prometheios*

(the far-seeing, a name given to the eagle as a bird of augury), men substituted the Titan, Prometheus, the eagle remained in the legend, but as executioner instead of victim.

(Reinach:1909, pp. 84–85)

Reinach, a good Hellenist like Nietzsche, knew that the name "Prometheus" derives from "*prometheia*" or "foresight." Prometheus can see the future of humanity and his own resurrection or unbinding; in this case, the theme of resurrection migrates from the bird to the hero's liver:

A divine animal when sacrificed never died completely; for after a few days of mourning a successor was found, another animal of the same kind, which remained sacred and intangible for a year. This explains the resurrection of so many gods and heroes, the fact that their tombs were shown, that they were honoured in a ritual, and represented as living among the gods.

(Reinach:1909, p. 85)

If these resurrected birds offer an image of immortality, we can also think of the relative immortality of the machines, with their endlessly replaceable parts. Here is, as Günther Anders puts it, the world of technology, a world that according to mythology, we owe to Prometheus' gift (see Müller:2016).

Freud quotes Reinach in his 1912 postscript to his analysis of the Schreber case. In most of the legends concerning Prometheus, the hero's regenerated liver is gnawed endlessly by an eagle, but in a few other versions, the bird is a vulture. If the eagle comes day after day to feed from this bloody substance, it is because, as Reinach had explained, the Greeks associated eagles with the heavens, with the sun, and with lightning. Eagles were distinguished by one feature: their ability to look at the sun without being dazzled—a point mentioned by Freud in his Postscript (Freud:2003, pp. 68–70). In Greek mythology, eagles were rumored to test their offspring; if the young were unable to withstand the glare of the sun, they would be cast out of the net, in a premonition of the medieval "ordeal," as Freud writes. There cannot be a starker contrast than darkly pulsating viscera linked with divination and a paternal "truth" so blinding that almost nobody will be able to withstand it.

However, when Freud developed his analysis of the Prometheus myth in 1932 in a dense paper on "The Acquisition and Control of the Fire," he insisted on one detail of the legend: Prometheus would have hidden the stolen fire in fennel stalks, in which one might recognize penis-like objects. Freud starts looking at other legends, myths, and rituals about micturition in which urine is used to quench fire and extinguish flames. The acquisition of fire calls up images of homosexual urination: here would be the exact opposite of the generous theft of fire by the Titan. What matters is that the act is at root a criminal gesture, the crime being directed at Zeus, the main god, a paternal figure. Freud continues:

> We know that in myths the gods are granted the satisfaction of all the desires which human creatures have to renounce, as we have learnt from the case of incest. Speaking in analytic terms, we should say that life of the drive (*Triebleben*)— the id—is the god who is defrauded when the quenching of fire is renounced: in the legend, a human desire is transformed into a divine privilege. But in the legend the deity possesses nothing of the characteristics of a super-ego, he is still the representative of the paramount life of the drives (*Trieblebens*).
>
> (Freud:1953,XXII, p. 189, modified)

If the jealous and cruel gods allegorize the unleashing of the drives, the myth conveys clearly that the renunciation to the pleasures they enjoy, a renunciation demanded by culture, cannot but be painful. Here is why the liver is chosen as the point of impact of the cruel punishment:

> In ancient times the liver was regarded as the seat of all passions and desires; hence a punishment like that of Prometheus was the right one for a criminal driven by the drives, who had committed an offence at the prompting of evil desires. But the exact opposite is true of the Bringer of Fire: he had renounced a drive and had shown how beneficent, and at the same time how indispensable, such a renunciation was for the purposes of civilization. And why should the legend treat a deed that was thus a benefit to civilization as a crime deserving punishment? Well, if, through all its distortions, it barely allows us to get a glimpse of the fact that the acquisition of control over fire presupposes a renunciation to the drive, at least it makes no secret of the resentment which the culture-hero could not fail to arouse in men driven by their drives.
>
> (Freud:1953, XXII, p. 189)

What has been renounced in this case? Not just the fire of love, or a "symbol of the libido," but also a transgressive fire. Freud goes on:

> When we ourselves speak of the 'devouring fire' of love and of 'licking' flames—thus comparing the flame to a tongue—we have not moved so very far away from the mode of thinking of our primitive ancestors. One of the presuppositions on which we based our account of the myth of the acquisition of fire was, indeed, that to primal man the attempt to quench fire with his own water had the meaning of a pleasurable struggle with another phallus.
>
> (Freud:1953, XXII, p. 190)

Freud needs a third element to go beyond the couple fire and water:

> In the antithesis between fire and water, which dominates the entire field of these myths, yet a third factor can be demonstrated in addition to the historical factor and the factor of symbolic phantasy. This is a physiological fact, which the poet Heine describes in the following lines: *Was dem Menschen dient zum Seichen/ Damit schafft er Seinesgleichen.* (With what serves a man for pissing / He creates creatures in his image).
>
> (Freud:1953, XXII, p. 192)

Heine rediscovers what had amused Hegel when he pointed out that Nature conflated the high and the low in its outrageous combination of fire and urine: "... the same conjunction of the high and the low which, in the living being, Nature naïvely expresses when it combines the organ of its highest fulfilment, the organ of generation, with the organ of generation" (Hegel:1977, p. 210). Freud develops a similarly ironical view of the micturating penis:

> The sexual organ of the male has two functions; and there are those to whom this association is an annoyance. It serves for the evacuation of the bladder, and it carries out the act of love which sets the craving of the genital at rest. The child still believes that he can unite the two functions. According to a theory of his, babies are made by the man urinating into the woman's body. But the adult knows that in reality the acts are mutually incompatible—as incompatible as fire and water.
>
> (Freud:1953, XXII, p. 192)

In his turn, Freud offers an almost grotesque image of drive-based enjoyment presented as the mindless interaction of mutually masturbating Titans who have not even discovered the difference between urination and ejaculation! Re-reading Freud's interpretation of the legend, Mignotte counters this version with a feminist twist: for her, Prometheus' liver is an equivalent of the placenta, "an interface between the matrix void and the void that is intrinsic to the egg" (Mignotte:2020, p. 79). Of course, even in the male version, this is not the end, for *Prometheus Unbound* comes after *Prometheus Bound*.

4.4 Kafka's solution: Obsolescence as exhaustion

The Prometheus myth held a huge appeal for Franz Kafka. As a seeker for autonomy who considered love as a form of torture by other means (mostly epistolary, as we see in his letters to Felice), he found in the bound Greek Titan a model for his doomed struggle against a domineering and powerful father. More often than not, his Oedipal struggle aborted, or he lost himself in sado-masochistic games. Self-hate helps if one wants to achieve the freedom required to be a writer. This freedom unmoored him from the ground of the family. It was above all freedom from the blood links he would search. He was disgusted by the blood proximity of the family, of all that evoked his parents' abhorred sexuality, a thought that was unbearable for him. He recognized a bond of blood, but hated it: "But I come from my parents, am bound to them and my sisters by blood…" (Kafka:2022, p. 427). This insight betrays a deep ambivalence that should not be reduced too quickly to an Oedipal urge:

> At times I pursue this too with my hatred, the sight of the marriage-bed at home, the used bedclothes, the carefully laid out shirts can nauseate me, can turn me inside out, it is as if I were not been definitively born (*als wäre ich nicht endgültich geboren*), came again and again into the world from this musty life in this musty room, were compelled again and again to seek confirmation for myself there…
>
> (Kafka:2022, p. 428)

Like the good lawyer he was, Kafka argues that he had ground to hate his family (*es gibt übergenug Grund zu zolchem Haß*) (Kafka:1988, p. 375). Such hate is, of course, accompanied by shame, the shame of not having been born once and for all, which generates another torture, the torture of having to be born again and again.

Günther Anders, one of the best commentators of Kafka, coined the term "*Promethean shame*" in an essay that uses Freud's idea of the "birth trauma":

> Philosophically speaking, Sigmund Freud's discovery of the 'Trauma of Birth' cannot be rated highly enough: for what more incisive event could happen to life than being torn from the 'ground?' The feelings Freud brought into view ('Oceanic Feeling;' 'Death Drive') are metaphysical in every respect, even if Freud's language was masked by the scientific vocabulary of his century. This is equally true of the "Trauma of Birth" with which he described the *shock of individuation*, no matter how well he disguised it. In an analogy with our question 'who is ashamed?' the question to ask in relation to this trauma is the following: '*Who* is actually shocked here?'
>
> (quoted by Müller:2016, p. 375)

The death drive refers to the individual's wish to get rid of the "agony of being an individual" that for Anders underpins a deeper link between shame, birth, and original trauma. The shock of individuation should be compared with "being torn from the ground." Prometheus, who is responsible for the creation of tool-making humanity against the wishes of the higher gods like Zeus, can relinquish his individuality and merge with the ground, the rock he has been chained to. Kafka's story rewriting of Prometheus was originally without a title. Max Brod decided to modify the original order and turned the last paragraph into the first; he assumed that the examples had to come first, before the statement of a general law. Kafka imagined this differently, as we can see from my literal translation:

> The legend tries to explain the inexplicable; as it comes out of the ground of truth (*Wahrheitsgrund*), it has return to the inexplicable in the end.
>
> There are four legends concerning Prometheus: According to the first he was clamped to a rock in the Caucasus for betraying the secrets of the gods to men, and the gods sent eagles to feed on his liver, which was perpetually renewed.
>
> According to the second Prometheus, goaded by the pain of the tearing beaks, pressed himself deeper and deeper into the rock until he became one with it.
>
> According to the third his treachery was forgotten in the course of thousands of years, forgotten by the gods, the eagles, forgotten by himself.
>
> According to the fourth everyone grew tired of the groundless affair. The gods grew tired, the eagles grew tired, the wound closed tired.
>
> There remains the inexplicable mass of rock.[1]

Kafka begins by presenting legends in general; he defines their function as a poetic account of natural phenomena; for the Greeks, any spring, tree, river, could give rise to a myth or legend that accompanied some form of metamorphosis. Niobe wept and turned into stone, Io jumped to escape and created the Ionian sea, etc. Kafka's riddle posits a link between myth and nature on the one hand, and myth and human suffering on the other. Prometheus' legend condenses this universal principle by following a sequence of four moments that end up in exhaustion. The hero turns into stone and all the participants have forgotten whatever happened. Nobody escapes from such a pervasive exhaustion. No reason can be given for the cruelty of the gods that returns to the indifference of Nature. The main issue becomes: what is the truth in these legends?

What remains unshakeable for Kafka is a principle of truth; here is why he searches for an indisputable *Wahrheitsgrund*, a "ground for truth," a solid grounding. The positive aspect yielded by the exhaustion of the myth is the possibility of finding truth. Truth requires a secure grounding. In the end, this ground is reduced to an old rocky mountain, for indeed such a substratum does not need any explication or verification: it is just there, when all the rest has been invented in order to make sense of the mountain. This does not mean that Kafka wants us to believe in a grounding in the natural world. The mass of rock that we call "mountain" functions as a primordial empty site, the *chora* I mentioned, a space defined by pure potentiality, which sends us back to Winnicott's void as Mignotte argues.

The primal void is not so empty as it seems, for it keeps fossilized traces, organic remainders situated in bodies, either in blood or the liver, that testify to an endless torture, for life itself is an eternal torture. The liver survives to allow the renewed torture predicated on Prometheus' immortality, the immortality of endless suffering. We can thus understand Kafka's desire for a cessation of this immortality by turning into stone and making one with the mountain. Only then will the absurdity of the torture end. When the liver turns into stone, it somehow lives on, but the pain has vanished for good.

In the human body, the skin and the liver share a common feature: both heal by reconstituting their tissues. If the Greek *hepar* keeps a link with the seat of pleasure and affects, the Germanic *lifere* that gave *liver* is cognate with "life." It calls up "courage." Another writer, James Joyce, connected the courage to write with the ability to face a never-ending torture, given his tendency to identify with a "crying Jesus." In that context, he mentions the city of Trieste in which he spent years writing *Ulysses*, but also battling rampant alcoholism and struggling with decaying liver, teeth, and eyes: "And Trieste, ah Trieste ate I my liver!" (Joyce:1939, p. 301). Such a literary autophagy was the condition required for achieving the monuments of *Ulysses* and then *Finnegans Wake*, a book written in seventeen years, the duration of what Joyce called his "cruelfiction," blending crucifixion, cruelty, and fiction: "O, you were excruciated, in honour bound to the cross of your own cruelfiction!" (Joyce:1939, p. 192). Let us move on to encounter a more contemporary crucifixion.

Note

1 Here I translate from Kafka's manuscript text in *Oktavheft* G., III (18 October 1917 - January 1918) as reproduced in Kafka:1992, II, p. 69–70. Slashes indicate paragraph breaks.

Bibliography

Deleuze, Gilles (1991). *Coldness and Cruelty*, and Leopold von Sacher-Masoch, *Venus in Furs*. trans. Jean McNeil, New York, Zone Books.

Derrida, Jacques (2002). *Without Alibi*, trans. Peggy Kamuf, Stanford, Stanford University Press.

Derrida, Jacques (2017). *The Death Penalty, Volume II*, edited by Geoffrey Bennington and Marc Crépon, Chicago, University of Chicago Press.

Freud, Sigmund (1953). *Three Essays on the theory of sexuality*, in Standard Edition: VII, p. 125–243, "Thoughts for the times on war and death," Standard Edition, XIV, p. 273–300, and "The Acquisition of Fire," Standard Edition, XXII, p. 185–193.

Freud, Sigmund (2002). *The "Wolfman" and Other Cases*, trans. Louise Adey Huish, London, Penguin.

Freud, Freud (2003). *The Schreber Case*, trans. Andrew Weber, New York, Penguin Books.

Hegel, G. W. F. (1970). *Philosophy of Nature*. trans. A. V. Miller, Oxford, Oxford University Press.

Hegel, G. W. F. (1977). *The Phenomenology of Spirit*. trans. A. V. Miller, Oxford, Oxford University Press.

Joyce, James (1939). *Finnegans Wake*, London, Faber.

Kafka, Franz (1988). *Tagebücher 1910–1923*, Frankfurt, Fischer.

Kafka, Franz (1992). *Nachgelassene Schriften und Fragmente*, II, edited by Jost Schillemeit, Frankfurt, Fischer.

Kafka, Franz (2022). *The Diaries*, trans. Ross Benjamin, New York, Schocken.

Lacan, Jacques, Lacan (1992). *The Seminar, Book VII, The Ethics of Psychoanalysis*, trans. Dennis Porter, New York, Norton.

Mignotte, Touria (2020). *Cruelty, Sexuality, and the Unconscious in Psychoanalysis: Freud, Lacan, Winnicott, and The Body of the Void*. trans. Andrew Weller. London: Routledge.

Müller, Christopher John (2016). *Prometheanism: Technology, Digital Culture and Human Obsolescence*, London, Rowman and Littlefield.

Nancy, Jean-Luc (2002). *Hegel: The Restlessness of the Negative*, trans. Jason Smith and Steven Miller, Minneapolis, University of Minnesota Press.

Nancy, Jean-Luc (2021). *Cruor*, Paris, Galilée.

Nancy, Jean-Luc (2023). *Cruor*, translated by Jeff Fort, in *Corpus III, Cruor and Other Writings*, New York, Fordham University Press, p. 7–44.

Nelson, Maggie (2011). *The Art of Cruelty: A Reckoning*, New York, Norton.

Nietzsche, Friedrich (1974). *The Gay Science*. trans. Walter Kaufmann, New York, Random House.

Nietzsche, Friedrich (1995). *Unpublished Writings from the period of Unfashionable Observations*, trans. Richard T. Gray, Stanford, Stanford University Press.

Reinach, Salomon (1909). *Orpheus: A general History of religions*, trans. Florence Simmonds, London, W. Heinemann.

Semm, Markus (1994). *Der springende Punkt in Hegels System*, München, Boer.

Wrangham, Richard (2019). *The Goodness Paradox: The Strange Relationship Between Virtue and Violence in Human Evolution*, New York: Pantheon Books.

Chapter 5

Irritating Kant with Sade, irritating Sade with Kant

5.1 A not so kind cruelty: Ferrari's crucifixions

In the Spring of 2022, visitors to the Centre Pompidou's permanent collections could stray into a temporary exhibition of works by an Argentinian artist, León Ferrari. They would come face to face with a huge statue that looked like a gaudily painted crucifixion with the difference that the cross was replaced by an American army jet. The work was the most important piece in a retrospective dedicated to Léon Ferrari, *León Ferrari: A Kind Cruelty (1920–2013)* (Liuci-Goutnikov and Wain:2022). The huge crucifixion of the jet, *La Civilización occidental y Cristiana*, caused a scandal in 1965 and was again met with an uproar in 2004. Even Francis, soon to be Pope, declared that the work constituted a real "blasphemy." Ferrari reproduced an American bomber with the letters "USAF" quite visible on the wings and fuselage. To this US jet, a Christ in pain is nailed; his knees, feet, and hands are bloody. This is presented in a naive manner that evokes the polychrome wooden sculptures often seen in South and Central American churches. The title of the show is at first counterintuitive, for there is little kindness or amiability in the paintings, sculptures, collages, and installations gathered; on the contrary, the dominant mood is a fierce critique of the Argentine dictatorship, whose abuses were at one time covered up by the local Catholicism.

Visiting the huge room that housed the show, my attention was caught by a 1965 piece, a big blackboard covered with childishly drawn words entitled *Milagro en la OEA* ("Miracle at the Organization of American States"). The word *irrités* in French stood out. I looked closer. A caption explained that Ferrari was denouncing the conference in which President Johnson had reinstated the 1948 Bogotá Charter, a charter allowing the US government to control the South American continent and fight against left-wing regimes. The first text quoted is a newspaper's review taken from the Argentine daily *La Nación*. According to the journalist, the conference was a "miracle" that would bring freedom to Argentina. The word *milagro* ("miracle") is handwritten in letters whose size increase. Then the text switches to French: Ferrari reproduces

DOI: 10.4324/9781032715834-6

verbatim a long passage from Sade's *Justine*, without naming the source. Readers who know Sade have no trouble finding the text, that stages a scene of blasphemy. Murderous Libertines force a ten-year-old girl called Florette to pretend that she has been blessed by a miracle. Threatened with tortures and disguised as the Blessed Virgin, she raises her arms at the instant the priest consecrates the host. The public believes in an authentic miracle; all agree to increase their donations. Seeing the success of the farce, the libertines take the transubstantiation travesty a step further in the evening:

> Aroused (*irrités*) by this initial crime, the sacrilegious ones go considerably further: they have the child stripped naked, they have her lie on her stomach upon a large table; they light candles, they place the image of our Savior squarely upon the little girl's back and upon her buttocks they dare consummate the most redoubtable of our mysteries. I swooned away at this horrible spectacle, 'twas impossible to bear the sight. Séverino, seeing me unconscious, says that, to bring me at heel, I must serve as the altar in my turn. I am seized; I am placed where Florette was lying; the sacrifice is consummated, and the host ... that sacred symbol of our august Religion ... Séverino catches it up, and thrusts it deep into the obscene locale of his sodomistic pleasures ... crushes it with oaths and insults ... ignominiously drives it further with the intensified blows of his monstrous dart and as he blasphemes, spurts, upon our Savior's very body, the impure floods of his lubricity's torrents ...
>
> (Sade: 2014, p. 524, and Sade: 1965, p. 613)

The passage is in French; then the text returns to Spanish: "como la misa como el milagro como la misa que regaran en la catedral milagrosa de la OEA" ("like the mass, like the miracle, like the mass, they made rain (but also: they made a mess) in the miraculous cathedral of the OAS"). The political satire targets the alliance between Catholics and the CIA-sponsored torturers who were launching a bloody repression then. The idea of a political "miracle" led Ferrari to look for a scene of profanation, with that child abused by Sade's ferocious molesters.

Ferrari has caught Sade's version of cruelty brought about by irritation nicely. The parodic staging hinges around the slippery nature of the term "irritation." It shifts from anger, true or faked, displayed to announce tortures punishing an innocent victim, to sexual arousal that always culminates in orgasm. Sade's cruelty pushes the irritation to a climax, which triggers Ferrari's own political anger intensified by the hidden political denunciation. Sadean cruelty is exacerbated when aimed at the knot between religion and politics. One of the most systematically reviled objects of Sade's scorn is any reference to the deity. Whoever calls up the name of God triggers murderous irritation among the Libertines. Ferrari is conscious of the dubious role played by the Catholic church in Argentina during its "dirty war," a moment in which state sadism was condoned by those in power. Such a hyperbolic cruelty then returns in his works to play a satirical role. The name of Sade is enough to suggest an array of tortures, blasphemous acts, and sexual orgies. They call into question humanist or Christian pretexts used to cloak the exactions of torturers sanctioned by repressive regimes in a self-righteous veil. A similarly critical function underpins Lacan's reference to Sade: as we will see, Lacan uses Sade above all to "irritate" Kant.

5.2 Kant and Sade: Parallel pathologies

In his 1959 seminar on the Ethics of Psychoanalysis, Lacan discusses an anecdote used by Kant to discuss moments when one might be ready to lose one's life for some cause. He first imagines a man who is looking at the gallows upon which he is to be condemned to death should he have sex with a woman he desires. Kant deduces that any man in his right mind would abstain from sex. The little story appears at the beginning of the *Critique of Practical Reason* when Kant examines the links between freedom and moral action. The vignette should exemplify rational behavior:

> Suppose that someone says his lust is irresistible (*wollüstigen Neigung*) that, when the desired object and opportunity are present. Ask him whether he would not control his passion if, in front of the house where he has this opportunity, gallows were erected on which he would be hanged immediately after gratifying his lust (*nach genossener Wollust*). We do not have to guess very long what his answer would be.
>
> (Kant: 1949, p. 141)

One should not forget that the vignette belongs to a diptych: the second half sketches the moral deliberation of a man who is threatened with death if he does not denounce an innocent man. In this case, Kant argues, one might accept death in order to avoid committing a terrible felony. The outcome of the comparison between the two situations, both of which Kant says are met with in common experience, is to state the fundamental law of pure practical Reason: one must act in such a way that the maxim of one's will is capable of being taken as a principle of universal legislation.

As Lacan objects, Kant concludes too quickly that no one would be foolish enough to risk death in order to accede to erotic bliss. Kant assumes that if the aim of concupiscence, one of the translations of *Wollust*, is punished by death, this suffices to cancel the erotic desire. At this point, Lacan betrays some impatience with the philosopher of Koenigsberg's rationalism and even suggests that his "passions" may have been somewhat weak (Lacan: 1992, p. 108). Alluding to Freud's concept of the "overevaluation" of the object displayed by passionate lovers, Lacan mentions Hamlet, the Minnesingers, the sublimated exaltation of lovers in courtly love; one could also think of Tristan and Isolde, who know quite well that their tryst will be punished by death if they are found out. Lacan argues that there are people who are either driven or insane enough to accept the challenge, and states:

> ... it is not impossible that this man coolly accepts such an eventuality on his leaving—for the pleasure of cutting up the lady concerned in small pieces, for example. The latter is the other case that one can envisage, and the annals of criminology furnish a great many cases of the type. (Lacan: 1992,

(p. 109)

Kant thought he could rely on the reality principle: reality would be founded upon universal fear of death, so much so that anyone rejects the transgressive pleasure. Lacan takes into consideration another type of excess capable of subverting the rule of reason, and that is exemplified by Sade's excessive jouissance. Sade's passionate irritation presented in close proximity with death appears as the exact antithesis of Kant's deluded universalism. For Sade, perverse desire enacts the savage parody of the ethical law. Beyond its subversive aspect, Sade poses an *a priori* problem: he puts in question the foundations of Kant's universal law.

From the point of view of psychoanalysis, Kant's practical reason is only an offshoot of a purified reason. In his second Critique, Kant begins by systematically ruling out the "pathological" element. This is the term systematically used in the *Critique of Practical Reason*—from the start, there is a categorical distinction between "pure" reason in its capacity to determine the will, and feelings or affects: "In the will of a rational being affected by feeling (*pathologisch-affizierter Wille*), there can be a conflict (*Widerstreit*) between the maxims and the practical laws recognized by this being"(Kant:1949, p. 130, trans. modified). For Kant, the "pathological" refers to the way feelings and emotions like love, desire, pleasure, any empirical motivation, tend to sway human actions—they make subjects wish to get personal gain or look for their private interest. Kant multiplies examples to show that, each time, one must deduce that wishes to accrue personal gain fall into contradictions, for they fail the test of the generalized transformation into a universal law or maxim.

Lacan's scathing critique puns on "pathological," a Greek term implying "being affected by pathos." Here a professional "pathologist" opposes his cynical knowledge to Kant's blithe efforts at grounding morality in the domain of the "pure" by discarding all affects. The medical pathologist has acquired a hard knowledge gained observing sadistic perverts and unrepenting psychopaths in the wards of psychic hospitals. From the start, Lacan suggests that there is another Reason at work in a pervert's unreason. Here is why Marquis de Sade is called for.

The names of Kant and Sade are linked in Lacan's discussion of the death drive; he explains that the ethics of psychoanalysis can be "illustrated through a confrontation, or heightening of the difference by contrast, of Kant and Sade, however paradoxical that may seem" (Lacan: 1992, p. 207). For Sade, Nature thrives on destruction; it is through crime that humans bring about a regeneration of Nature. Murder is a social equivalent of what takes place on a larger scale in the universe. A passage that attracts Lacan's attention deploys the idea of a "second death":

> Murder only takes the first life of the individual whom we strike down; we should also seek to take his second life if we are to be even more useful to nature. For nature wants annihilation; it is beyond our capacity to achieve the scale of destruction it desires.
>
> (Lacan: 1992, p. 211)

The character who speaks here is a perverse and libidinous Pope instrumental in ushering in a principle of annihilation parallel with Freud's death drive. Like Dante's sacrilegious popes who are in Hell, like Ferrari's compromised Argentine priests, he wants to inflict an eternity of tortures.

Instead of merely enjoying the pantheistic energy released through human actions and spontaneous natural formations, Sade and Freud tend to substitute "a subject for Nature" (Lacan: 1992, p. 213). Like Hegel meditating on blood, as we have seen, Sade and Freud animate Nature, which is underpinned by a struggle between opposed principles: Good and Evil, Light and Darkness, Love and Death, Eros and Thanatos. Lacan knows Sade well and quotes the last volume of the Pauvert edition of *Juliette*, in which a libertine exclaims that even if God existed (but this is not the case!), then God can only be conceived as a supremely evil Being: "If it were true that there was a God, master and creator of the universe, he would indubitably be the most bizarre, the most cruel, the most evil and the most sanguinary being..." (Sade: 1967, p. 210). By a curious contradiction, only God would have to be abhorred, insulted, and rejected. Meanwhile, an evil or indifferent Nature (Sade hesitates on this moot point) simply provides a model: one must imitate its ravaging excess, its recurrent catastrophes, natural disasters like floods and volcanic eruptions.

Georges Bataille intuited this when he presented himself as a Sadean volcano. His earlier texts appear as systematic irritations of the system of symbols displayed by Groddeck, only he goes further in his wish to subvert bourgeois rationality: "A man who finds himself among others is irritated because he does not know why he is not one of the others" (Bataille:1985, p. 6). The solution he finds is to become Nature in its most destructive aspects: the speaker says, "I am the *Jesuve*," the portmanteau-word combining Vesuvius and Jesus. Indeed, Bataille would enact the fantasy of sex followed by death as it had been called up by Kant's vignette; he writes: "Love, then, screams in my own throat: I am the *Jesuve*, the filthy parody of the torrid and blinding sun. // I want to have my throat slashed while violating the girl to whom I will have been able to say: you are the night" (Bataille:1985, p. 9).

Bataille used the works of Sade to promote his own rebellious attitude, and I will return to his interaction with Lacan. Lacan focuses on the tenacious Sadean fantasy of going beyond the first death of the body. Beautiful victims are subjected to excessive tortures, but apparently can keep suffering forever. Once they are dispatched, they are replaced by identical victims. In novels like *Juliette, Justine*, or the *Hundred and Twenty Days of Sodom*, victims are destroyed in huge quantities that follow a serial pattern—their number has been the object of obsessive calculations well analyzed by Marcel Hénaf (Hénaf:1999, pp. 27–40). Hénaf shows the principle of a systematic logical saturation that presupposes a Leibnitzian cosmology aiming at overthrowing the "lyrical body." The victims' quasi-immortality is accompanied by a blurred indistinction: they all exhibit beauty, the grace of youth, the "touching" vulnerability provided by poverty or naiveté, exciting or irritating bodies upon which Sade's Libertines exert terrifying rages. However, irritation must be transformed into its opposite: for when they unleash their murderous furor, the aim is to reach the indifference of a godlike apathy or ataraxia.

The parallel between Sade and Kant allows us to understand what is at stake. Sade's fantasies stop before visualizing graphic dismemberment, with the exception of the ending of *120 Days of Sodom*. Kant and Sade would share a concept of beauty as pure form offering a limit. Lacan sums up the issue in these terms:

> Proclaiming the law of jouissance as the foundation of some ideally utopian social system, Sade expresses himself in italics (...): "Lend me the part of your body that will give me a moment of satisfaction and, if you care to, use for your own pleasure (*et jouissez, si cela vous plaît, de celle du mien*) that part of my body which appeals to you."
>
> (Lacan: 1992, p. 202)

This statement echoes almost literally Maurice Blanchot's analysis of Sade's "unreason" in a book that Lacan knew well, *Lautréamont and Sade*, which begins with a meditation on rationality and irrationality. Blanchot then condenses Sade's teeming contradictions in a magisterial manner:

> At every moment [Sade's] theoretical ideas set free the irrational forces with which they are bound up. These forces both excite and upset the thought by an impetus of a kind that causes the thought first to resist and then to yield, to try again for mastery, to gain an ascendancy, but only by liberating other dark forces by which, once again the ideas are carried

away, side-tracked and perverted. The result is that all that is said is clear but seems at the mercy of something that has not been said. Then, a little further on, what was concealed emerges, is recaptured by logic but, in its turn, obeys the movement of a still further hidden force.

(Blanchot: 1995, pp. 75–76)

Having grasped the rationale of this perverted logic, Blanchot formalizes the paradox of Sade's doctrine: it boils down to a parody of the Declaration of Human Rights:

[H]e draws up a kind of Declaration of the Rights of Eroticism, with for a fundamental principle this idea, applying equally to men and women. "What harm do I do, what offence do I commit, if I say to a beautiful creature I meet: 'Lend me the part of your body that can give me an instant's satisfaction, and enjoy, if so pleases you, the part of mine you prefer.'" To Sade such a proposition is irrefutable.... But what does he conclude from that? Not that it is wrong to do violence against anyone and use them for pleasure against their will, but that no one, so as to refuse him, can plead as excuse an exclusive attachment or "belonging to anyone."

(Blanchot:1995, pp. 76-77)

The idea of an impossible reciprocity of enjoyment is predicated upon its very excess. For Sade, nobody can put a halt to erotic enjoyment. Enjoyment, or "jouissance" more precisely, leads to all sorts of bad treatments for the others; indeed, jouissance cannot find a limit; it entails both the ecstatic erotic enjoyment of an object of desire and the complete possession of that object. Sade reiterates the "law" of jouissance at various points in his novels. His thought can be summed up as this statement by one of his Libertines: "*Jouissons: telle est la loi de la nature*" (Let us enjoy—such is the law of nature) (Sade:1967, vol. 20, p. 181). Lacan sees in this maxim the formulation of the "fundamental law" of Sade's philosophy. One can posit a Sadean law in terms that are almost identical to Kant's categorical imperative. Kant and Sade posit a formalist Reason whose principle is affirmed irrespectively of the object to which it applies.

This parallel underpins the part of Lacan's Seminar on the Ethics of Psychoanalysis in which he asks why traditional morality fails to acknowledge its foundation in desire. Kant's moral imperative cannot be concerned with objects, as we saw, but only with the assertion of the Law as Law: the Law becomes an unconditional "Thou shalt." One can replace Kant's "Thou shalt" with Sade's fantasy of excessive jouissance; both become a supreme imperative (Lacan: 1992, pp. 315–316). This is the main insight that underpins "Kant with Sade," the essay Lacan published in *Critique* in 1963, one year after the demise of the review's founder, who was Bataille. The name of the journal was propitious, for it is echoed in the constant references to Kant's three "Critiques" and to Sade's relentless critique of morality. Lacan had been asked to write a Preface to Sade for his collected works in Editions du Cercle Précieux. His preface to the "Philosophy in the Bedroom" was rejected as being too opaque. In it, Lacan's central point was to argue that a pure and almost derisory fantasy of absolute jouissance could be elevated to the status of a universal law. He writes: "*Philosophy in the Bedroom* came eight years after the *Critique of Practical Reason*. If, after showing that the former is consistent with the latter, I can demonstrate that the former completes the latter, I shall be able to claim that it yields the truth of the *Critique*" (Lacan: 2006, p. 646). Lacan promises his readers that, thanks to Sade, he will add the erotic spices lacking in Kant's moral philosophy. This entails unleashing some humor or comedy. The issue comes to the fore in "Kant with Sade":

> But aside from the fact that if the deductions in the *Critique* prepared us for anything, it is for distinguishing the rational from the sort of reasonable that is no more than resorting in a confused fashion to the pathological, we now know that humor betrays the very function of the "superego" in comedy. A fact that—to bring this psychoanalytic agency to life by instantiating it and to wrest it from the renewed obscurantism of our contemporaries' use of it—can also spice up (*relever*) the Kantian test of the universal rule with the grain of salt it is missing.
>
> (Lacan: 2006, p. 648)

Sade's subversion would bring in the missing spices capable of irritating Kant's universalism. His formalism is condensed in his categorical imperative. Kant's strategy was to make the object of desire disappear as such. Desire arouses unwholesome interest. Only the recognition of an inner moral law can achieve universality. Such a law, as he painstakingly demonstrates, can never be given a phenomenal object as its correlate. Kant's position thus leads to something like a tautology: the law is the law because, if it was not the law, there would be no law. Such an empty reiteration of principles is derided by Lacan who compares it with Jarry's famous quip in *Ubu Roi*: "Long live Poland, for if there were no Poland, there would be no Poles" (Lacan:2006, p. 647).

The point is that Sade's maxim can be summed up in terms that call up Kant's maxims: "I have the right to enjoy your body," anyone can say to me, "and I will exercise this right without any limit to the capriciousness of the exactions that I might wish to satiate with your body" (Lacan: 2006, p. 648). Black humor is at work here, for we recognize an inevitable sliding from the rational to the merely reasonable and then to the pathological. The subversive impact of the formulation lies in its debunking of any "reciprocity" that would be mistaken as an ethical basis for intersubjectivity. As we saw, Sade denounces the role conferred to reciprocity in the formation of intersubjectivity. According to Sade, one will never deduce a rule of reciprocity from subjectivity, a point on which Lacan would agree since for him, desire is desire of the Other. This Other, the Unconscious, is unfathomable, which entails that subjective inter-positioning has to be mediated by language, castration, and the law of the prohibition of incest. Any resort to a trust in intersubjectivity, or reciprocal mirror-images, appears as a delusion. Accordingly, Kant's and Sade's maxims entail that the Other is placed in a position of domination over the subject. Such an overarching domination discloses the truth of a divided or split subject. "In coming out of the Other's mouth, Sade's maxim is more honest than Kant's appeal to the voice within, since it unmasks the split in the subject that is usually covered up" (Lacan: 2006, p. 650). Sade's debunking gets at the heart of the Rights of Man by parodying all universalist ethical systems. Lacan equates the subjectivity of a "second" person who owns the law with a pun in which the wish to kill the other appears. If I say "*Tu es...*" (You are), I also expose my wish to murder the other in the echo of "*Tuez!*" (Kill!) (Lacan: 2006, p. 650).

Kant and Sade convey the idea that pain and death accompany any moral experience. A limit to torture would be the Stoician contempt of the body that Kant discusses at some length in the second Critique. If like Epictetus, I exclaim coolly: "See, you broke my leg," when I am subjected to the tortures meted out by my master, my indifference will make the master lose his perverse jouissance. If, however, the Sadean torture is inflicted on subjects to destroy or rape their modesty, what is achieved is a dereliction of the human subject facing an enjoying Other. The enjoying Other returns in Sade's fantasy of an evil God. One cannot expel the ghost of an evil God condensing jouissance in a position evoking Freud's Father of the horde, an uncastrated Father who deprives the sons of their will. Sade's scenes of perversion only fleetingly suggest pleasure. Jouissance is predicated on the absence of desire; it needs teeming perverse fantasies to be sustained.

Lacan adds that he will adduce Sade in order to torure Kant:

> Thus Kant, being questioned and tortured (*mis à la question*) with Sade—that is, Sade serving here, in our thinking, as in his sadism, as an instrument—avows what is obvious in the question "What does he want?" which henceforth arises for anyone.
>
> (Lacan: 2006, p. 654, modified)

The question leads to need for a rationale in the forest of dark fantasies that crowd the works of Sade. They also point to the subjective moment of disappearance, or *aphanisis*, that Ernest Jones introduced into Freudian theory. This disappearance is postponed by the imagination that needs the fantasy of a fully enjoying subject. However, the enjoying subject reveals that he or she cannot meet the excessive level of enjoyment displayed by the evil God. The deaths of the victims inscribed in serial combinations reach libidinal saturation. And on the other side, subjects of the fantasy like Justine tend to be monolithic. There is no character progression in Sade's novels. Justine and her friends learn nothing but the invention of new tortures, thus producing the object of fantasy as a metamorphic and plastic object. ˙

In consequence, Lacan rejects the common idea that Sade's subjects would "negate the other." On the contrary, their desire is based on a recognition of the Other as Other. In his Seminar on Anxiety, Lacan returned to Sade's jouissance of the Other, and in March 1973, he analyzed the anxiety created in the victim by the tormentor. This strong affect would be the true aim of Sade's reiterated scenes of humiliation and torture:

> I will leave it to you to look up in *Juliette*, even in *The 120 Days...*, the few passages in which the protagonists, entirely absorbed as they are in satisfying their avidity for torments on their chosen victims, enter the strange, peculiar and bizarre trance that is expressed in these odd words, which I really do have to voice here—*I triumph*—exclaims the tormentor—*cunt-skin!*
>
> (Lacan: 2014, pp. 164–165).

A slightly different rendering by Cormac Gallagher comes closer to the original text: "I had," cries the tormentor, "I had the skin of the cunt." Lacan glosses this curious moment of enthusiasm in which the supreme trophy is brandished to say that at that very moment, the Libertine discovers "the reverse of the subject" (*l'envers du sujet*). The subject or victim is turned inside out like a glove, which echoes with the general Sadean fantasy: it aims at turning the subject inside-out in the name of the Other's enjoyment.

Sade's Libertines exhaust themselves trying to realize the jouissance of God. This is the conclusion of "Kant with Sade": if desire is the other side of the law, Sade ends up betraying his absolute submission to the law. Lacan makes the point cogently:

> Sade thus stopped at the point where desire and the law become bound up with each other. // If something in him let itself remain tied to the law in order to take the opportunity, mentioned by Saint Paul speaks, to become inordinately sinful, who would cast the first stone? But Sade went no further. // It is not simply that his flesh is weak, as it is for each of us; it is that the spirit is too willing not to be deluded. His apology for crime merely impels him to an oblique acceptance of the Law. The Supreme Being is restored in Evil Action.
>
> (Lacan:2006, p. 667)

Ironically, this point seems to be confirmed by the final scene of the "Philosophy in the Bedroom." The Mother, Madame de Misteval, is condemned by the perverted daughter Eugénie to be raped: she will be infected with syphilis and her sex will be sewn up. However, such a ferocious attack on the Mother's body only leaves it even more intact than before. The Law says: do not touch the Mother, at any cost! Sade cannot help but let Reason speak, even when he believes that he can subjugate all the others as subservient victims complacently offered to the predator he thinks he is, just because of the unleashing of transgressive sexual excess. This critical insight underpins Adorno's reading of Sade.

5.3 The unreason of reason and its cruel morality

Did Lacan read Adorno and Horkheimer on Kant and Sade, as Roudinesco assumes, or is the pairing of Kant and Sade already provided by a philosophical tradition that has been misread, as Monique David-Ménard suggests? (David-Ménard:1997). Adorno's and Horkheimer's ground-breaking parallel between Kant and Sade in their *Dialectic of Enlightenment* first published in 1944 (Horkheimer and Adorno:1987) predates Lacan's analysis. Their main thesis is relatively simple: Kant's Reason emerges as the culmination of the cult of reason that accompanied the rise of the bourgeoisie in the eighteenth century. This was the time when the bourgeoisie was conquering the world in the name of science and progress; the bourgeois world finds its counterpart in the mechanization of tortures deployed by Sade's perverse utopias. *The Critique of Practical Reason* stresses the autonomy and self-determination of the moral subject and defines a pure form for any ethical action. The philosophy of Enlightenment meets global capitalism with a vengeance. Any human concern must be ruled out: what matters is only the conformity of Reason with its own laws. This supreme Reason must appear devoid of any object, human affects being elided from its self-referential domain.

It is conceivable that Lacan did not read the *Dialectic of Enlightenment*. He states in "Kant with Sade" that the link between the two contemporary thinkers had never been "noted, to our knowledge, as such" (Lacan:2006, p. 645). Lacan loves parading his erudition. If the book, not yet translated into French then, had been available to him, my guess is that he would have acknowledged the source. In fact, there was another source closer to him—and that he fails to mention—that might have shown him the way. It is Simone de Beauvoir's essay on Sade provocatively entitled "Must One Burn Sade?" (Beauvoir:1951). De Beauvoir, who had befriended Lacan at the time of writing *The Second Sex*, and who has a female psychoanalyst play the leading feminine role in her *roman-à-clef* or disguised autobiography *The Mandarins*, has pointed to illuminating similarities between Sade's philosophy of excess and Kant's notion of freedom when she writes: "With a severity similar to Kant's, and which has its source in the same puritan tradition, Sade conceives the free act only as an act free of all feeling. If it were to obey emotional motives, it would make us Nature's slaves again and not autonomous subjects" (Beauvoir:1987, p. 55). Sade would invert Kant's philosophy ironically by disturbing it and provoking it. Sade enacts revolutionary terror in literature and thus makes philosophy play the role of an evil demon. Philosophy unleashed a Cartesian *malin génie* whose critique of morality becomes hyperbolical. Sade gives universal reason the task of proclaiming atheism; he finds materialism on a rejection of morality and offers a sanction to the most extreme forms of debauch.

Moreover, as noted by Michel Delon who edited the first volume of Sade in the prestigious Pléiade series, educated contemporaries had perceived parallels between Sade's thought and Kant's morality. Delon quotes an essay published in 1801 in which *Justine* is presented as more logical than any strict moralism:

> If the pleasure given to me by the exercise of virtue is of the same nature as my physical enjoyment (*jouissances physiques*), if the approbation of my conscience is only a pleasant trickling of my nerves, what will I say to those who prefer one pleasure to another? What will I say to the brigand and the thief who take pleasure in their crimes, if it is not just that they should be careful not to be caught and punished? And, since we have to show in its most horrible light this awful system, what will its devotees reply to the author of *Justine*? Will they not have to agree that he is the most logical among those they have adopted? If one posits as principle that everything depends upon sensation, there will be no difference between a hero who saves his fatherland and a monster wallowing in mud and blood.
>
> (Sade:1990, p. 24)

As we have seen, Lacan's analysis follows a similar parallel. Moreover, his reading of Sade does not betray any trace of the neo-Marxist denunciation of the bourgeoisie that presides in Adorno and Horkheimer's book. For Horkheimer, who was the actual writer of the Sade chapter, Juliette was indeed more logical than Kant: she draws the conclusions that Kant denies namely that bourgeois order of the world sanctions crime. Crime is regulated by the same rationality that ordains the activities of the happy few. Sade's "apathy" functions like an equivalent of Kant's "disinterestedness," for both underpin the brutal efficiency of the bourgeois conquest of the world. Their "right to enjoyment" includes an absolute extension of its field, up to the right to enjoy the bodies of others as one saw in slavery.

The counterpart of this globalized rationality would be the systematic mechanization of perverse pleasures that culminates in the Sadean orgy. Roland Barthes had noted how Sade's orgies functioned like perfectly oiled machines; in these well-ordered mechanisms, everyone has a part to play, and nobody can be left idle (Barthes:1976, pp. 152–153). Similarly, Kant's Law would aim at ushering in a sadistic bachelor machine that transforms us into "subjects" and reduces the moral law to abstract ownership. Indeed, Kant's *Metaphysics of Morals* seems to demonstrate hat the role of ownership comes to the fore when it comes to sexuality, which yields hilarious definitions of sexual reciprocity:

> *Sexual union (commercium sexuale)* is the reciprocal use that one human being makes of the sexual organs and capacities of another (*usus membrorum et facultatum sexualium alterius*). (…) For the natural use that one makes of the other's sexual organs is *enjoyment*, for which one gives itself up to the other. In this act a human being makes himself into a thing, which conflicts with the right of humanity in his own person. There is only one condition under which this is possible: that while one person is acquired by the other *as if it were a thing*, the one who is acquired acquires the other in turn…
>
> (Kant:1996a, pp. 428–429)

This evocation of marriage as a mutual commodification relies on Kant's rigid formalism: the law is the law only if it is devoid of content since what matters is the conformity of practical reason to its universal maxims. Here, the thing is a mere thing, and not the Thing of Lacan's sublime.

Kant's formulation resembles Sade's law as formulated by Lacan:

> Proclaiming the law of *jouissance* as the foundation of some ideally utopian social system, Sade expresses himself in italics (…): "Lend me the part of your body that will give me a moment of satisfaction and, if you care to, use for your own pleasure (*et jouissez, si cela vous plaît, de celle du mien*) that part of my body which appeals to you'.
>
> (Lacan:2006, p. 202)

The subject of the fantasy approximates the jouissance of God but this God is closer to the *Dio boia* mentioned by Joyce in *Ulysses*: he is a "hangman god," a God unsurpassable in evil. In this negative theology, Sade would enact a "reversion" of a subject that is opened up and gutted in the name of the Other.

Pierre Klossowski, who is often quoted by Lacan, underlined the kinship between Sade's thought and the heresiarchs of gnostic descent. A similar hatred for the body linked with a mystical cult of the orgasm underpins a fantasy of a lost original light. Klossowski points to links between a negative theology of jouissance and a jouissance of writing. Sade's writing would be the writing of excess and pure exteriority. Klossowski saw Sade not as a "pervert" or a monster but as a writer; an excruciatingly boring and repetitive writer, for sure, but whose writings, nevertheless, allow us to glimpse crucial links between fantasies deployed by a perverse imagination and the law in which the jouissance of the Other is hidden. Klossowski writes:

> The parallelism between the apathetic reiteration of acts and Sade's descriptive reiteration again establishes that the image of the act to be done is re-presented each time not only as though it had never been performed but also as though it had never been described. This reversibility of the same process inscribes the presence of nonlanguage in language; it inscribes a foreclosure of language by language.
>
> (1991, p. 41)

Sade's symptom would thus not be sadism but writing, a bad writing that hesitates between the repetitive fantasy of an outrage to a Mother Nature and a reiterated questioning of the Other's jouissance. If Lacan owed a key insight to Simone de Beauvoir, he also had read Freud on the parallels between sadism and masochism, which sends us back to our discussion of cruelty. Freud's 1924 essay on "The economic problem of masochism" presented Kant's categorical imperative as a philosophical expression of the cruelty typical of the super-ego. Freud writes:

> This super-ego is in fact just as much a representative of the *id* as of the outer world. It originated through the introjection into the ego of the first objects of the libidinal impulses in the *id*, namely, the two parents, by which process the relation to them was desexualized, that is underwent a deflection from direct sexual aims. Only in this way was it possible for the child to overcome the Oedipus-complex. Now the super-ego has retained essential features of the introjected persons, namely their power, their severity, their tendency to watch over and to punish. (...) The super-ego, the conscience at work in it, can then become harsh, cruel and inexorable against the ego which is in its charge. The categorical imperative of Kant is thus a direct inheritance from the Oedipus-complex.
>
> (1961, pp. 157–170)

According to Freud, this is how a perverse couple is created that replaces the couple of Sade and Sacher-Masoch. It is the sadism of the super-ego that generates the masochism of the ego. This moral sadism is exemplified by "Russian character types"—Freud is thinking here both of his Russian patient the "Wolf-man" and of Dostoevsky's characters. These persons multiply sinful acts just to be punished by their sadistic conscience. If in 1924, Kant is designated by Freud as the accomplice of Sade, their unlikely coupling poses a huge problem because this ends up questioning the moral ways in which civilization deals with aggression. The renunciation to immediate instinctual gratification comes first; then this creates morality; and finally, it is morality that creates cruelty and not the reverse as is often assumed.

Before Freud, Hegel's critique of Moses in "The Spirit of Christianity" (1798–1799) paved the way by providing a negative appraisal of Kantian morality. For Hegel, Kant appeared as the successor of Jewish lawgivers like Abraham and Moses because they "exercised their dominion mercilessly with the most revolting and harshest tyranny, (...) utterly extirpating all life; for it is only over death that unity hovers" (Hegel:1971, p. 188). A stranger to love, Abraham would have taken the whole world as his opposite. He created a terrifying God who was a merciless stranger, the Master of a people he reduces to religious slavery. Hegel anticipates Freud when the latter presented Moses as more Egyptian than the Egyptians, the founder of an "oriental" system of absolute and ferocious domination. The "Spirit of Christianity" sketches the genesis of the castrating Father, anticipating Freud's *Moses and Monotheism* by 150 years.

Hegel accuses Kant of having imported Jewish formalism in morality, religion, and philosophy, thus misunderstanding the Christian commandment of love. Reducing love to a command was the root of cruel perversions of the law. According to Hegel, "in love all thought of duties vanish" (1971, p. 213). Against Moses, Hegel extols Jesus for having raised love above morality. Jesus does not praise reverence for the law but promotes self-annulling love. It is love that "exhibits that which fulfils the law but annuls it as law and so is something higher than obedience to law and makes law superfluous" (Hegel:1971, p. 212).

A similar animus against Kant is felt in Lacan's 1972 essay entitled "*L'étourdit.*" Lacan uses stern terms when he mentions "the inept topology that Kant bodied forth by establishing firmly the bourgeois who cannot imagine anything but transcendence in aesthetics and dialectics" (2001, p. 480). By that time, indeed, Lacan may have heard of Adorno's and Horkheimer's strictures. At least, he betrays a neo-Marxist irritation resembling the debunking of the two philosophers. Lacan also suggests that Sade's critique of morality is not much funnier than Kant's but more logical, a theme discussed by Horkheimer.

When one superimposes Hegel's theological critique of Jewish slavery in the name of an oriental monotheism incapable of love with Hegel's subsequent evocation of the Terror during the French Revolution in the *Phenomenology of Spirit*, the circle linking the universality of an absolute Law with revolutionary "Terror" and death seen as the absolute master is completed. Whether inspired by Kojève's neo-Marxist reconstruction of Hegel's system or by Jean Hyppolite's balanced assessment—Hyppolite's commentary on the *Phenomenology of Spirit* presides over the idea of desire as "desire of the Other." Before participating in Lacan's seminar, he has detailed the Hegelian notion of Alterity in Desire (Hyppolite:1945, pp. 156–162). In fact, Lacan's reading of Kant has remained Hegelian since the beginning. Critiquing Kant as a Hegelian, he sees Sade's merit lying in the negativity he deployed: Sade would thus be the truth of Kant when he exhibits the cruelty

hidden behind the moral law. The cruelty of the Other returns as baleful jouissance, a bad version of the jouissance of the Other that turns into another
categorical imperative; Sade's imperative forces the subject to go beyond
pleasure and the limits of the ego. An excessive jouissance is the dominant
affect in Sade's works—it could have been construed as revolutionary, as
Bataille and his neo-Surrealist friends believed, or it could have remained at
the level of a deep and persistent irritation.

5.4 Irritation or revolution?

In fact, "Kant with Sade" presents less a psychoanalytic or philosophical
critique of Kant's moral philosophy than a game of double irritation. Lacan's
appeal to Kant allows him to reject the fashionable fascination for Sade that
was dominant then among intellectuals. Eric Marty has documented the
extent of Lacan's involvement in "Lacan and the Sadean thing" (Marty:2011,
pp. 171–267). The reference to Sade had been a mainstay of Bataille's philosophy of revolutionary excess. Sade's name has been forever linked with the
French Revolution, but some commentators see him as a remainder from the
ancient regime, with its perverse nobility too satisfied with its privileges, and
others with the revolutionary abolition of all these antiquities. The second
option was defended by the first serious English commentator of Sade,
Geoffrey Gorer whose book on *The Revolutionary Ideas of the Marquis de
Sade* dates from 1934.

I will focus on Gorer's interpretation, which is historical and political.
Gorer highlights Sade's unleashing of revolutionary energy and his critique of
the rapacity of the powerful tyrants who oppress the people, to contrast it
with Lacan's more reserved assessment. Gorer praises Sade not only for having been one of the forces of dissolution of the *ancien régime* that ushered in
the French Revolution but also for having been disillusioned with its outcome, its own murderous excess, all the while refusing to collaborate with
Napoleon once he had seized power. To show how Sade incited revolutionary
violence, Gorer's narrative begins on July 2, 1789. That day, Sade, who had
been incarcerated in the Bastille, began screaming through his high and
barred window that prisoners were executed in the Bastille. The disturbance
he created led to his transfer to the insane asylum at Charenton on July 4.
The governor of the Bastille stated that if "Monsieur de Sade was not removed
tonight from the Bastille, I cannot be answerable to the King for the safety of
the building" (Gorer:1934, p. 53). He was to lose his life during the storming
of the Bastille, his head carried on a pike during the storming that followed
ten days later, on July 14. The first bloody event that ushered in the French
Revolution had been anticipated by Sade.

A second moment discussed by Gorer is when Sade, who was the speaker
for the section des Piques (in which the infamous Marat sat), refused to take
revenge on the Président and Madame de Montreuil, his father-in-law and

mother-in-law, even though they had persecuted him for three decades. Sade who refused to sign their death warrant, which was interpreted as a weakness, soon found himself in jail with the moderates (Gorer:1934, pp. 57–58). This fact had also been pointed out by Simone de Beauvoir in her essay "Must We Burn Sade?" Indeed, de Beauvoir had noted that Sade could have had a good opportunity to unleash his alleged "sadism." He could have become one of those revolutionary delegates who had the power to condemn to the guillotine, to torture and kill whoever they wanted. He refused to do this because he rejected the logic of revolutionary Terror, the Terror that Hegel discussed at length in the *Phenomenology of Spirit*, presenting it as the reign of abstract death. For Sade, this Death had nothing to do with the "cruelty" he extolled. Here was a dehumanized mass murder committed in the name of the law. As de Beauvoir writes, Sade's concept of cruelty was on the contrary predicated on the intensity of life and singularity. Her existentialist vocabulary manages to seize an important feature: Sade's cruelty was meant to "reveal to him particular individuals and his own existence as, on the one hand, consciousness, and freedom, and on the other hand, as flesh. He refused to judge and condemn, or to witness anonymous death from afar" (Beauvoir: 1987, p. 15).

Like de Beauvoir, Gorer has read Freud and thus refuses to apply the epithet of "sadist" to Sade himself. For Gorer and de Beauvoir, Sade was above all a writer who used his texts to express his darkest fantasies; he was carried away by a wish to study sexual passions, which included all the perversions:

His aim is no less than strip every covering, both mental and physical, off man and expose him to our disgusted gaze as the mean and loathsome creature he is. It is the supreme blasphemy. Our gods you may attack, individuals you may show to be monsters, but to attack the human race is unforgivable. Even the paler "scientific" exposures of the Viennese psychoanalysts have called forth the most indignant remonstrances; no wonder de Sade, with his cold and objective exhibition of the most carefully hidden corner of our unconscious minds, of our daily weaknesses and meannesses, has been tracked and pursued by authority all over the world.
(Gorer:1934, p. 88)

Gorer highlights a feature missed by most readers: they do not see that the evil characters presented as diehard libertines can be understood satirically, as a critique of the powerful leaders of the world. Their freewheeling exactions, their unleashed domination, their enjoyment of cruel abuse, all evoke an ancient regime systematically denounced by Sade's narratives. Like Maurice Heine, the first accurate biographer of Sade, Gorer insists that the "ghastly projects" expressed with glee by his reactionary and even "fascist characters" should not be taken to represent the author's wishes. Sade saw himself as a playwright who liked to toy with radical ideas. His Libertines prove *ab absurdo* the mistakes one can make about freedom and sexuality. Sade's works would produce an anti-fascist machine, an insight developed at the time by Bataille in "The Use Value of D.A.F. de Sade (An Open Letter to My Comrades)," a text dating from 1930 (Bataille:1985, pp. 91–102). Like Bataille, Gorer reads a double message in Sade's novels: a call for insurrection in the name of amoral excess, and self-defeating parodies of the delirious megalomania of proto-fascist speakers.

Gorer quotes the Preface to *Justine* in which Sade argues that writers have the right to say anything. Sade's critique of sexuality did not spare religion. Like Lacan, Gorer praises his "elegant" *Dialogue between a Priest and a Dying Man* and presents it as offering a "well-reasoned piece of dialectic" that sounds "moderate and dignified in its language" (Gorer:1934, p. 119). Gorer even compares Sade's Juliette with Lenin: both saw in religion the "opium of the people." The novel *Juliette,* in which we discover a series of corrupt leaders and legislators, "exposes a system of corruption and intrigue which often reads like a description of the United States today, together with a hard-heartedness and sanctimonious cynicism which might have served as a model to Hitler's Germany or our own National Government" (Gorer:1934, pp. 132–133).

In Gorer's view, Sade announced the social and ethical dystopias of Kafka, which is enough to ensure a certain modernity to his rather bland way of writing: "The astounding feature of the book is its modernity; it is difficult to realize that it is the eighteenth century and not the twentieth century he is describing" (Gorer:1934, p. 133). When Saint-Fond explains that he plans to multiply criminal exactions because he fears the onset raid of a popular revolution, his strategy announces those of Hitler and Mussolini. Gorer never doubts that Sade was an authentic revolutionary, a republican disgusted with the system of the ancient regime and shocked by the mechanized murder deployed by revolutionary Terror in 1793.

As we have seen, this was not the road taken by Lacan, perhaps because it was too close to the position of his friend Bataille. Lacan's main effort was to introduce Sade in a dialectical balancing of jouissance and the law; to achieve this, he had to posit a theoretical excess that encompassed both Kant and Sade, each undermining the other. As Jacques Nassif has showed, Lacan and Bataille remained quite close after World War II (Nassif: 2019, pp. 36–57). They spent whole nights drinking, exchanging ideas, and discussing the lives of Sylvia, Bataille's first wife and Lacan's second wife, as well as of Laurence Bataille, the daughter of Georges and Sylvia, who became a psychoanalyst in Lacan's school. Laurence Bataille worried Lacan and Bataille when she became the mistress of Balthus as she was barely sixteen. Balthus, Balthasar Klossowki, was the brother of Pierre Klossowski who wrote so well on Sade. Balthus was a famous artist who liked painting pubescent girls half-undressed.

When Lacan discussed Sade next to Kant in his seminar on ethics, Bataille was still alive. This was not the case when the essay derived from it was published in Bataille's review *Critique*, which may explain its ironic tone. Ten years later, the *Encore* seminar attempted to deliver a philosophy of love. Lacan unpacked his maxims about the *"jouissance* of the Other" that is not the sign of love (Lacan:1998, p. 4). Opposing starkly love and jouissance, he returned to Hegel's starting point when calling Kant "Sadean," which he did when he revisited "Kant with Sade." Lacan concluded that he proved that "morality admits that it is Sade" (Lcan:1998, p. 87). This joke can be heard in English as "a sad thing":

> You can write Sade however you like: either with a capital *S*, to render homage to the poor idiot who gave us interminable writings on that-subject—or with a lower-case *s*, for in the final analysis that's morality's own way of being agreeable (...)—or, still better, you can write it as *çade*, since one must, after all, say that morality ends at the level of the id (*ça*), which doesn't go very far.
>
> (Lacan:1998, p. 87)

The off-hand dismissal of the "poor idiot" signals that Lacan had put more distance then between his ethic of desire and that of Sade. Here is why Lacan had jumped from Sade to Blanchot and then to Klossowski and Bataille. For Bataille, Sade represented the pinnacle of the literature of evil. Lacan accepted that this constituted a breakthrough and a radical subversion whose diamond-like edge he intended to preserve, as we saw in the seminar on Ethics. At that time, Sade's boring and repetitive language was not an obstacle: "The fact that the book falls from one's hands no doubt proves that it is bad, but literary bad-ness here is perhaps the guarantee of the very badness (...). Sade's work belongs to the order of what I call experimental literature" (Lacan:1998, p. 201). In his first approach, Lacan agreed with such an experimental and even revolutionary project, for here was a writing that explores its very limits and staged the possi-bility of its own foreclosure, as Blanchot and Klossowski argued.

5.5 Foreclosed writing and humor

For Klossowski, the foreclosed language of Sade's fictions looked to its out-side, which would correspond to a pragmatism of fantasy: fantasy dictates its laws and limns its own realm. Sade's novels investigate how fantasy is deter-mined from the Outside by the Law. Also, Sade testifies to the division of a desiring subject who has to deploy immense efforts to placate the Other. The Libertines who imagine themselves as the Masters because they torture vic-tims treated as slaves are enslaved to the law of excess, to the norm of an abhorred divine jouissance. Moreover, Sade would be too much "in love with truth" (Lacan: 2007, p. 76). This love of truth makes him write terribly and locks him up in his symptom. The terrible style derives from the repetitive nature of the symptom.

Like Deleuze who, as we saw, had presented Sacher-Masoch's humor as the opposite of Sade's irony, Lacan understand Sade's writing as tending toward its exhaustion (and this might be related with the Kafkaian aspects of Sade's writing pointed out by Gorer). Sade's text exhausts himself in a bewildering accumulation of murders and transgressions, but only approaches absolute jouissance asymptotically, for the Libertine will always feel inferior to it. Meanwhile, Sacher-Masoch's humor would imply that the masochist does not need God, for he or she is happy just dealing with God's lowest servants. Unlike Sacher-Masoch, who is often entertaining, Sade is boring because he remains a theoretician; his novels are stuck in the groove of an all-too theoretical but rather absurd demonstration. It is his love for truth that made him to become, in his life, a "martyr." This explains why his works attract the passionate hagiography of the specialists.

One way of overcoming Sade's dead-end would be to return to Kant, provided one be in a position to appreciate Kant's humor. Freud did, at least in his discussion of the Schreber case; there he makes a lot of a moment of humor in Kant. Freud reminded us that Kant provided a solid model for theoretical elaborations at a point when he introduced a "genetic" approach. Freud meant to rationalize Schreber's "feminine attitude towards God" and make sense of the President's delusion that he turns into a woman who will be sexually abused by God. Schreber, too, has turned into a passive slave of God's *jouissance*. Freud concludes by quoting Kant's famous Irish bull:

> Or else our attempts at elucidating Schreber's delusions will leave us in the absurd position described in Kant's famous simile in the *Critique of Pure Reason*:—we shall be like a man holding a sieve under a he-goat (*Bock*) while someone else milks it.
>
> (Freud: 1963, p. 132)

This witty reference brings us back full circle to the *Critique of Pure Reason*, in which the "Division of General Logic into analytic and dialectic" begins with a momentous but simple question: "What is truth?" Kant attempts to demonstrate that such a question is absurd. According to him, the question presupposes one has attained to the universality of criteria of knowledge by which one could answer it. He thus writes:

> For if the question is in itself absurd and demands answers that are unnecessary, then it not only embarrasses the person raising it, but sometimes has the further disadvantage of misleading the incautious listener: it may prompt him to give absurd answers and to provide us with the ridiculous spectacle where (as the ancients said) one person milks the ram while the other holds a sieve underneath.
>
> (Kant: 1996b, p. 112)

Lacan was right to think that some "fun" appears in Kant's writings, and also that Kant, on the whole, might be funnier than Sade: "Kant could very easily make us lose our serious demeanor here already since he hasn't the slightest sense of comedy (this is proved by what he says about it when he discusses it). //But someone who has no sense of comedy whatsoever is Sade, as has been pointed out" (Lacan:2006, p. 661). Lacan may not have thought that Kant was a true entertainer, although the philosopher was reputed to be a great wit in Koenigsberg. This was Sade's reputation as well. More than Sade, however, Kant had a keen sense for the absurd, which emerges in a minor text in which he surveys the "diseases of the head."

This essay written in 1764, when Kant had just turned forty, hesitates between social banter and medical analysis. Kant begins by locating afflictions like stupidity and madness in the head. Kant had read news of the discovery of an old man living in the woods in the company of a young boy. This man was insane and claimed to be a "goat prophet" who shunned the rest of the humans; thisevent led Kant to meditate on madness. He began by distinguishing between derangement (*Verrückung*), madness (*Wahnsinn*), and insanity (*Wahnwitz*). He attacks his decadent society in which the heart is forgotten: only the head, that is the intellect, is recognized. People prefer having a scoundrel as a friend to being hampered by a moron or dimwit. Then in order to introduce order into these unhealthy transformations, Kant sketches a whole "onomastic of the frailties of the head" that moves from "imbecility" (*Blödsinnigkeit*) to madness (*Tollheit*) via idiocy (*Dummköpfigkeit*) and foolishness (*Narrheit*) (Kant: 2011, p. 206).

If the "dull head" lacks wit, the idiot lacks understanding for "wit" is defined by the agility of the mind, the facility in finding adequate expression; some people are not stupid but dull, as was Clavius, a genius in mathematics who was failed in school because he could not write verse. A person who lacks the capacity to produce accurate judgments is called either a ninny, a simpleton, or an idiot. When such a limited person is simple, even if his heart is estimable, he ends up as a "H-" (Kant's discrete abbreviation for *Hahnrei*, "cuckold"). The truly "foolish person" is one whose judgment and understanding, even when they are sound, are never applied to his own person. Kant sketches a typology of perverse passions deriving from "reversed reason" that is comparable to Sade's taxonomy of passions in the *120 Days of Sodom*. Is Kant pointing to himself when he sketches the psychology of the fool? "The *fool* (*Narr*), however, is at the same time rendered so stupid by his passion that he believes only then to be in possession of the thing desired when he actually deprives himself of it" (Kant: 2011, p. 208).

For Kant, a typically Sadean personage would be the emperor Nero: Nero represents the type of a fool who is so arrogant that he ends up destroying himself (Kant: 2011, p. 209). The delusion leading to willful arrogance is found in silly men and inflated fools. All depends upon "whether silly inconstancy or rigid stupidity has taken possession of the empty head" (Kant: 2011, p. 209). Kant's nomenclature is long and sarcastic, and he provides an exhaustive survey that paves the way for an analysis of madness and enthusiasm. Enthusiasm is the delusion that Kant castigated in his debunking of the apocalyptic visions of a mystic like Swedenborg (we will return to Swedenborg and Boehme later), and the corrective to enthusiasm is given by an author Kant was fond of, Jonathan Swift, who analyzes the foolish utterances of poetry, and thinks that silly as they are, they do have a cathartic function. Bad writing provides a regular purgation for stupid authors, and thus bad poetry is necessary to the body politic. It should be tolerated as a necessary evil, because thanks to its operation, one avoids "disturbing the commonwealth" (Kant: 2011, p. 217): we are back to Aristotle's theory of catharsis, but this time applied to poetry and in a comic mode.

Laughter at pure stupidity would have a political function. More than tragedy, guffaw produced by reading atrocious poems purges the community of its evil humors and even of its dangerous passions. Kant had read a 1733 German translation of Swift's *Peri Bathou or Anti-Sublime*, a hilarious satire on bad writing. Its third chapter sketches a physiological account of poetic writing, which would derive from a "natural or a morbid secretion from the brain." One cannot prevent bad poets from indulging in "poetical evacuations." Here is how Swift talks about writing:

> I have known a man thoughtful, melancholy, and raving for divers days, who forthwith grew wonderfully easy, lightsome, and cheerful, upon a discharge of the peccant humour in exceeding purulent metre. Nor can I question, but abundance of untimely deaths are occasioned for want of this laudable vent of unruly passions: yea, perhaps, in poor wretches (which is very lamentable) for mere want of pen, ink, and paper! From hence it follows, that a suppression of the very worst poetry is of dangerous consequence to the state.
>
> (Swift:1801)

That awful poetry denotated by oxymorons, *vivacité de pesanteur* (vivacity of heaviness), or "alacrity of sinking," matches Kant's decision to situate the diseases of the mind in the head as opposed to the heart. The point is to present the writing as a literal catharsis, that is, as a purgation of the bowels. Having touched on the notion of the excremental sublime via writing in a manner that brings us back to Sade, Kant then develops the trope of a sublimity verging on stupidity: both disclose a sense of the infinite. Stupidity and infinity play the same cathartic function for the "head," not to speak of the bowels or sex. Kant borrows Swift's satire because he adheres to a purgative theory of humor aligned with the ideas of Aristotle and Freud. If we follow Kant, the reverse of rationality would not be madness, or perversion, as Sade demonstrates, but stupidity.

To get a whiff of Kant's sense of humor, which was pervasive, one can look at Robert R. Clewis's *Kant's Humorous Writings, An Illustrated Guide* (Clewis:2021). Clewis details Kant's sophisticated explanations of the causes of laughter and provides witty vignettes and funny stories all illustrated by drawings. Clewis argues that Kant ended up blending the incongruity theory and the relief theory of the comic. Kant announces a Freudian logic of the joke. His gallery of jokes includes the story of the man who cannot have sex because he sees the gallows erected in front of the bedroom in which the woman he covets is sleeping (Clewis: p. 177). It is true that the vignette has the structure of a *Witz*. Clewis reminds us that the point, for Kant, is not to prone abstinence or to stress the domination of reason over passions; in fact, his example meant to suggest that there are moments in a person's life when one can accept the idea of dying. It is better, he argues, to die for moral reasons, like the wish to avoid perjury, or causing an innocent man's terrible torture and death, that for a one-night stand.

Sade's Libertines would accept death in both cases: first to have sex and kill the woman, then by complying with the iniquitous request just to see an innocent man squirm. Sade's subversion entails obeying an unjust law and taking pleasure in this. This awareness justifies Lacan's final diagnosis facing Sade, which sounds like a debunking. As we have seen, at the end of the "Philosophy in the Bedroom," Madame de Mistival, the archetype of the "good mother," tries to save her daughter Eugénie from the evil influence of the Libertines. However, she is horribly tortured by Eugénie, whose name means "well-born." Because Eugénie has discovered an excessive jouissance in crime, she lashes back at her mother and makes her suffer. The mother is raped by a servant who has syphilis, after which her sex is sewn up. The irony is that such a ferocious torture wreaked upon the mother's body ends up generating a paradoxical revirginization. Full of scorn for Sadean enthusiasts, Lacan scoffs, derides, and deflates. Here is how he concludes his essay:

> My verdict is confirmed regarding Sade's submission to the Law. //There is thus precious little here—in fact, nothing—by way of a treatise that is truly on desire/ / What is announced about desire here, in this mistake (*travers*) based on an encounter, is at most but a tone of reason.
>
> (Lacan:2006, p. 667)

If the meaning is clear—Sade is condemned for not having any sense of the law of desire, which sounds like a Freudian Kantianism—Lacan's words are opaque, ambiguous, if not tortuous, when he writes *"dans ce travers pris d'une rencontre."* Usually, *travers* means a minor fault, or wrongness in direction. Is Lacan playing on the idea of *"traversing"* the fantasies exhibited in the works of Sade, this time by taking a *chemin de travers*, a "sideways path," a detour via Kant? Have Kant and Sade met obliquely or squarely, at crossways or at a true intersection?

Is Lacan confessing here that he might have misread both Kant and Sade, both *pris de travers* (taken in bad part, or misunderstood)? All the maxims, theses, concepts, speeches, harangues, diatribes, and fictions spun by those writers have met the fate of Oedipus who faced the Sphinx but was unable to avoid his terrible destiny, even though he had been warned by the oracle that he was to kill his father at a three-ways crossroads.

Whatever the outcome, murder or interpretive triumph in the solving of the riddle, there has nevertheless been a *rencontre*, even if it is a partly missed encounter. Did Lacan manage to marry Kant and Sade for good? Have they become an ideal couple, as žižek surmises (Zizek:1998)? Thanks to Lacan's reciprocal irritation of Kant by Sade and of Sade by Kant, we can at least avoid the orthodoxy that would be defined by the tyranny of goodwill and would be buttressed by morality, a morality opposed by Lacan's ethics of desire. Facing the daily miracles of a godless religiosity marked by perversion, as Sade wished, or by the formalism of the conformity of Reason with its own laws, whose maxims Kant posited, we might only be saved by avoiding the stark alternative, hence going sideways in what I would call Lacan's specific "traversion," that is, a negotiation with perversion that eschews the moralistic overtones of the word.

Traversing Reason and Madness tied together in their Gordian knot, we can choose instead to follow Heidegger in his amble through his *Holzwege* (Heidegger:1950, 2002). The term *Holzwege* is glossed in this way: "In the wood there are paths, mostly overgrown, that come to an abrupt stop where the wood is untrodden. They are called *Holzwege*." Those hidden country paths full of detours and winding roads leading off the beaten tracks may not take us anywhere in particular, although they lead us to a philosopher who was both influenced by Heidegger and who had a change of mind and heart about Lacan: Jean-Luc Nancy.

Bibliography

Barthes, Roland (1976). *Sade, Fourier, Loyola*, trans. Richard Miller, New York, Hill and Wang.

Bataille, Georges (1985). *Visions of Excess, Selected Writings 1927–1939*, edited and translated by Allan Stoekl, Minneapolis, University of Minnesota Press.

Beauvoir, Simone de (1951). "Faut-il brûler Sade?" *Les Temps Modernes* (n. 74, December 1951, p. 1002–1033, and n. 75, Jan. 1952, p. 1197–1230, republished in *Privilèges*, Paris, Gallimard, 1955.

Beauvoir, Simone de (1987). "Must We Burn Sade?" trans. Annette Michelson, in Marquis de Sade, *The 120 Days of Sodom & Other Writings*, New York, Grove Press, Evergreen, 1987, p. 3–64.

Blanchot, Maurice (1995). *The Maurice Blanchot Reader*, ed. Michael Holland, Oxford, Blackwell.

Clewis, Robert (2021). *Kant's Humorous Writings, An Illustrated Guide*, New York, Bloomsbury.

David-Ménard, Monique (1990). *La Folie dans la Raison Pure*, Paris, Vrin.

David-Ménard, Monique (1997). *Les Constructions de l'Universel*, Paris, Presses Universitaires de France.

Freud, Sigmund (1961). "The Economic problem of Masochism," *SE*, XIX, 1961, p. 157–170.

Freud, Sigmund (1963). *Three Case Histories*, New York, Colliers.

Gorer, Geoffrey (1934). *The Revolutionary Ideas of The Marquis de Sade*, London, Wishart & Co.

Hegel, G. W. F. (1971). *Early Theological Writings*, trans. T. M. Knox, Philadelphia, University of Pennsylvania Press.

Heidegger, Martin (1950). *Holzwege*, Frankfurt, Vittorio Klostermann.

Heidegger, Martin (2002). *Off the beaten track*, trans. Julian Young and Kenneth Haynes, Cambridge, Cambridge University Press.

Hénaf, Marcel (1999). *Sade: The Invention of the Libertine Body*, trans. Xavier Callahan, Minneapolis, University of Minnesota Press.

Hyppolite, Jean (1945). *Genèse et Structure de la Phénoménologie de l'Esprit*, Paris, Aubier.

Horkheimer, Max, and Adorno, Theodor W. (1987). *Dialectic of Enlightenment*, trans. J. Cumming, New York, Continuum.

Kant, Immanuel (1949). *Critique of Practical Reason and other writings*, trans. Lewis White Beck, Chicago, The University of Chicago Press.

Kant, Immanuel (1996a). *Practical Philosophy*, trans. Mary J. Gregor, Cambridge, Cambridge University Press.

Kant, Immanuel (1996b). *Critique of Pure Reason*, trans. W. S. Pluhar, Indianapolis & Cambridge, Hackett.

Kant, Immanuel (2011). *Observations on the Feeling of the Beautiful and the Sublime and other writings*, trans. Hollis Wilson, Cambridge University Press.

Klossowki, Pierre (1991). *Sade My Neighbor*, trans. A. Lingis, Evanston, Northwestern University Press.

Lacan, Jacques (1992). *Seminar VII, The Ethics of Psychoanalysis*, trans. Denis Porter, New York, Norton.

Lacan, Jacques (1998). *Seminar XX: On Feminine Sexuality. The limits of love and Knowledge 1972–1973*, trans. Bruce Fink, New York, Norton.

Lacan, Jacques (2001). *Autres Ecrits*, edited by Jacques-Alain Miller, Paris, Seuil.

Lacan, Jacques (2006). *Ecrits*, translated Bruce Fink, New York, Norton.

Lacan, Jacques (2007). *The Other Side of Psychoanalysis, The Seminar Book XVII*, trans. Russell Grigg, New York, Norton.

Lacan, Jacques (2014). *Anxiety*, Seminar X, trans. A. R. Price, Malden, Polity.

Liuci-Goutnikov, Nicolas and Wain, Andrea, curators (2022). *León Ferrari: L'aimable cruauté (1920–2013)*, Paris, Centre Pompidou, April 20-August 29, 2022.

Marty, Eric (2011). *Pourquoi le XXe siècle a-t-il pris Sade au sérieux?* Paris, Seuil.

Nassif, Jacques (2019). *Pour Bataille*, Paris, Editions des Crépuscules.

Sade, D. A. F. de (1965). *Justine, Philosophy in the Bedroom and other writings*, trans. Austryn Wainhouse and Richard Seaver, New York, Grove Weidenfeld.

Sade, D. A. F. de (1966). *The 120 Days of Sodom and Other Writings*, trans. Austryn Wainhouse and Richard Seaver, New York, Grove Press.

Sade, D. A. F. de (1967). *Histoire de Juliette ou Les Prospérités du Vice*, in *Oeuvres Complètes*, vol. 24, Paris, Pauvert.

Sade, D. A. F. de (1990). *Oeuvres*, I, Paris, ed. Michel Delon, Gallimard, Pléiade.

Sade, D. A. F. de (2014). *Justine et autres romans*, ed. Michel Delon, Paris, Gallimard, La Pléiade.

Swift, Jonathan (1801). *Works*, vol. 17, Martinus Scriblerus, or the Art of Sinking In Poetry – Wikisource.

Zizek, Slavoj (1998). "Kant and Sade: The Ideal Couple," *Lacanian Ink*, n° 13, p. 12–25.

Chapter 6

Lacan's quarrel with Nancy and posthumous victory

I have discussed the critique of Lacan that Philippe Lacoue-Labarthe and Jean-Luc Nancy elaborated on the issue of translation; I then linked Nancy and Derrida on the theme of blood and cruelty. I now return to Nancy, who, in his work with Lacoue-Labarthe first, then on his own, has produced one of the most powerful and comprehensive critiques of Lacanian psychoanalysis. I will try to show that this critique aimed at a new foundation taking, as Lacan did, Freud as the Author of a particular type of discursivity. Since the 1970s, Nancy has touched eloquently and creatively on the discourse of psychoanalysis and revisited some of its concepts. His critical conversation with Freud and Lacan, his two major interlocutors, generated strenuous and disinterested departures devoid of any partisan stakes. In the last decade, Nancy seemed to acknowledge a more capacious understanding of psychoanalysis that led to visible agreement with the insights of the later Lacan.

I will follow Nancy's evolution. Some points are well known: first, Nancy and Lacoue-Labarthe deconstructed or dismantled Lacan's system because they saw it predicated on an unstable synthesis of Freud, Heidegger, and Saussure. In a second moment, Nancy offered a new combination of Freud and Heidegger as one sees in *Sexistence*, a 2017 book in which he sums up most of his previous analyses. All the while, Nancy sustained a life-long dialogue with Derrida, first through his critique of Freud's "speculations" and of Lacan's Hegelianism, then by questioning Heidegger's blindness about the issue of sexual difference, which had come to the fore in seminars on "*Geschlecht*" brought to our attention by Derrida. Psychoanalysis, for Nancy as for Derrida, is everywhere in their attentive dialogue. If psychoanalytic issues are disseminated in various contexts, what looms large is the question of sexuality. Symptomatically, an excellent *Nancy Dictionary* announced that an entry on "Psychoanalysis" would be found in page 136 (Gratton and Morin:2015, p. 136). However, at that spot, readers find nothing between the entries "Presentation" and "Relation." If one looks up the latter entry, one is simply sent to "Sexual Relation." Here is an emblematic progression: from a vanishing psychoanalysis to a concept of relation that reveals its truth

DOI: 10.4324/9781032715834-7

as being sexual. Peter Gratton discusses the idea of "Sexual Relation" in his *Nancy Dictionary*, and as we will see, the term *relation* can be used to introduce Nancy's post-Lacanian thinking about sexuality (Gratton and Morin:2015, pp. 215–217).

6.1 Obstacles and Instances

Nancy and Lacoue-Labarthe began with a fanfare in 1973; both being barely thirty, they published *The Title of the Letter: A Reading of Lacan* (Nancy and Lacoue-Labarthe:1992), a book that was seen as a pamphlet against Lacan. I have discussed their critique of Lacan "translations" in Chapter 1. In fact, *The Title of the Letter* presented itself simply as a close reading of one single essay by Lacan, the 1957 "The Instance of the Letter in the Unconscious, or Reason Since Freud" in *Écrits*. Lacoue-Labarthe and Nancy scrutinized Lacan's theoretical program by focusing on a text published at a tumultuous moment in its founder's career.

Lacan had been caught between two institutional "excommunications" when he launched the journal *La Psychanalyse* in which his piece was published along with the translation of Heidegger's "Logos." His *"écrit"* is dense, allusive, and makes huge claims for psychoanalysis. Freud remains the main reference when Lacan formalizes the modes of the dream-work as condensation and displacement equated with poetic metaphors and the metonymy of desire. Ferdinand de Saussure is an important reference for his formula that any sign is made up of a signifier and a signified provides one major theoretical key. And then Heidegger looms large in the essay-manifesto. We have seen how Lacan had paraded his friendship with the philosopher with the proud declaration: "When I speak of Heidegger, or rather when I translate him, I strive to preserve the sovereign significance (*signifiance*) of the speech he proffers" (Lacan:2006, p. 438). Unpacking one by one Lacan's network of concepts and allusions, *The Title of the Letter* proposes a critique of all these terms, above all questioning expressions like "sovereign significance."

When *The Title of the Letter* was published, it was perceived as a wholesale attack on Lacanian doctrine that came directly from the school of Derrida. Lacan voiced his ambivalent reaction to the publication in his seminar. Conceding that here was an example of solid philosophical commentary, admitting that none of his own students had been able to read him as thoroughly, he suggested nevertheless that the two authors were motivated by the worst intentions. Amusingly, Lacan made a point of never naming the philosophers who, in his irritated response, only appear as *"sous-fifres."* They are reduced to being Derrida's stooges, his underlings, his minions, his peons, thus mere subalterns. These slavish disciples had acted at the behest of a master whose name, likewise, remains unmentioned, even though everyone knew that it was Derrida. The fact was that Nancy and Lacoue-Labarthe, the

goon squad of deconstruction, had been shooting up Lacanian psychoanalysis and almost succeeded in destroying its foundations.

The philosophers' commitment to a reading of Lacan's text literally, word
for word, patiently, philosophically, and rigorously, could not but attest to a
certain love. As Lacan quipped, that love was the flipside of hatred. Such
love-hate ambivalence generated some irritation in Lacan, although he recognized that the *Title of the Letter* had performed an extraordinary task.
Although the authors were never named, Lacan recommended that everyone
should buy their book. His followers would decide whether *The Title of the
Letter* was right. Did they have a point when concluding that Lacan had created a hopeless muddle by combining Saussure's structural linguistics, Freud's
Unconscious, and Heidegger's *aletheia?* In one curious passage, Lacan even
praises the amazing prescience of his two readers, who, as he stated, had
anticipated his forthcoming explorations. Lacan had planned to use Aristotle's
concept of *enstasis* when developing the "formulas of sexuation" he had
begun presenting. Uncannily, Nancy and Lacoue-Labarthe seemed to have
guessed that move and its outcome:

> They even discover the *enstasis*, the Aristotelian logical obstacle that I had
> reserved for the end. It is true that they do not see the relationship *(rap-
> port)*. But they are so used to working well, especially when something
> motivates them—the desire, for example, to obtain their Master's, a truly
> serendipitous term here—that they even mention that in the footnote on
> pages 28 and 29."
>
> (Lacan:1998, p. 69)

This snide remark introduces the loaded term *rapport* to which I will return
later. Lacan denigrates the level of their work when he suggests that the philosophers were graduate students writing an MA thesis, which refers to the
idea of the discourse of the Master in his theory of the "four discourses" (see
Introduction p. 3). Such an accusation does not seem justified by the note on
Aristotle in which Nancy and Lacoue-Labarthe comment on the word
"instance" used in the title of Lacan's essay.

Nancy and Lacoue-Labarthe were quoting Émile Benveniste, who in 1956
suggested using the term *"instance of discourse"* in order to describe the
insertion of a speaker in speech, before moving on to Roman Jakobson's
shifters and following the term *enstasis* that was used in several places by
Aristotle. It is true that, in the first French edition, that note was made
unreadable because a typographical mistake permutating two lines, which
might have given Lacan trouble deciphering it. However, this cannot explain
why Lacan accuses Nancy and Lacoue-Labarthe of not having "seen the rapport" (made the connection). Here is the end of the footnote by Nancy and
Lacoue-Labarthe, an endnote in the English translation:

But one will not forget that for Aristotle, ενστασις (*enstasis*), in the theory of refutation, designates the obstacle which one opposes to the reasoning of an adversary (*Rhetoric* II, 25, 1402a); cf. *Prior Analytics* II, 26, *Topics* VIII, 2, 157ab. This "agency" is, in particular, what the exception opposes to a universal prediction. An example of this *topos* happens to be the following, to be appreciated according to its most "proper" meaning: "it is honourable in some places to sacrifice one's father, for example amongst the Triballi, but it is not honourable in an absolute sense" (*Topics* II, 11, 115b).

(Nancy:1992, p. 24, note 4)

What is remarkable indeed is that Nancy and Lacoue-Labarthe had found in Aristotle an anticipation of Freud's theory of the murder of the Father. This point resonates with remarks that parallel Lacan's readings of Hegel and Aristotle with those of Bataille. In any event, their note's content and tone hardly warrant Lacan's accusation that they "do not see the relationship." It looks as if Lacan had feared that Lacoue-Labarthe and Nancy had seen the value of the concept of *enstasis* that runs through Aristotle's *Analytics*, *Rhetoric* and *Topics*.

The term *enstasis* used by the two philosophers as a key concept in Aristotle ushers in the key concept of "exception," a term that became a conceptual cornerstone in Lacan's theory of sexuation. Indeed, *enstasis*, which literally means any obstacle opposed to an argument, turns for Lacan into the idea of a singular exception to a universal logical predicate. Thus, *enstasis* would allow one to posit a couple composed of the universal and its exception. Here is the logical couple that led Lacan to set in place a mechanism through which he would establish that "there is no sexual relationship," a motto to which I will return.

In seminar XX, Lacan who continues offering acid praise to the two philosophers guides his audience to passages culled from Aristotle's *Rhetoric* and *Topics*. He announces that *enstasis* will later introduce the formula of sexual difference in terms of "all" and "not-all" (S 20, pp. 70–72). What is quite curious is that when Lacan explained his formulas, unpacking them, dividing the process of sexuation into four logical formulas, which he did in the following meeting (Lacan:1998, p. 78), he did mention Aristotle's *Nichomachean Ethics* (Lacan:1998, p. 82) but never returned to *enstasis*. If the term had played a useful logical function for him, it was then muted. It looks as if Lacan had left it to professional philosophers like Nancy's and Lacoue-Labarthe. This testifies to the impact of their commentary on Lacan. Such an impact would reverberate forty years later in the texts that Nancy devoted to sexual enjoyment.

Lacan went on with his formalization of sexuality via Aristotle; he took as a starting point the idea that the negative particular would provide an exception that proves the rule of the affirmative universal. To be more precise, he thinks here of the exception constituted by the Freudian farther of the horde, the mythical father who has not been castrated but castrates and enjoys the possession of all the women of the group. This figure entails that by contrast there will be one universal rule for all other men: all men are submitted to castration if they are inscribed on the male side of the formula of sexuation.

For serious philosophers who have examined Lacan's borrowings from Aristotle, this specific twist on Aristotelian logic is glib and not very rigorous. This is the opinion of Pierre-Christophe Cathelineau who does not mention the concept of *enstasis* once in his excellent book on *Lacan Reader of Aristotle* (see Cathelineau:1998, pp. 276–281). Cathelineau insists on the "torsion" brought by Lacan to Aristotle's categories. Lacan's logic is more Freudian than Aristotelian: in Aristotelian logic one cannot admit that a universal positive judgment depends upon the negative particular to be affirmed as the rule justified by an exception. In fact, Lacan may have been wise to leave the term *enstasis* to Nancy and Lacoue-Labarthe.

In spite of this, it would be exaggerated to reduce Lacoue-Labarthe's and Nancy's book to an attack mounted by professional philosophers eager to redress or denounce conceptual blunders and hurried appropriations in Lacanian theory. One of the conclusions of their multifaceted reading, nevertheless, insists that there is a gap between the post-Saussurean linguistics of the signifier (a terminology that seems, on the other hand, quite correct if one wishes to introduce some order in Freud's mechanisms of dream formation) and Heidegger's theory of language. Even when Lacan suggests something like negative theology of truth reduced to a "hole" in knowledge through which both jouissance and the Real appear, *The Title of the Letter* proves that mixing Saussure and Heidegger cannot yield a good cocktail.

On the other hand, it was by showing how Lacan was torn between flaunting his scientific credentials and his ultimate philosophical goals that his commentators have saved his doctrine from closing itself and turn into an all too rigid system. They acknowledge Lacan's urge to promote poetic creation, a point that see a saving grace given the inconsistencies and contradictions of his theory. To do so, Nancy and Lacoue-Labarthe must go beyond the textual limits they had fixed, as a passage states:

> the formulas of 'congruence' which *The Instance* gives for metaphor and metonymy, as well as the entire algorithmic process and all the calculations it may engender, are to be taken between the game and the feint, Lacan himself forbidding that one be taken in by them.
>
> (Nancy:1992, p. 119, trans. modified)

If Nancy and Lacoue-Labarthe fault Lacan for misguided attempts at blending structuralist linguistics and Heidegger's ontology, it is because they take seriously Heidegger's rejection of any positive science of language—language has to remain a constellation of poetic signs always pointing elsewhere.

This was not Lacan's idea, and on this point, he was not a disciple of Heidegger. Moreover, as we have seen, Lacan presented his own translation of Heidegger's "Logos" as a way of proving that he did not suffer from the disease of "Heideggerianism" or "neo-Heideggerianism" (Lacan:2006, p. 438). Nevertheless, Lacoue-Labarthe and Nancy still think that Heidegger's "logos" had turned into a "master word" for Lacan (Nancy:1992, p. 134). Such a mastery would derive from Lacan's wish to own truth. Here is why Lacan could send back to them the accusation of working toward the acquisition of a Master's degree.

6.2 The truth of sexual relation(ship)s

The question of truth in psychoanalysis remained an open issue for Nancy. It sketched a theoretical program to which he returned after 2001 when he wrote The "There Is" of Sexual Rapport. In fact, in spite of the title that seems to announce a flat rejection of Lacan's theory predicated on the motto that "There is no sexual rapport," Nancy does not pursue the deconstruction of Lacanian psychoanalysis begun in 1973. On the contrary, reading both Freud and Lacan in a more positive manner, his evolution evinces a deeper agreement, along with a quest for a stable and robust foundation. When Nancy presented the works of Freud to a Japanese audience, he insisted on two main elements: the key to Freud's doctrine was the theory of the drives; Freud's system was the most non-religious thought of the twentieth century.

Working at the cusp between poetics and deconstruction, Nancy cleared a new path for French phenomenology whose edges he sharpened without falling prey to the "religious turn" lying in wait for phenomenologists like Emmanuel Levinas or Jean-Luc Marion, an evolution eloquently denounced by Janicaud (see Janicaud:2001). Indeed, it looks as if Nancy's reading of Lacan owes something to Freud's distance from religion when he quipped: "The Freudian invention is the most clearly and resolutely unreligious of modern inventions. It is also for this reason that it cannot even believe in itself" (Nancy:2010). One might even argue that Nancy tried to help Lacan not to believe in himself. It seems to me that Nancy brought a welcome corrective to Lacan's hubristic drift in the last decade, that is the time when Lacan started referring to himself in the third person. As Nancy's work testifies, it is when psychoanalysis starts to believe too much in itself that it becomes imperative to make it aware of its own delusions.

A delusion is not the same as a mythology. Nancy points out the need for a Freudian mythology, for he knew that Freud had called his theory of the drives a "mythology" in New Introductory Lectures on Psycho-analysis: "The theory of the drives is so to speak our mythology. The drives are mythical entities, magnificent in their indefiniteness" (Freud:1965, p. 118, modified). Alluding to the theory of the Triebe, Freud added in the same lecture XXXII that Trieb was a good term: it calls up the image of a strong pressure:

"We picture it as a certain quota of energy which presses in a particular direction. It is from this pressing that it derives the name of *Trieb*" (Freud:1965, p. 120). While taking over the concept of the drive, Nancy refused the Lacanian idea that everything depends upon the primacy of the *Unbewußt* (Unconscious). As we saw about the issue of translation, Nancy and Lacoue-Labarthe refused to take the Unconscious as an undisputed source or fountain of truth. They rejected the view that there would be an unconscious truth out of reach of discourse, language, and rationalization.

However, when their friend and colleague Alain Badiou called Lacan's theory an "anti-philosophy," Nancy would reject this dismissive solution for he wanted to keep thinking and philosophizing with Freud and with Lacan. As Nancy explained later, it would be wrong to think that Freud had discovered a "dark continent," as he himself imagined, a continent equated with the Unconscious. In fact, Freud merely provided a new narrative—here was his real invention:

> …there is no Freudian discovery and … the unconscious is not an organ. But Freud did make an invention: he invented man's narrative. Before, it was a Creator or Nature that had created Man, before, man was promised a celestial afterlife or the survival of his species, but instead, Freud gives man another origin and another destination. Man comes from a momentum [*élan*] or a surge [*poussée*] which surpasses him, which surpasses in any case much of what Freud designates as the "self" [*moi*]. He calls this momentum or surge the *Trieb*.
>
> (Nancy:2010, n.p.)

Nancy inherits from Lacan a rejection of any form of ego-psychology; indeed, the foundation he is looking for exceeds the human self, even any kind of subjectivity; at times, it looks quite close to a Bergson's *élan vital* or even Groddeck's *It*:

> The notion of *Trieb*—or of the *Triebe* complexes—signifies a movement that has come from elsewhere, from the non-individuated, from what is the hidden archaic state of our origins, proliferating and confused—and that is: nature; the world; the whole of humanity behind us, and behind it what makes it possible; the emergence of the sign and the gesture; the call of all of us to the elements, to forces, to the possible and the impossible; the sense of infinity lying ahead of us, lying behind and amongst us; the desire to answer to this call, and to expose oneself to it. We originate from this movement, from this momentum, from this surge. In the final analysis, it is within this movement and as such a movement that we can *grow*—as we say in French when talking about plants: it is thanks to this movement that we rise and become what we are capable of being.
>
> (Nancy:2010. n.p.)

Freud provides a strong conceptual lever for Nancy because he allows him to rethink Heidegger's ontology. The upsurge of the Freudian drives would lead to the sense of the "thrownness" (*Geworfenheit* for Heidegger) of all human subjects:

> This surge comes from elsewhere than us. It makes of us a grown individual, a being which has not been "produced" by a set of causes, but led, launched, projected, or even "thrown" (to reuse a word of Heidegger's). This "elsewhere" is not a "beyond", it is neither a theological transcendence, nor a simple immanence as some atheistic negative theologies have understood it to be. This "elsewhere" is inside us: it forms within us the most creative and the most powerful engine driving this momentum, which is what we are.
>
> (Nancy:2010, n.p.)

Refusing any religious reading of Heidegger or Freud, Nancy insists on the double character of the drive. What is remarkable is that the Freudian drives stand both outside and inside the subject:

> This is because it (this elsewhere) is nothing less than our being, or it is being in itself once it has detached itself from its ontological moorings. It is "being" considered in the meaning of the verb "to be": it is a motion, a movement, an emotion, the shock and rise of desire and fear, waiting and attempting, trying, accessing, even crisis and exaltation, exasperation or exhaustion, the forming of forms, the invention of signs, the incoercible tension moving to an unbearable point where it fragments or lays itself down.
>
> (Nancy:2010, n.p.)

The point is not to launch a new ontology but to rethink the nexus between being and sexuality—one of the key points of the Freudian intervention in culture. Paradoxically, this move will entail a "return to Lacan" for Nancy.

Such a "return" occurred when Nancy began once more to read Lacan closely. This time it was neither as "text" or as "discourse" but as the production of an idiosyncratic thinker-poet stringing cryptic one-liners. One of them was the motto: "There is no sexual relation." Denying this flatly in *The "There Is" of the Sexual Relation* (Nancy:2013, pp. 1–22), Nancy tackles head-on Lacan's paradoxical statement. An orthodox Lacanian might be tempted to see in Nancy's title nothing more than a rejection. Lacan repeatedly stated since the end of 1960s that "there was no sexual relation," and then Nancy affirms the exact opposite: "there is a sexual relation." As the translator observes, the key here is the term *rapport*. Lacan keeps referring to "*rapport sexuel*," which means both "relation," "relationship," and "having sex" (Nancy:2013, p. 109). Nancy began his examination with a battery of observations that sounded highly critical, especially when he remarked that Lacan's expression, "There is no sexual relation," has an air of deliberate provocation; it is a paradox because it flies in the face of common sense: after all, what we call "sexual relations" happen every day (Nancy:2013, p. 2). Lacan's motto was meant to shock, and because it states something like: "What there is, is not." Such a sweeping negation might be inscribed in a philosophical genealogy, for it sounds like similar claims made by Hegel and Heidegger when they assert that, somehow, Being is not. In fact, a Heideggerian logic would have no problem in accepting the idea that the "sexual relationship" is a "being" (small b) that is and whose "Being" (capital b) is not. The real Being coupled to the human subjects engaged in an active sexual life would be hidden; it would never allow itself to be seen, counted, or even defined.

Being as such can be approached via a word that can be read either as a verb or as a noun, a word that sounds quite vulgar in French; Nancy uses the verb *baiser* (to fuck) (Nancy:2013, p. 2). Deriving from an archaic term, *baiser*, which meant "give someone a kiss," the verb has since the middle of the twentieth century taken the slang meaning of "to fuck" or "to shack." This noun-verb would condense the Lacanian paradox provided it can be conjugated both in the active and in the passive voice. Psychoanalysis seems to imply a huge reversibility in sexual matters. Nancy nimbly concludes his semantic overview as follows: "the foundational expression of psychoanalysis is that I am kissed every time I kiss, fucked every time I fuck" (Nancy:2013, p. 3). What does Nancy mean? Deploying a logic that looks more Freudian than Lacanian—one might think of the letters Freud sent to Fliess while they were exploring the inversion and multiplication due to bisexuality—this utterance implies that, according to psychoanalysis, I am severely mistaken if I believe in any sexual "relation." One would have to believe that there is such a thing as the One—that is union or fusion—when in fact there are always only two—that is, separation. Nancy adds then a second critical intervention: reflecting on passivity and activity, he concludes that the provocative force of the Lacanian motto is meant to do more than shock: it should also prohibit and interrupt. The pragmatic effect of this prohibition would be tantamount to a *coitus interruptus* (Nancy:2013, pp. 3–4), which is not so surprising in view of the incest taboo, the castration threats, and the panoply of Freudian concepts. A certain castration in sexuality would correspond to the renunciation to straightforward empirical evidence.

Having reached this point, Nancy expects that Lacanian analysts will cry foul play. Indeed, his reading seems to be partisan or to present a deliberate misreading. However, after a few detours through Aristotle and Kant on the concept of "relation," a concept that never refers to a thing but to rapports between entities, Nancy reconciles himself with the idea of a "there is no." Lacan made of "love" the means by which men and women overcome the fateful "There is no…" Noticing that he has strayed from the letter of Lacan's text, Nancy backtracks to tackle the concept of "relation" that he presents as the key to sexuality. Hence, relation will become Nancy's main concept when discussing the bodily aspects of sexuality.

Relation, whether sexual or not, cannot be reducible to an "act," even if common French usage treats them as synonyms. Nancy ends up approaching Lacan's original meaning. If common usage assumes that relation is something, whereas in fact, it is an action, not a product, one must unpack the intertwined meanings knotted together in Lacan's motto that "There is no sexual relation." Nancy explains that the claim that there is no sexual relationship means that there is no return, no report, no conformity, no preestablished proportion for what is involved whenever a couple mates. If the claim is about the relation of two subjects in the sexual act, this act asserts, as Lacan stated, that *rapport* as a measured homology between two beings is impossible.

Finally, moving from Hegel to Heidegger, Nancy reiterates the critique of *homoiosis* that I had presented about translation, but this time, he applies it directly to sexuality:

> The sexual is not a variety of the genre known as relation, but in the sexual we see the extent of relation and see it fully exposed. I could say that the sexual relates (*rapporte*) what there is of relation (*rapport*), but its report— its account and its narrative—is not totalizing and does not close the circle. (...) The sexual is not a predicate, for it itself is no more a substance of a thing than relation is a substance or thing. The sexual is its own difference, or its own distinction. Being distinguished as sex or sexed is what makes sex or sexed-ness.
>
> (Nancy:2013, p. 9)

Earlier criticisms facing Lacan tend to fade away. In fact, Nancy offers a profound and subtle philosophical commentary of Lacan's sentence, one that remains entirely in accord with its original logic. Whether we stress the beginning of the sentence ("*There is* no sexual relationship") or its end ("There is no sexual *relationship*")—in other words, whether we stress the ontology (the being of the relationship) or the epistemology (the nature of this relationship, or the possibility of calculating the relationship by framing it as a fraction or as complementarity, as the homology between the two sides of a straightforward and clear-cut opposition, i.e. masculine-feminine, active-passive, lover-beloved, etc., namely pairs of opposites that must, of course, be applied to subjects of the same biological sex)—we always presuppose a dialectical relationship between two terms, "no" and "sexu*al*.

Nancy suggests that one should think through the negativity and restlessness implied by the maxim of "there is no sexual relationship." If "relation" leads to sexual difference, it is because it shatters any belief in a pre-existing "One." Whereas Lacan made a place for the One by giving it the name of "Love," for Nancy the shattering brought about by the experience of sex is such a disruption and breakthrough that there is no need to sublimate it or elevate it in the name of love. Quite systematically, Nancy remains down to earth and close to bodies: talks of sexuality as "fucking," he introduces jouissance and defines sexual enjoyment as "coming." This sexual climax entails a specific encounter with finitude. As he notes, Lacan never excluded this idea: "The finitude of relation or jouissance (which is, after all, what Lacan wants to make us understand) must be understood as what punctuated (finishes, terminates, *and fines*, that is, refines) sexual infinity" (Nancy:2013, p. 15). Following Lacan's lead, Nancy also introduces limits. The Other jouissance or the jouissance of the Other cannot be infinite, he asserts. These should not be reserved to women and mystics, as Lacan suggested in his seminar on love (Lacan:1998, p. 76), for it is divided and predicated upon its impossibility. Concluding with a rephrasing of the initial statement (*"the sexual" is the "there is" of relation*), Nancy adds that there is no "there" there: in other words, no subject, no *Dasein*, is given or available to recuperate such an enjoyment (Nancy:2013, p. 21).

Nancy makes the same point explicitly in a dialogue with Adèle van Reeth about the sexual sense of "coming":

> I don't think that what Lacan says about feminine *jouissance* means it's only the woman who *jouit*. If I were to rephrase it in my own words, I would say of feminine *jouissance* that it is neither the possession nor appropriation of something, but rather openness to an alterity, since the woman is in the position of what Lacan calls "the Other," the big Other. *Jouissance*, then, would make woman into that big Other, that is, that which remains outside language and meaning, and which for that reason escapes any capture by a subject.
>
> (Nancy:2017, p. 21)

The concept of jouissance deployed here would lie beyond satisfaction and bring us closer to an ecstasy, an ecstasy capable of differing from itself, thus lacking a stable site and remaining absolutely ungraspable. Nancy reiterates this analysis in *Sexistence*, ironically pointing out that Lacan had anticipated this move in a February 1973 seminar when telling his audience There is a jouissance, since I am confining myself here to jouissance, a jouissance of the body that is, if I may express myself thus—why not make a book title out of it? it'll be the next book in the Galilée collection—"beyond the phallus." That would be cute, huh? (Lacan:1998, p. 74) Rebounding on this allusion to the *Title of the Letter*, Nancy quips that his present book could have been "cute" enough to please Lacan (Nancy:2017, p. 143, note).

Finally, in a move that was somewhat predictable, we reach the idea that the concept of jouissance itself turns into an equivalent of Derrida's *différance*. The point is underlined in a note to *The "There Is" of Sexual Relation*, when Nancy alludes to Derrida's unfinished treatment of *Geschlecht* (sexuality in German, along with other meanings) in Heidegger: "Derrida's *différance* must therefore be sexual. (...) Therefore being is sexed and/or sexing" (Nancy:2013, p. 109). Sexual difference has turned into ontological difference. Here, finally, and momentously, Freud and Hegel merge with Heidegger.

In all these discussions, Nancy distinguishes himself both as a brilliant commentator and a sharp critical reader. He is able to read Lacan closely and critically at once in an effort to understand why psychoanalysis still matters today. He rejects the vulgar philosophy of jouissance taken as simple and immediate enjoyment deployed by a very bad but quite successful French philosopher like Michel Onfray; Onfray attempted to debunk Freud in many ways while claiming that Freud should be exposed as a fraud. Moreover, Onfray promoted an idea of a jouissance that would be obtained without social repression (Onfray:1991). Against this type of non-thought, Nancy remains closer to Derrida, whose books on the concept of *Geschlecht* introduced the wedge of sexual difference into the heart of Heidegger's philosophy.

Thus, by a curious historical twist, Nancy ended up recombining the two main references of Lacanian discourse, Freud and Heidegger, that he had worked to disjoin so ferociously in *The Title of the Letter*. What emerges from the confrontation between Freud and Heidegger in Lacan's theory bridges the gap between a science of the Unconscious and a new mythology. If the Unconscious is the modern equivalent of the ancient soul, we need to return to that obscure hinge and make better sense of the links knotting language and body, drives and pleasure, life and death, culture and individuals. One of these knots will be provided by Lacan's theory of the letter as pertaining both to human activities and to the natural world.

Bibliography

Cathelineau, Pierre-Christophe (1998). *Lacan, lecteur d'Aristote: Politique, métasphysiaue, logique*, Paris, Editions de l'Association freudienne internationale.

Derrida, Jacques (2020). *Geschlecht III: Sex, Race, Nation, Humanity*, trans. Katie Chenoweth and Rodrigo Therezo, Chicago, University of Chicago Press.

Freud, Sigmund (1965). *New Introductory Lectures on Psycho-analysis*, New York, Norton.

Gratton, Peter and Morin, Marie-Eve, editors (2015). *The Nancy Dictionary*, Edinburgh, Edinburgh University Press.

Janicaud, Dominique (2001). *Phenomenology and the theological turn: the French debate*, New York, Fordham University Press.

Lacan, Jacques (1998). *On Feminine Sexuality, The Limits of Love and Knowledge, 1972–1973, Encore, The Seminar of Jacques Lacan, Book XX*, trans. Bruce Fink, New York, Norton.

Lacan, Jacques (2006). *Ecrits*, trans. Bruce Fink, New York, Norton.

Nancy, Jean-Luc, and Lacoue-Labarthe, Philippe (1992) *The Title of the Letter: A Reading of Lacan*, trans. François Raffoul and David Pettigrew, Albany, SUNY Press.

Nancy, Jean-Luc (2010). "Freud—so to speak. Introduction to the Japanese edition of S. Freud's Complete Works", trans. Gianmaria Senia, *European Journal of Psychoanalysis*, https://www.journal-psychoanalysis.eu ' freud-so-to-speak

Nancy, Jean-Luc and van Reeth, Adèle (2017). *Coming*, trans. Charlotte Mandell, New York, Fordham University Press.

Nancy, Jean-Luc (2017). *Sexistence*, Paris, Galilée.

Nancy, Jean-Luc (2013). *Corpus II – Writings on Sexuality*, trans. Anne O'Byrne, New York, Fordham University Press.

Onfray, Michel (1991). *L'art de jouir*, Paris, Grasset.

Chapter 7

"Perpetual translation made language"

Lacan's response to deconstruction in "Lituraterre"

I have mentioned the seminar in which Lacan discovered with some irritation and annoyance *The Title of the Letter*. At first, Lacan seemed paralyzed by the precision of those close readings allied with a sharp critique of his philosophical synthesis. In fact, such reproaches missed their aim, he thought, because he had anticipated the attack and already given his response to deconstruction. What was needed was a clearer distinction between Derrida's concept of writing and his concept of the Letter. Here is why Lacan moved on in his seminar, for what mattered most at the time was his new forays into the logic of sexuation. In fact, his response on the letter was rarely mentioned or discussed, because, quite simply, the text is too hard to read. Indeed, Lacan's new theory of the letter was presented in a difficult, opaque, and highly allusive essay entitled "Lituraterre."

Like most of Lacan's "*écrits*," this essay began as an occasional piece in response to a prompt. The invitation to introduce a special issue on "literature and psychoanalysis" came from the editorial board of *Littérature* at the university of Paris-VIII Vincennes. Their tri-quarterly had been launched in February 1971 and that special issue dated October 1971 was its third instalment. The published version reproduced in *Autres écrits* (Lacan:2001, pp. 11–20) evinces discrepancies with the oral version that Lacan read in his Seminar on May 12, 1971, a few months in advance of the publication. One can read his "Leçon sur *Lituraterre*" in book XVIII of the *Séminaire, D'un discours qui ne serait pas du semblant* (Lacan:2007, pp. 113–127).

The board of the new journal was the department of French Literature at Paris VIII, that notorious "experimental" university founded in the wake of May 1968 that was called "Vincennes" for its location. "Vincennes" had a department of psychoanalytic studies, which was unheard of at the time in France, and it was in the hands of Lacanians like Jacques-Alain and Judith Miller. It was in this context that Lacan gave a memorable lecture on politics to an unruly crowd of students on December 3, 1969 (see Lacan:1990, pp. 117–128). It seems that he accepted the invitation to write an introduction for *Littérature* as a gesture of collegiality. However, what he published

DOI: 10.4324/9781032715834-8

is not at all an "introduction." It is an original text marked by strongly auto-biographical features.

Lacan had been encouraged to be creative by a close friend of his, Hélène Cixous, one of the founders of Paris-Vincennes. Cixous published a section of *Portrait du Soleil* on Freud's Dora in the same issue. Bernard Mérigot, one of the editors, asked pointedly: "Must psychoanalysis be taught in universities?" (Bellemin-Noël:1971, pp. 116–120). Merigot reminded his readers of Lacan's "Analyticon" of December 3, 1969, later added as an appendix at the end of seminar XVII. In this lecture, Lacan addressed the Vincennes students and reproached them for making excessive and contradictory political demands.

In fact, not everyone in that issue was Lacanian. Jean Bellemin-Noël, a member of the editorial committee who worked on the links between psycho-analysis and literature, was not close to Lacan. André Green, also a contrib-utor, was by then a major contradictor, as we have seen about affects. The authors of the Postface insisted that if they did not aim at being exhaustive in their exploration of the links between psychoanalysis and literature, they shared one common presupposition: they refused to "apply" psychoanalysis to literature, a point made by Lacan repeatedly at the time (see Bellemin-Noël:1971, p. 121).

7.1 Unleashing the letter

It is evident that Lacan is given pride of place in number three of *Littérature*. Not only is his essay the first, but it is printed in a much larger font than the rest. "Lituraterre" remains an atypical essay, for this was the single time Lacan would take a whole seminar to read a text he was going to publish independently. As an *écrit*, it has extra theoretical weight. In it Lacan pro-poses a new theory of the letter. Jacques-Alain Miller was entirely justified when he placed the text at the beginning of *Autres Écrits*: "Lituraterre" plays the same inaugural role that Lacan's seminar on Poe's "Purloined Letter" held in *Écrits* in 1966. It is not by chance that Lacan revisits his own reading of Poe in this text about Dupin's handling of a famous letter whose content we will never know. However, in "Lituraterre," the letter acquires a new autonomy and a distinctive agency. The letter cannot be reduced to the "logic of the signifier." Lacan had heard objections coming from the school of Derrida.

In this playful and literary text, Lacan performs what his title suggests. His witty spoonerism brings *literature* as literally as possible down to the earth, thus *à terre*. This allows him to propose an ontology of the letter as material and belonging to the earth (*terre*). Some effects of this are terrifying (*atterrer* means to appall, to terrify, and we will see that a moment of sub-limity is needed to reach the main insight); other consequences are matter of fact, if not lowly materialist (*terre à terre*). In the end, we will be saved if we know how to land safely (*atterrir*). Such interwoven linguistic games are hard to render in English. By repeating Lacan's permutation, one could yield echoes between "light" or "lite," or literature and erasure. Sticking to the theme of the earth, Dany Nobus has suggested two translations, "erasure-land" and "stainearth" (Nobus:2013, p. 337). Lacan himself gives a hint about possible translations when he quotes Joyce, whose coining of "litter-age" (*Finnegans Wake*, 292. 16) condenses *letter* and *litter*, as we find in "The letter! The litter!" (Joyce:1939, p. 93) or "letter from litter" (Joyce:1939, p. 615). Joyce linked the idea of writing as a material process linked with the physicality of the revolving orb of the earth: "This ourth of years is not save brickdust and being humus the same rotourns. He who runes may rede it on all fours" (Joyce:1939, p. 18). In fact, Lacan offers us his own "runes" to read thanks to his identification with Joyce, a proof of his own experimental modernism.

Even if Lacan calls his title a "spoonerism" (*contrepet*), meaning that two syllables are inverted, the word "lituraterre" does not mean much in French; this is not the case with usual *contrepèteries*, a genre that the left-wing satirical weekly *Le Canard Enchaîné* has illustrated in each of its issues. A *contrepeterie* works on a sentence that looks banal enough, but whose permutations of letters and syllables yield obscene meanings. François Rabelais had illustrated the genre in his *Fourth Book* when Panurge, the irrepressible joker, puns on "*femme folle à la messe*" (woman who is mad about mass) in which he hears "*femme molle à la fesse*" (woman who is soft in the ass, see Rabelais:1552, p. 175). Lacan was reading Rabelais next to Joyce at the time, as we see from an allusion (Lacan:2001, p. 12). Reading Rabelais's fourth book, Lacan would discover the word "*symptomates*," a plural meaning "symptoms" (Rabelais:1552, p. 155). The word, glossed by Rabelais in authorial endnotes as an "accident caused by diseases" like coughing, difficulty in breathing, or headache, reappeared as a key to understand Joyce, for soon after Joyce would be called the "sinthome," or the symptom of literature.

A simple example of what would be a purely Lacanian *contrepeterie* is the rather innocuous "*Salut, Fred!*" (Hi, Fred!), except that one can hear in the greeting: "*Phallus raide!*" (Erected phallus!). Freud discussed similar tongue-twisters under the category of verbal jokes. He quoted Lichtenberg who laughed at a friend who was such a classicist that he automatically read *Agamemnon* instead of *angenommen* ("assumed") (Freud:2003, p. 88). If the word "lituraterre" does not hide any obscenity as far as I can see, its scrambled syllables are replete with suggestions that enact the operation of "rature": it is a crossing out and an erasure of words like "*lit*" (bed), "*rater*" (to fail), or "*terre*" (earth). Indeed, the pun joining "*rature*" (crossing out, erasure) and "literature" is not unusual in French. Lacan may have remembered that Surrealists friends named their first journal *Littérature*—it was launched by André Breton, Philippe Soupault, and Louis Aragon. *Littérature* lasted from

1919 to 1924 and saw the evolution of Dadaists turning into Surrealists. Breton added that the title was chosen in a spirit of derision: like the Dadaists, the Surrealists detested "literature," which is why the first Surrealist manifesto includes a debunking of "literature." Offering advice to would-be writers, Breton extols the practice of writing without any preconception and never revising anything, adding ironically: "Be convinced that literature is one of the saddest ways that lead to everything" (Breton:1988, p. 332). In spite of the distance, Lacan echoes the Surrealist attack on literature in a spirit of playfulness that sends up the journal's serious title, given the formalist agendas of his literary colleagues. The frolics of unhinged signifiers reinstate the primacy of the Freudian Unconscious. In the same way, Aragon and his Surrealist friends played on the signifier, multiplying puns on "*littérature*" reduced to "*lis tes ratures*" (read your erasures). The phrase "*Lis tes ratures*" has been used and abused for names of literary gatherings, conferences, bookstores, and collections of texts (see Doucoudray et al.:2000).

Lacan's playfulness is, nevertheless, indissociable from his idea of writing, as we see in the seminar of January 13, 1971. Lacan discloses his intention to explore the idea of writing taken absolutely as he thinks Derrida did, that is, writing distinguished from its being embodied in written texts:

> ... we are entering here, with that, into the heart of what is involved in l'*écrit*, indeed even l'*écriture*, so now imagine it is the same thing, people speak about l'*écriture*, like that, as if it were independent of l'*écrit*. This is what sometimes greatly embarrasses discourse. Moreover, this term, "*ure*", like that, that is added on, allows you to clearly sense the funny sort of drunkenness (*biture*) that is involved on this occasion.
>
> (Lacan:1971b)[1]

"*Biture*" is an old slang word referring to drunkenness, as in "*J*"*ai pris une biture*" (I got drunk). In this passage, we sense Lacan's impatience with Jacques Derrida and the latter's promotion of writing as new and powerful conceptual lever. Reminding his audience that writing depends from the fact that someone will use it as a tool, a means of inscription in a text, Lacan moves beyond the fight for recognition and originality to let a sense of poetic enthusiasm, if not drunkenness, pervade "Lituraterre."

However, just at the moment when the text seems to veer into drunk concatenations of puns, Lacan changes tack and parades his philological credentials: he justifies his pun by the etymological dictionary of the Latin language of Ernout and Meillet; the dictionary links the word *lino* with *liturarius* via *litura*, terms derived from the verb *lino*, meaning to erase; thus, *liturarius* also means "having ratures, marked by corrections" (Ernout and Meillet:1959, p. 360). Let's recall Freud's "Mystic Writing Pad" that I presented in connection with Derrida. Freud concluded by saying that one hand is writing whereas the other is erasing what has been inscribed.

This is only one of the many times Freud compared the Unconscious with a text full of erasures. We find a detailed treatment in the later essay on "Psychoanalysis terminable and interminable." In that belated survey of the limits of psychanalysis, Freud compared the psyche to a sacred text marred by distortions. He refers to Robert Eisler who, in 1929, had proved that Christian censors had distorted Flavius Josephus's famous testimony about Jesus. Josephus was presented as having witnessed miracles performed by Jesus and then acknowledged his divine essence. Examining the manuscripts, Eisler discerned blanks and gaps in the original Hebrew, from which he concluded that the text had been first erased, then revised. Freud summarizes Eisler's findings eloquently:

> ... the writings of Flavius Josephus must have contained passages about Jesus Christ which were offensive to later Christendom. (...) One way would be for the offending passages to be thickly crossed through so that they were illegible. In that case they could not be transcribed, and the next copyist of the book would produce a text which was unexceptionable but which had gaps in certain passages, and so might be unintelligible in them. Another way, however, if the authorities were not satisfied with this, but wanted also to conceal any indication that the text had been mutilated, would be for them to proceed to distort the text. Single words would be left out or replaced by others, and new sentences interpolated. Best of all, the whole passage would be erased and a new one which said exactly the opposite put in its place. The next transcriber could then produce a text that aroused no suspicion but which was falsified.
>
> (Freud:1964, XX, p. 236)

The Freudian unconscious thus appears as a forged text marked by erasures, deletions, blackenings, corrections, rewritings, mutilations, and falsifications. A patient analysis of the erasures should allow one to discover the truth; the truth is always reconstructed from gaps and distortions, whether in texts or in the psyche. James Joyce was aware of this process combining the history of civilization and the history of each individual; he exemplified it when he made forgery a key theme in *Finnegans Wake*: a central character is called Shem the forger. Joyce alludes to a historical forgery meant to destroy the political career of the man he admired most, Charles Steward Parnell. Joyce alludes to this incident with the theme of "Hesitency," a misspelled word concealing the titular hero (HEC). It was through the misspelling of "Hesitency" that Richard Pigott was exposed as a forger in 1889. He had forged incriminating letters signed "Parnell." Lacan was engrossed in Joyce then, slowly identifying himself with the Irish writer. Four few years later, he would devote an entire seminar to him.

Here is why Lacan calls up a well-known moment in Joyce's life. In 1918, while penniless in Zurich, Joyce met a rich heiress, Mrs. Rockefeller

McCormick. She was willing to subsidize him but under one condition: he was to start a psychoanalysis with Carl Jung, who was training her as a psychoanalyst at the time. Joyce refused indignantly; of course, he lost her financial support. He made light of the incident when writing to his more reliable patron, Harriet Weaver:

> A batch of people in Zurich persuaded themselves that I was gradually growing mad and actually endeavored to induce me to enter a sanatorium where a certain Doctor Jung (the Swiss Tweedledum who is not to be confused with the Viennese Tweedledee, Dr. Freud) amuses himself at the expense (in every sense of the word) of ladies and gentlemen who are troubled with bees in their bonnets.
>
> (Joyce:1975, p. 282)

Lacan puns in a Joycean manner, calling Mrs. McCormick a "messehaine"—a portmanteau word combining *mécène* (benefactor), *messe* (mass), and *haine* (hatred)—and agrees that Joyce was right to refuse to undergo psychoanalysis under those conditions: "In the game I called up, he would not have gained anything, instead went straight to what one can expect from the conclusion of a psychoanalysis" (Lacan:2001, p. 11). How did Joyce reach such a "conclusion" on his own? A whole seminar devoted to Joyce four years later will reveal that it was by inventing a new writing, and turning symptoms inherited from his father (drunkenness, financial irresponsibility, inability to lay down the law in his family) into the *sinthome*, turning himself into pure literature. Joyce paved the way with his insistent punning on letter/litter in *Finnegans Wake*. Lacan was also remembering an in-joke, a little game played by Joyce's friends when they published a collection of essays on *Work in Progress*, the title under which *Finnegans Wake* was known for a while.

The collection *Our Exagmination Round His Factification of Work in Progress* includes two mock letters of protest. One of them, signed by Vladimir Dixon, is addressed to "Mister Germ's Choice" and entitled "A Litter" (Beckett:1972, pp. 194–195). Dixon alluded to the way Joyce's disciples had learned to imitate the polyglottic idiom invented in *Finnegans Wake*. Dixon is worried that such excessive punning might become silly, dangerous, or overintellectual. In fact, it had created some sycophancy among Joyce's "apostles": "… so much travail from a man of your intellacked must ryeseult in somethink very signicophant" (Beckett:1972, p. 194). In a similar manner, Lacan's essay becomes more and more Joycian as it progresses. He invents curious coinages like "papeludun" (more or less equivalent to *pas plus d'un—* not more than one) and "Hun-En-Peluce" (standing for *Un-en-*plus with *peluche* added to it, like an "extra-One" that would also be a "plush-One"), both of which are used systematically in the 1971 seminar. Such portmanteau-words condense meaning imaginatively.

In 1971, Lacan was exploring the later Joyce an experimental writer whose bold creation of a new language made up of more than sixty actual idioms had paved the way for French contemporary experiments in the "unreadable" (*illisible*) and "intransitive" mode. This was the kind of writing produced at the time by Lacan's close friend Philippe Sollers. *Finnegans Wake* stages a clash between speech and writing, a clash embodied by the rival characters Shem and Shaun, the warring sons of the archetypal family. Shaun the postman carries letters but does not write; he only speaks and sings. Shaun leaves writing to his antagonist, his brother Shem the Penman. By an association that generated the concept of the *sinthome* in 1975, Joyce calls up Aquinas, the philosopher quoted by Stephen Dedalus in *Ulysses*, because Joyce and Aquinas both identified the "letter" of literature with "litter," waste and garbage.

Lacan had quoted an anecdote about Aquinas's surprising rejection of writing in the last years of the theologian's career in the first issue of *Scilicet*, "Proposition of 9 October 1967 on the Psychoanalyst of the School." In that essay about clinical issues, Lacan compares the end of analysis with what happened to Aquinas. The analysand who "concludes" often experiences a moment of un-being, a *désêtre* marking the termination of a psychoanalysis. In 1967, Lacan had stated this, letting a purely hypothetical psychoanalyst speak: "Let him learn from what I didn't know about the being of desire, what happens to his being, once he has reached the being of knowledge, and let him erase himself. *Sicut palea*, as Thomas said about his work at the end of his life—like manure" (Lacan:1968, p. 25). By 1971, Lacan had seen that his previous translation was forced; Latinists will remember that *palea* means "straw, chaff, dross, husks," not really manure. The very anecdote is quite baffling. In 1268, Aquinas returned to Paris to teach, trying to complete his *Summa theologiae* along with his commentaries on Aristotle, but could not finish. He had to move to Naples in 1272, where again he frantically tried to finish the *Summa theologiae* and his commentaries. After a year and a half, he stopped writing completely: he had had a mystical vision. In 1273, during a mass, he heard a voice coming from a crucifix saying: "Thou hast written well of me, Thomas; what reward wilt thou have?" He replied: "None other than thyself, Lord." His confessor urged him to resume writing, but Aquinas replied: "All that I have written seems to me like straw (*sicut palea*) compared with what has now been revealed to me." Indeed, Aquinas never wrote again. A few months later, on March 7, 1274, he died in the abbey of Fossanova. In 1971, Lacan more accurately refers to a "litière" for *palea*; *litière* is a litter made up of straw in the bedding meant for cats, horses, or cows.

From the evocation of Aquinas and Joyce who are somehow twinned, Lacan moves to another modernist, Samuel Beckett. What links all four is the strong connection they establish between writing and garbage. Lacan writes mischievously: "I have to add that I was undoubtedly tired of the garbage bin to which my fate has been linked. It is well known that I am not the only one, to share it, in owning this" (Lacan:2001, p. 11). The verb used for "confess" is *avouer* that Lacan decides to pronounce "avouère" as we read it in the spoken version of the seminar (Lacan:2007, p. p. 114), going back to a seventeenth-century pronunciation of the word. Here is the almost untranslatable French version: "*L'avouer ou, prononcé à l'ancienne, l'avoir dont Beckett fait balance au doit qui fait déchet de notre être, sauve l'honneur de la littérature, et me relève du privilège que je croirais tenir de ma place*" (Lacan:2001, p. 11). Let me try to translate: "To own up, or, following the ancient pronunciation, to own the asset with which Beckett balances the 'I owe you' that turns our being into rubbish, here is what saves the honor of literature, and relieves me of the privilege I might believe to be mine from my place."

The name of Beckett is introduced by an allusion to the play *Endgame* in which we discover two characters stuck in "ashbins" or dustbins: they are Hamm's parents, Nagg and Nell. Their bodies are hidden, only their faces are visible. When they die after a few speeches and aborted efforts at reunion, the young Clov puts back the lid on top of them. Without any trace of emotion, Hamm asks him to "screw down the lids" (Beckett:1986, p. 103). Lacan, who often referred to a scene that struck a nerve in him, generalizes about the function of literature: "The question is whether what the textbooks seem to be demonstrating, which is that literature is a rehashing of leftovers, is a matter of collocating in written form [*l'écrit*] what would first have been chant, spoken myth, dramatic procession" (Lacan:2001, pp. 11–12). He evokes the invention of literature as an elaboration from poetry, comedy and tragedy, the three genres known in the ancient world. Literature is a belated form that slowly acquired the right to use all the other genres so as to cook and recook them; their leftovers are fused in the mix when literature prepares its universal stew.

Beckett may not have avoided the common fate of literature, that is recycling scraps of a dead culture. Nevertheless, he saves its honor by linking a private confession (*avouer*)—Lacan was aware of the importance of the psychoanalytic cure Beckett had with Bion in the 1930s, a cure that allowed him to overcome his writer's block—with his recurrent sense of duty and debt (*doit*). From this specific position, which is very different from that of Joyce, Lacan deduces that Beckett insisted on a duty to speak, on an imperative of expression in spite of its very impossibility. The Kantian imperative was strongly affirmed in Beckett's works, and he explained to Georges Duthuit that his aim was to convey "the expression that there is nothing to express, nothing with which to express, nothing from which to express, no power to express, no desire to express, together with the obligation to express" (Beckett:1983, p. 139). Beckett would show the way more than Joyce's hubristic claims, when he chose the way of humility (see De Villiers:2023). Such an attitude reminds Lacan that there is no privileged place from which one speaks or writes, even if one is a famous author or a psychoanalyst. In so far as he accomplishes the desperate task of writing, one will have to recreate a sense of tragedy that goes back to antique forms as song, dance, and dramatic ritual. In fact, in this brief historical survey, Lacan agrees fully with Derrida, who explained that, for him, literature was a relatively recent invention that had a political function:

> Literature is a modern invention, inscribed in conventions and institutions which, to hold on to just this trait, secures in principle its *right to say everything*. Literature thus ties its destiny to a certain non-censure, to the space of democratic freedom (freedom of the press, freedom of speech, etc.) No democracy without literature: no literature without democracy.
>
> (Derrida:1992, p. 23)

Literature exhibits the qualities or defects of writing condemned by Plato: the mechanical tool prevents people from using their memory and mind actively. Moreover, given the power to "say everything" that, as we saw, had been posited as a preliminary condition of literature by Sade, then literature can blend all the genres while refusing to submit to the authority of kings or fathers. In that sense, literature does more than presuppose or include writing, it is an extension of the main features of writing: both writing and literature are predicated on the possibility of an anarchic freedom. Here is why literature can be considered as progressive; it anticipates historical movements toward democracy. Are these broad features also perceptible in what Lacan calls "lituraterre"? To the optimistic program aiming at more democracy, with which Lacan is in global agreement, he adds a darker twist but suggesting that true literature gets lost in an age of unleashed consumption, with a market swamped with bad books. This is the situation Lacan alludes to with the term of "poubellification." It is not the first time that Lacan identifies publication with "poubellification" or the act of throwing one's texts to a garbage can by publishing them. "Poubellification" was already mentioned in a seminar on the object of psychoanalysis on December 5, 1965, and another twist was added when Lacan appeared on television in 1973. In *Television*, Lacan compared the role of the psychoanalyst with that of the saint: the saint's particularity is that he wishes to become identical with trash: the saint "acts as trash: his business being *trashitas*" (Lacan:1990, p. 15). "Lituraterre" will thus play with the "trashitas" of writing.

7.2 Lacan picks holes in Derrida's writing

After the dense prologue of the first page, the rest of the essay is divided into two parts. A first section (Lacan:2001, pp. 12–14) tackles the topic of "literature and psychoanalysis" by way of the concept of the "letter," and a second section beginning page 15 provides a concrete example taken from a recent trip to Japan, a country evoked in its specific attitude to letters and calligraphy. Lacan begins by criticizing Freud's own forays into literature, especially his psycho-biographical essay on Dostoevsky, the 1928 text "Dostoevsky and Parricide," and seems to understand why psychoanalytic criticism never got any good press among academics. Even if psychoanalysis is founded upon a literary text, Sophocles' *Oedipus Rex*, the fact does not grant any psychoanalyst a deeper wisdom facing literary analysis.

Lacan meditates on what it meant to open *Ecrits*—whose title, he confides, was "more ironical than what one has thought" (Lacan:2001, p. 12)—with a reading of a literary text by Poe, "The purloined letter." Wasn't this an admission that he had a hand in literary criticism as well? He sums up the general argument of his first *"écrit"* insisting once more that Poe's tale describes the trajectory of a letter that was purloined twice, once by the Minister, once by Dupin, without our being aware of what is written in it. The lack of content for the reader is redoubled by the fact that the letter's major effect is to "feminize" whoever possesses it. This is sufficient to distinguish the letter from the signifier: if the letter carries signifiers, we never know the content of its message, even if we deduce that it reaches its destination in the end. The genius of Poe had consisted in remaining rigorous in his demonstration. Such a decision should not be explained by his biography. Lacan reiterates the criticism he had addressed Marie Bonaparte's psychobiography of Poe, adding that he presents another facet of the letter, a structural pattern different from previous accounts: he now sees the letter as constituted by a hole.

Lacan alluded to the Enlightenment on the cover of *Ecrits*, but the light implied in "enlightenment" turns into a hard glare thrown on psychoanalysis. This then allows it to make a hole: "... *quand j'invoque ainsi les lumières, c'est de démontrer où elle fait trou*" (Lacan:2001, p. 13, literally "when I thus call upon the Enlightenment, it is in order to demonstrate where psychoanalysis pierces a hole"). The meaning seems clear enough: psychoanalysis makes a hole in knowledge and lets truth speak through it. As such, the process redoubles the function of the letter. The couple truth/knowledge is established then carefully, and the letter is defined as the edge of the hole made in knowledge: it is a *littoral* (the edge of the sea-shore) that is also a *littéral* (literality, one might say). What remains to be studied is how the Unconscious organizes the circuit of the letter. Without naming it, Lacan is alluding to Jacques Derrida's critical readings both of Freud in "Freud and the scene of writing," an essay published in *Tel Quel* in 1966, the same year as *Ecrits*, and of himself, the attack on his reading of Poe in the seminar on "The Purloined Letter."

In "Le facteur de la vérité," an essay published first in *Poétique*, then in *The Post Card* (Derrida:1987, pp. 413–496), Derrida developed his critical program facing Lacanian psychoanalysis, a program he had sketched in *Positions*. In that book originally published in 1972 Lacan was taken to task for his glib use of Hegelian categories and for an undeclared idealism at the same time as he was flaunting the "materiality of the signifier." Lacan incurred the double reproach of "phonocentism" and idealism (Derrida:1982, pp. 107–113). In 1975, Derrida renewed his attack: Lacan was accused of simplifying Poe's text and missing literary nuances, glossing over the intertextual plays elaborated in the Dupin stories of detection (see Muller and Richardson:1988). One objection was that Lacan translated the absence of content of the letter into a Freudian "truth" that would be the truth of psychoanalysis according to Lacan. This truth always disclosed its main object, the phallus, a phallus hidden in the empty signifier of the letter. The letter would ultimately allegorize castration (Derrida:1987, pp. 413–496).

Indeed, as we have seen, Lacan's argument cannot be dissociated from his analysis of letters. For Lacan, a letter remains a single entity no matter what happens to it. As he reiterates in the Seminar on "The Purloined Letter," letters are uncuttable and uncountable entities: "Cut a letter into small pieces, and it remains the letter that it is..." (Lacan:2006, p. 16). In French, one can speak of "letters" in the plural, but one cannot say: "there is letter," or "we have here some letter," as one might say "there is time" or "there is butter." In the sense of missive, a letter, be it singular or plural, cannot be counted or divided. Here is why, in Poe's plot, the police are mistaken in their assumption that the Minister's room must be divided into smaller units, objects, books, frames, table legs, etc. They repeat Zeno's paradox: if a line is endlessly divisible, then movement is impossible, which means that intelligence dies.

Similarly, a "letter" in French and English is a term predicated on a homophony that does not work in German, where we have to distinguish between *Brief* and "letters" as written signs (*Buchstaben*) that may be used to write a *Brief*. Even if a letter has been lost or destroyed, it remains present by its absence as a letter. Lacan refuses to distinguish these two meanings. The action of the police proves *a contrario* that the indivisibility of the letter creates its invisibility. Since their categories cannot assimilate the idea of a reversed and re-signed paper, for them the letter "is missing in its place," the expression by which librarians notify that a book has been lost as soon as it has been misplaced. Seeing only what they can divide into smaller units, they miss the letter spread out in front of their eyes.

Derrida's objections to the letter's economy as a circuit determined by an ideal teleology are rather damaging. Indeed, why should a letter "always" return to its original place? Is Lacan implying that all mislaid letters end up in their rightful owners' hands? An answer to this query can be given if I see that I need to take into account how I relate to the letter. In some way, I am always the answer, which is another manner of stating that readers who read the "letters" of literature are their (or its) addressees. Lacan's generalizations make better sense when we add to his sayings the qualification "in psychoanalysis," and understand that psychoanalysis implies a relational interaction between subjects. Slavoj Žižek has expanded this argument cogently in *Enjoy your Symptom!* Against Derrida's accusations of idealism and teleology, Žižek explains that Lacan's formula functions at different levels defined by the registers of the Real, the Imaginary, and the Symbolic. At an imaginary level, the idea that a letter always reaches its destination means that "its destination is wherever it arrives" (Žižek:1992, p. 10). In order for anyone to mention any letter, that letter must have had a recipient, even if she or he was not the original addressee. At a symbolic level, the circuit of the letter is an economy, but not a meta-language. It relies on a theory of fate: Fate is entirely contained within the letter itself, whether one sees its possession as tragic, gendered, or a blessing. At the level of the Real, the letter often figures death as its hidden message. This derives from its very materiality; what could be more "dead" than these inert little signs of a piece of paper, as Derrida himself has often stressed? The letter has become a "dangerous supplement" that has to be put to rest, while pointing to an excess enjoyment, a free-floating jouissance that has no name and no function (Žižek:1992, p. 22).

As we have seen earlier, Derrida questioned the logic of representation implied by Freud's and Lacan's images for the unconscious. In his critical reading of Freud's "Mystic Writing Pad," Derrida acknowledged the powerful impact of the allegory of writing to describe the unconscious but saw that there was a remainder of idealism (Derrida:1978, pp. 199, 217–218, and 221). On the other hand, Lacan felt that he had been the first, historically speaking, to point out the crucial role of Freud's letter 52 to Fliess, by which he meant the December 6, 1896, letter in which Freud compared the psychic mechanism to a series of inscriptions or "retranscriptions" (Freud:1985, pp. 207–214).

In the 1971 Seminar, Lacan appears preoccupied by Derrida's attacks. He explains that he has read several books about writing, James Février's *Histoire de l'écriture (Hisrtory of writing)*, and a whole collection *On Writing*. He pays homage to Freud's key insights and distances himself from what he understands as a mystical theory, the concept of Derrida's "arche-writing," that is, a writing that would pre-exist to any verbal utterance. Lacan mentions a patient who symptomatically kept calling his wife "mother" and comments:

> He called her what he should have called her. So then there is only a lapse with respect to what? With respect to what the authors of *archiécriture*, the writing that is in the world from all time prefigures the word. A funny exercise, right? I don't mind… it is a function of the university discourse, to confuse things like that.[2]

The issue was whether the patient who took his wife for a mother was making a *lapsus linguae* or a *lapsus calami*. Was the patient spoken by his written unconscious, determined fully by a written script that he followed blindly? Lacan found a clearer way of expressing himself on the following page when he affirmed that "there is no lapse except *calami*, even when it is a *lapsus linguae*" (Lacan:2007, p. 90).

Finally, in order to dispel the conceptual confusion, Lacan take the bull by the horns, and reiterates, against Derrida, or what seemed to be Derrida's position at the time, that the speaking subject remains the main foundation: "I am therefore going to try to indicate the essence of what seems to produce the letter as a consequence, and of language, precisely in what I say: that who speaks inhabits it" (Lacan:2001, p. 15). The terms are quite clear: human beings inhabit language because they speak; the letter appears as a consequence of there being this language.

"Lituraterre" had to go further and exemplify the abstract analysis by offering a personal vignette. The proof of the theory would lie in auto-fiction, and in this case, in a carefully crafted narrative. Spinning an autobiographical story will allow Lacan to self-consciously reflect on the style he uses: "One will not be astonished to see me proceed by a literary demonstration, since this would amount to falling in with the step from which the question issues. Thanks to which, however, a certain demonstration can be asserted" (Lacan:2001, p. 15). The issue being how literature pertains to psychoanalysis, and conversely, Lacan shows that both are intimately knotted.

Thus, the second part of the essay provides an allegorical travelogue to Japan. Lacan ends up rewriting Roland Barthes's *The Empire of Signs* and uses key insights on Japanese language contained in the lecture he gave in Tokyo on April 21, 1971 (Lacan:1971a). However, the main discovery was made during the return flight. Because of an enforced detour of the plane's trajectory, Lacan explains that the Russian army had forbidden international airlines to fly over Siberia, he witnessed a magnificent spectacle: huge clouds emptying their stormy rains onto the vast expanse of the tundra underneath. Lacan displays a rare talent for description here, while splicing two scenes: what he has seen in Japan, mostly its practice of calligraphy, without bypassing its industrial aspect as when he mentions the interlocking ribbons of superposed highways in Osaka, and what he sees from the plane, this godly downpour that calls up a paradoxical writing effect. Here is a good example of what one might call the Lacanian sublime:

> So it appeared to me, invincibly, this circumstance is no small matter: through-parting-clouds, the streaming of waters, only trace to appear, by operating there rather than indicating the plain's relief in this latitude, on what of Siberia forms the plain, a plain desolate of any vegetation other than reflections, reflections that push into shadow what does not mirror back from it.
>
> (Lacan:2001, p. 16)

The *ruissellement* (streaming) calls up the double movement of the hand at work in Freud's Mystical Writing Block, for it both generates a trace and erases it. It is all at once writing and the *rature* (erasure) of writing.

What has been erased? Lacan's allegory becomes more ambitious, for he asserts that what has been erased, and will be erased again and again, is only semblance:

> What is revealed by my vision of the streaming, in so far as erasure dominates, is that in being produced from between the clouds, it joins its source, for it is indeed to the clouds that Aristophanes hails me to make me find what the signifier is about: that is to say semblance par excellence, if indeed it is through its rupture that rains falls from it, the effect of what it precipitates, precipitating matter that had been in suspension.
>
> (Lacan:2001, p. 17)

Note how Lacan puns on "precipitate" to refer to rain. The vision of a rupture of the perceptual continuum breaks with the usual reassurance we derive from the patina of everyday appearances. When slick and deceptive appearances are gutted and opened up, what is revealed is a jet, a downpour, and a rush of energy. It is as if the Freudian drive suddenly admitted that it came from nature. We might be back to Heidegger's "storm of Being," that flickering flash of lighting we glimpsed at the end of "Logos": "Once, however, in the beginning of Western thinking, the essence of language flashed in the light of Being— once, when Heraclitus thought the Λογοσ as his guiding word, so as to think in this world the Being of beings" (Heidegger:1984, p. 78). We have seen that Heidegger concluded that Heraclitus was not faithful to his initial intuition, which is why he ended up reducing Logos to rational thought and decided that the task of the moderns is to retrieve the lost vision: "We see this lightning only when we station ourselves in the storm of Being" (Heidgger:1984, p. 78). If the clouds have been rent by lightning, this "clearing" in the sky can happen again. Lacan's clouds allegorize a cosmic energy by generating a diluvian downpour, but he grafts on the Heideggerian landscape a classical reference. This brings in the dimension of laughter: Lacan also alludes to Aristophanes' *The Clouds*, a sarcastic comedy in which Socrates, accused of being a Sophist, replaces the gods with mere philosophical obfuscation and reduces the gods to mere clouds. Aristophanes' satire would prove quite damaging to Socrates when the time of his trial came; however, Socrates was reputed to have attended the performance and laughed at his own derisive portrayal. Lacan pushes this analogy while re-introducing truth as *jouissance*:

> This bursting that dissolves what made form, phenomenon, meteor (and I have said that science is generated when these features are made sense of), is it not also the case that by dismissing the jouissance in such bursting we can then constitute a world *(le monde)* or filth *(l'immonde)*, and thereby reach the drive in which life is figured?
>
> (Lacan:2001, p. 17)

We can organize a world as a cosmos ruled by beauty and order only if we exclude the excessive jouissance that those orgasmic moments embody; by the same token, the other side of the world is constituted as its negative, as *immonde*, or pure abjection. Science is created when phenomena like meteors and storms are given a definite shape or form. Lacan continues his meditation on the jouissance that comes from the Real as the destruction of semblance:

> What is evoked of jouissance as the rupture of a semblant is what presents itself in the real as a furrowing (*ravinement*). // It is from the same effect that writing is in the real left by the furrowing of the signified that has rained down from the semblant, and thus constitutes the signifier. Writing does not copy the signifier, but only its language effects, effects forged by whoever speaks.
>
> (Lacan:2001, p. 17)

The density of the syntax and the allusiveness of the associations should not blind us to the fact that Lacan returns to common sense; wishing to dispel Derrida's cloudy disquisitions about an "original trace" located in an "arche-writing," he keeps his gaze fixed on those torrential rains that inscribe traces in the landscape. To Derrida's mystique of writing, Lacan opposes an ontology of writing seen both as a remainder of *jouissance* and as a material furrowing of localized traces.

Lacan's allegory developed in "Lituraterre" provides an image capable of summing up previous insights presented in his Tokyo speech under a more vivid and dramatic form. In Tokyo, Lacan compared his texts, his *écrits*, that is, to the small stones that are often scatttered in the raked and furrowed sand of a traditional Zen garden. This led him to reproach Derrida for having borrowed the concept of material writing inscribed in the psyche without crediting him. Derrida was accused of disseminating his traces in the void; against this, Lacan would re-inscribe writing in an immanent landscape and a desiring body capable of enjoyment. He explains to his Japanese friends from the use of Chinese radicals, *kanji*, among Japanese written characters, that writing cannot be defined as a transcription of vocal sounds; however, that should not lead one to conclude that writing is anterior to any spoken language as Derrida did. Lacan stated:

> Writing is quite different from articulating with one's voice. This contrasts with some people, who have taken their materials from what I teach and who are articulating in a really nonsensical fashion that written language is primary with regard to spoken language. It's absurd.
>
> (Lacan:1971a)

Here is one of the rare admissions that Derrida had a point, even if he pushed it to an extreme position.

7.3 A trip to Japan

Derrida was not the only butt of Lacan's debunking for he also takes to task Roland Barthes who in 1970 published with Albert Skira's press a superbly illustrated edition of his book on Japan, *The Empire of Signs*. After a few rapid visits to Tokyo, Barthes wrote a mock guide displaying his fascination for a culture in which, as he surmised, empty signs dominated in everyday life and culture. Lacan had studied Chinese for several years, and he had begun learning Japanese. More competent linguistically, he insinuated that Barthes, like Derrida, remained imprisoned in pure semblance:

> In other terms, subjects are divided as everywhere by language, but one of their registers can satisfy itself with the reference to writing, the other with speech.
>
> This is no doubt what has given Roland Barthes the inebriated feeling that in all their customs Japanese subjects envelop nothing. The empire of signs, he entitles his essay, wanting to say: empire of semblances.
>
> The Japanese, I have been told, hate this idea. For nothing is more distinct from the void hollowed by writing than the semblant. The former is a bucket always ready to receive jouissance, or at least to invoke it by its artifice.
>
> (Lacan:2001, p. 19)

Barthes would exhibit the same "inebriated" delusion that was evinced by Derrida: both reduce signs to an ontological void. Here, Lacan discusses *bunraku*, the popular puppet theatre, one of the main examples that had been analyzed semiotically by Barthes. According to Barthes, the Japanese puppet theatre is a distinguishing genre in Japanese culture because it reveals purely empty signs; *bunraku* would be subject to a complete exemption from meaning. This hollowing out of sense appears throughout all Japanese theatre, revealing that its essence is emptiness (Barthes:1982, 1982, p. 62).

Rejecting Barthes's disquisitions based on an inadequate understanding of Japanese language and culture, Lacan refuses to transform Japan into a utopia of a freedom from sense, a re-enactment of the void following Zen mysticism. Against this mystical drift, Lacan reads *bunraku* in a more down-to-earth manner. He notes more accurately that in *bunraku* "all that is said might be read by a narrator" (Lacan:2001, p. 20), adding this: "You are an element amongst others of the ceremonial where the subject is composed precisely by being able to decompose itself" (Lacan:2001, p. 20). If Japan reveals a certain utopia of language, it has nothing to do with the alleged emptiness of signs—indeed, Lacan sees in Japan a proliferation of meaning. He concludes beautifully that Japan "is perpetual translation made language" (Lacan:2001, p. 20).

Finally, in order to illustrate the fact that translation is always possible, even if one doesn't know the language, Lacan gives a last anecdote from Japan. During his visit, a Japanese biologist tried to bypass the language barrier by writing mathematical equations on a blackboard. If Lacan had been fluent in that mathematical language, he would have followed the demonstration without knowing any Japanese. Hence the recurrent display of mathemes and formulae in his later seminars that all began with handwritten equations or cryptic one-liners on a blackboard. The conclusion of the travelogue is abrupt and gnomic. Lacan needed a similar blackboard to disclose his concept of writing fully: "It seems to me that an ascesis of writing is only capable of being accepted if it merges with the 'it's written' upon which sexual relationship would be founded" (Lacan:2001, p. 20). The spoken version makes better sense of Lacan's drift. The oral performance ended with:

> An ascesis of writing, that subtracts nothing from the advantages we may get from literary criticism. To close the loop on something more coherent, it seems to me, taking into account what I have stated so far, that such ascesis will only be capable of being accepted if it merges with the impossible "it's written" upon which sexual relationship might one day be founded.
>
> (Lacan:2007, p. 127)

The insertion of "impossible" is key here, for indeed the next session of the seminar will be devoted to a lengthy account of why sexual rapport cannot be written: it is said to be "uninscriptible" (Lacan:2007, p. 132). Is Lacan contradicting himself or is he still groping toward an impossible writing? In fact, he suggests that there is a possible writing, which is why he mentions writing as an ascesis. It is indeed a psychoanalytical discipline that will produce an erasure where there was no trace before. All this sends us back to Freud's paradoxical temporality of the *Nachträglichkeit*, a deferred action in which the present-past of trauma zigzags between unwritten rupture and constant rewriting. All the semblances will be broken, shot through; they leave the gaping void of an empty page to which the subject is welcome. No anxiety of the blank page here: the blank leads to the void of a *chora*, and prevents jouissance from exhausting itself in repetitive patterns. Psychoanalysts should take lessons from Japanese painters when they produce calligraphies; calligraphy combines the singular and the universal, which is the aim of any writing, that is, to offer a formula for the "singularity of the hand that crushes the universal" (Lacan:2001, p. 16).

A zigzagging calligraphy brought Lacan from arch-modernists like Joyce and Beckett to two antagonists, Derrida and Barthes, both of whom allow him to refine and expand his concept of writing. In the end, Lacan appears aligned with the position of Gilles Deleuze and Felix Guattari who describe the aim of literature as the production of objective affects (Deleuze:1996, p. 174). If Lacan's vision of a storm over Siberia discloses a new "Sibériéthique" (Lacan:2001, p. 15), it also becomes a springboard that ushers in a new view of writing predicated on an ontology of the outside. Discovering written words in a rainy downpour over Siberia, Lacan will then elaborate a theory of life as a written text, a theme I'll develop in the conclusion.

However, "Lituraterre" may have gone too far and too quickly. Two years later, Lacan expressed some regret in having divulged too much with these forays into personal anecdotes. When he revisited his essay in October 1973, he pointed out certain weaknesses and called "Lituraterre" a text that is "not without some imperfections." Nevertheless, he did not reject its conclusions. He commented it in those terms:

> "The cloud of language," I expressed myself metaphorically, "constitutes writing." Who knows whether the fact that we can read (*lire*) the streams I saw over Siberia as the metaphorical trace of writing isn't linked (*lié*)— beware, *lier* and *lire* consist of the same letters—to something that goes beyond the effect of rain, which animals have no chance of reading as such?
> (Lacan:1999, p. 120)

Restating the theory of the impossibility of writing sexual relationship, Lacan affirmed the need to write it; to do this, he used a complex syntax of terms that sound overdetermined:

> Writing is thus a trace in which an effect of language can be read. That is what happens when you scribble (*gribouillez*) something. // I certainly don't deprive myself of doing so, for that is how I prepare what I have to say. It is worth noting that one must use writing if one wants to be assured.
> (Lacan:1999, p. 120, modified)

Bruce Fink was right to quote the last words in French: "*Il est remarquable qu'il faille, de l'écriture, s'assurer*" (Lacan:1975, p. 110). The idea is double. One needs writing to assure oneself of one's existence, but one uses writing to reassure oneself that things exist. Writing is both the constitution of one's subjectivity and the mark of a relation with the otherness of the world, its objects, its traces, its drives flowing and streaming, and ultimately, the whole earth. Literature literalizes the words of the love letter that our unconscious keeps on writing, and at the same time inscribes the unavoidable and irreducible mediation of the outside world.

When literature is rewritten as *lituraterre*, I can grasp what the clouds are telling me thanks to signs inscribed by rain pouring down in endless streams. This provides a sense of the legibility of the world. Such a legibility, which is also a translatability of signifiers into other signifiers, allows us to land (*aterrir*) back onto the old earth we come from, the earth on which we were born. The final question becomes: do we need writing to be sure that we were born?

Notes

1 Lacan:1971, from the seminar of January 13, according to *On a discourse that might not be a semblance* translated by Cormac Gallagher from unedited typescripts, see https://www.valas.fr/IMG/pdf/THE-SEMINAR-OF-JACQUES-LACAN-XVIII_d_un_discours.pdf The same passage is dated March 10, 1971, in Jacques-Alain Miller's edition, see Lacan:2007, p. 80.
2 This is Cormac Gallagher's translation (Lacan:1971b). Jacques-Alain Miller's version in *Seminar XVIII* has *"les astucieux de l'archi-écriture"* (the all-too clever people who talk about archi-writing) (Lacan:2007, p. 89).

Bibliography

Barthes, Roland (1982). *The Empire of Signs*, trans. Richard Howard, New York, Hill and Wang.

Beckett, Samuel, and others (1972). *Our Exagmination Round his Factification of Work in Progress (1929)*, London, Faber.

Beckett, Samuel (1983). *Disjecta*, London, Calder.

Beckett, Samuel (1986). *The Complete Dramatic Works*, London, Faber.

Bellemin-Noël, Jean, editor (1971). *Littérature*, n. 3, Paris, Larousse, Octobre 1971.

Breton, André (1988). *Oeuvres Complètes*, ed. Marguerite Bonnet, Paris, Gallimard, Pléiade.

Deleuze, Gilles, and Guattari, Felix (1996). *What is Philosophy?* trans. Hugh Tomlinson, New York, Columbia University Press.

Derrida, Jacques (1978) *Writing and Difference*, trans. Alan Bass, Chicago, University of Chicago Press.

Derrida, Jacques (1982). Derrida, *Positions*, trans. Henri Ronse, Chicago, University of Chicago Press.

Derrida, Jacques (1987). *The Post Card: From Socrates to Freud and Beyond*, trans. Alan Bass, Chicago, University of Chicago Press.

Derrida, Jacques (1992). "Passions: 'An Oblique Offering," translated by David Wood, in *Derrida: A Critical Reader*, ed. David Wood, Oxford, Blackwell, p. 5–35.

De Villiers, Rick (2023). *Eliot's and Beckett's Low Modernism*, Edinburgh, Edinburgh University Press.

Doucoudray, Patrick, Leloup, Stéphanie and Robert, Francine, editors (2000). *Lis tes ratures*, Sarreguemines, Ed. Pierron.

Ernout, Alfred and Meillet, Antoine (1959). *Dictionaire Étymologique de la langue latine*, internet archive, p. 360, and *AE*, p. 11. https://archive.org/details/DictionnaireEtymologiqueDeLaLangueLatine

Freud, Sigmund (1924). "A Note Upon the 'Mystic Writing-Pad'" (1924) https://www.sas.upenn.edu/~cavitch/pdf-library/Freud_WritingPad.pdf

Freud, Sigmund (1964). "Psychoanalysis terminable and interminable," *Standard Edition of Freud's Collected Works*, vol. XXIII, London, Hogarth Press, p. 211–253.

Freud, Sigmund (1985). *The Complete Letters of Sigmund Freud to Wilhelm Fliess, 1887–1904*, ed. and trans. Jeffrey Moussaieff Masson, Harvard, Harvard University Press.

Freud, Sigmund (2003). *The Joke and Its Relation to the Unconscious*, trans. Joyce Crick, Penguin.

Heidegger, Martin (1984). *Early Greek Thinking: The dawn of Western philosophy*, trans. D. Krell and F. A. Capuzzi, San Francisco, Harper and Row.

Joyce, James (1939). *Finnegans Wake*, London, Faber.

Joyce, James (1975). *Selected Letters*, edited R. Ellmann, Faber, 1975

Lacan, Jacques (1968). "Proposition du 9 October 1967 sur le psychanalyste de l'école," in *Scilicet*, 1, Paris, Seuil, p. 14–30.

Lacan, Jacques (1971a). "Discours de Tokyo," April 21, 1971, available in French in Pas-tout Lacan, and translated by Dany Nobus and Jack Stone in parallel on www.freud2lacan.com. See also "Tokyo speech" p. 142–143, in https://lacanianworks.org/tokyo-discourse-21st-april-1971-jacques-lacan

Lacan, Jacques (1971b). *On a discourse that might not be a semblance*, translated by Cormac Gallagher from unedited typescripts, see https://www.valas.fr/IMG/pdf/THE-SEMINAR-OF-JACQUES-LACAN-XVIII_d_un_discours.pdf

Lacan, Jacques (1975). *Le Séminaire: Encore, Livre XX*, ed. Jacques-Alain Miller, Paris, Seuil.

Lacan, Jacques (1990). *Television*, transl. Denis Hollier, Rosalind Krauss and Annette Michelson, New York, Norton.

Lacan, Jacques (1999). *Séminaire XX, On Feminine Sexuality, the limits of love and knowledge*, trans. Bruce Fink, New York, Norton.

Lacan, Jacques (2001). *Autres Ecrits*, edited Jacques-Alain Miller, Paris, Seuil.

Lacan, Jacques (2006). *Ecrits*, translate by Bruce Fink, New York, Norton.

Lacan, Jacques (2007). *Le Séminaire, Livre XVIII, D'un discours qui ne serait pas du semblant*, Paris, Seuil.

Muller, John P. and Richardson, William J., editors (1988). *The Purloined Poe: Lacan, Derrida and Psychoanalytic Reading*, Baltimore, Johns Hopkins University Press.

Nobus, Dany (2013). "Annotations to Lituraterre," in *Continental Philosophy Review*, n. 46, p. 335–347.

Rabelais, François (1552) *Le Quart Livre*, https://fr.wikisource.org › wiki › Le... "Les moeurs et conditions de Panurge."

Žižek, Slavoj (1992). *Enjoy your Symptom!*, New York, Routledge.

Conclusion

"I am a poem, not a poet": Lacan's autopoiesis

In the Preface to the English translation of Seminar XI, *The Four Fundamental Concepts of Psychoanalysis*, the first of his seminars to be published and one of the most influential, Lacan develops the idea that no school certificate can provide adequate credentials for a psychoanalyst. Psychoanalysts should rely on themselves only to feel authorized to practice, even if a "hierarchy" or an institution is usually called upon to confirm their legitimacy. Surprisingly, perhaps because he is thinking that one can be born a psychoanalyst, Lacan offers an analogy with the birth certificate for his hypothetical analyst:

> What hierarchy could confirm him as an analyst, give him the rubber stamp? What a man from the North was telling me is that I was, indeed, born. I repudiate this certificate: I am not a poet, but a poem. A poem that is being written, even if it looks like a subject.[1]

Lacan had been questioned on the issue of "being born" by a psychoanalyst from Lille, here familiarly called a "Cht." The question seemed to beg an obvious answer: do I need a birth certificate to make sure that I was born? Is writing necessary for a subjective reassurance of my *Dasein*, a confirmation of my "being there"?

Documentary evidence of the kind required by a bureaucracy relying on verifiable written traces is usually required, and this defines a certain regime of truth as adequation not with "facts" but with stamped documents. In England the early modern concept of "truth," as Richard Firth Green has shown, replaced for good the older notion of "sooth" (credibility, honesty, deriving from a reputation established by friends and family) with a new "truth" linked with "evidence," which meant the presentation of legal documents in a trial (Green:1999). In fact, even if I may not know the exact date or place of my birth, or the official name under which I was registered, I cannot deny that I was born, and according to French syntax, still am. Lacan pushes the idea further when he adds an extra comma before *né*: "*Ce qu'un Cht me disait, c'est que je l'étais, né*" (Lacan:2001, p. 572). This entails that

DOI: 10.4324/9781032715834-9

"I was born" and still am born. French permits this play for "*Je suis né*" can be both construed as a present and a present perfect when English uses the preterit of *I was born*. The comma separating *je l'étais* from *né* stresses the fact of "being" in "having been born."

In the same way as psychoanalysts should not rely on official certificates delivered by schools, institutes, universities, any institution in fact, if they want to call themselves "psychoanalysts," human subjects do not need identity papers to verify that they were born. Of course, a birth certificate from the municipal records or a religious ledger brings a tangible proof and thus testifies to the importance of genealogies. Any subject is inscribed before birth among symbolic markers, ancestors, witnesses, strings of family names and first names. Here Lacan adds a new twist to the idea: even if I am being written, hence I can say that I am a poem, for all that, I should not call myself the author of the poem. I can consider my life, with all its myths and legends, as a "poem," because the Unconscious functions like a writing machine, even if its productions remain undecipherable. However, one should reject as a Romantic delusion the idea that I alone am the author of my life-poem.

The image found by Lacan at the end of his life is less sanguine or dramatic than the brief apologue he had sketched in 1960 when he described the subject of the Unconscious as a Heideggerian being-for-death: this subject runs along to his destination, unaware of the impending death sentence that was inscribed on his scalp while he was asleep:

> ... the subject—who, like the messenger-slave of Antiquity, carries under his hair the codicil that condemns him to death—knows neither the meaning nor the text, nor in what language it is written, nor even that it was tattooed on his shaven scalp while he was sleeping.
>
> (Lacan:2006, p. 680)

The new image of the subject as a poem was brought to Lacan by what he had intuited in "Lituraterre," this insight into a writing of the outside, as we have seen. Here was an image that allowed to circumscribe a Real both outside language as a symbolic code shared by all and insisting via material traces, this circumscription forming a letter, thus as he explains the rim of a hole through which the certainties gathered around us to make sense of the world, in a word "reality," are perforated.

In this new formulation, Lacan comes close to the view exposed by Virginia Woolf in "A Sketch of the Past." This autobiographical text was written in order to come to terms with the traumatic "blows" that had reverberated from Woolf's past while offering epiphanic revelations. Such ecstatic revelations had to be put into words in order to acquire consistency and reality: words are porous, but only writing can make these moments of being truly real. She writes: "... I make it real by putting it into words. It is only by putting it into words that I make it whole; this wholeness means that it has lost its power to hurt me..." (Woolf:1985, p. 72). Like Lacan discovering written words in a rainy downpour over Siberia, Woolf deduces from her intense raptures a philosophy of life as a written text, and the language she uses is one to which Lacan could subscribe:

> From this I reach what I might call a philosophy; at any rate it is a constant idea of mine; that behind the cotton wool is hidden a pattern; that we—I mean all human beings—are connected with this; that the whole world is a work of art; that we are part of the work of art. Hamlet or a Beethoven quartet is the truth about this vast mass that we call the world. But there is no Shakespeare, there is no Beethoven; certainly and emphatically there is no God; we are the words; we are the music; we are the thing itself.
>
> (Woolf:1985, p. 72)

What Woolf articulates is the link between the discovery of the self as a poem and the fact that such a text cannot have an author. As Gabrielle McIntire has shown, this occurs when an image from memory pierces the "cotton wool" of everyday life; by giving an "emotional blow" it disrupts the ordinary flow of perception. Such an interruption could be generalized to all subjects whenever they have moments of illumination thanks to which they feel they bare reborn. Then and only then can they know who they are truly. A traumatic shock asks of the subject to be written down, in order "to be explained and even contained via writing and narration to ease their unexpected disturbance." This makes of writing "a response to being" (McIntire:2008, p. 167). The importance of the moment does not derive from its content, which is often obscure, an anodyne, almost devoid of meaning, but from the personal value its occasion keeps for the subject. By suggesting the possibility of a "bio-graphy," or a writing of life, these moments heal and allow one to progress creatively. Here is why an "autopoiesis" coming from the outside and working by processing repeated irritations leads to the discovery that one is a "poem," albeit not a "poet." Hence, as Woolf states, "no Shakespeare, no Beethoven, no God," for we are the words, the music, and the thing itself: this discovery is an instant of triumph and humility at the same time.

Lacan's Preface is dated from May 17, 1976. One year later to the day he returned to the same idea in a slightly different key, for this time, he applied the formula to himself. It was during the last session of the seminar entitled *L'insu que sait de l'une-bévue s'aile à mourre* (Seminar XXIV), a title in which one recognizes the influence of Joyce's punning. The words can be rearranged as *L'insuccès de l'Unbewusst c'est l'amour*, which means that the failure of the Freudian unconscious is Love. These words also suggest something like: "The unknown that knows of the one-error takes wings to die." Close to the end of the seminar, Lacan explains that poetry is necessary because it keeps replenishing language with new meaning. Poetry helps psychoanalysts interpret slips of the tongue and the other unconscious productions presented by patients. He adds: "Only poetry, I have told you, makes interpretation possible, and this is why in my clinical practice, I am not able to make it cohere any longer. I am not enough of a 'poet,' I am not 'Poetassé'" (*"Je ne suis pas assez poète. Je ne suis pas poâte-assez."*) (Lacan:1977, p. 6).

Dany Nobus has given a wonderful and extended analysis of this passage (Nobus:2018, pp. 72–92) after he acquired the manuscript of an unpublished poem by Lacan owned by Jean-Michel Vappereau. In this later draft, Lacan began by reiterating: "As I am 'born' a poem, not a poet…" (see Nobus:2018, p. 85). Different transcripts of the seminar provide alternative forms for the last words. Most commentators noted that Lacan was quoting a quatrain by French poet Léon-Paul Fargue. In 1923, Fargue published a collection of short humorous poems entitled *Ludions* (little imps). The following year, they were set to music by his friend Erik Satie. The shortest of these poems entitled *Air du poète* ("The Poet's Tune") consists of four lines playing on the word *Papouasie* (Papua) that rhymes with a distortion of poetry as *Pouasie*, ending with: *"La grâce que je vous souhaite / C'est de n'être pas Papouète"* (I wish that you'll never have the distinction of being a poet). The punning element was not introduced by Lacan; it was already in the original. Fargue, a close friend of James Joyce and of Lacan, shared with the Irish writer a predilection for bad puns, invented words, and playful poetic riddles. Lacan was familiar with these verses and with Satie's song for he alludes to them several times in talks and seminars.

In *I Talk to the Walls* given in January 1972, Lacan commented on a poem by Antoine Tudal that he had quoted in "The Function and Field of Speech and Language in Psychoanalysis." This little piece of doggerel was written when Tudal was twelve. It posits love between man and woman, a world between man and love, and a wall between man and the world. Fargue's poem puns on the French name for Papua to play on the proximity between *pouasie* and *poésie*. Making fun of "poetry," Fargue has it rhyme with "*poux*" (lice) in *pouasie* and distorts the pronunciation of *poète*. His "*Papouète*" is both a "not-poet" (*pas-poète*) and an exotic Papuan. The distortion on "poet," often pronounced *poâte* or *pouet*, would suggest a bad and conceited writer. Indeed, until recently, the word *poète* was spelled with a tréma; Mallarmé always spelled it as "*Poëte*." Often distorted as *Pouet! Pouet!* to evoke either the sound of farting or an old bicycle horn, Lacan makes the word sound more funny than grandiose.

However, whereas the 1976 Preface to the translation of Seminar XI seemed to establish a general principle that all human subjects are not "poets" but "poems," one year later, Lacan himself asserted that he was not a poet. Was this statement meant to deplore a weakening of his inspiration, a crisis in his practice, or a loss of creativity? Can the two divergent formulations help us understand Lacan's attitude facing poetry? To try and answer this question, one should follow a chronological progression and go back to Lacan's lifelong fascination for poetry. Lacan took his point of departure in a Surrealist credo, the idea that poetry can be written by all. Poetry, for Breton and his friends, was written by all, especially by the hysterics, the deviant, and the insane. Lacan saw first in poetry a verbal proof of the link between creativity and the Freudian Unconscious. Lacan, even though he was close to Eluard, Breton, Aragon, Crevel, and Dalí, was not a proto-Surrealist poet. He was more a philosopher of psychoanalysis who produced a discursive synthesis capable of bridging the gap between the natural sciences and the humanities. One can verify this idea by examining the only poem Lacan ever published, a sonnet entitled "Hiatus Irrationalis," dated August 1929. One should be literal at this juncture: if Lacan feels that he can be represented by one poem, it might be this one. I will investigate whether this could disclose the origin of Lacan's "auto-poiesis," to use Luhmann's term.

The poem's main theme is an endlessly irritating mixture of fire and blood that shapes human desire. In other words, the sonnet provides a perfect allegory of irritation in the sense I have given to this term. The sonnet was published in the last issue of the short-lived Surrealist journal *Le Phare de Neuilly*, a journal that had only three issues from 1931 to 1933. Its editor was Lise Deharme, who figures as "The Lady of the Glove" in André Breton's novel *Nadja*. I tried to translate *Hiatus Irrationalis* in 2003, although I was aware of the difficulty of the task given the density and ambiguity of its language (Rabaté:2003, p. 21). Here, in an effort to help readers plumb its depths, I will provide a detailed commentary.

Hiatus Irrationalis begins by addressing "things," which is the poem's first word. This opening situates the meditation in a certain ontology, a point I insist on given the similarly ontological turn taken by "Lituraterre." Here, we immediately learn that "things" are not meant to refer to inanimate objects, for the poem's speaker wonders whether it is "sweat" or "sap" that traverses them: "things" include human and animal bodies, and also plants. Lacan later highlighted the motif of "*das Ding*" presented by Freud's *Project* in Seminar VII (Lacan:1992, pp. 101–114). In "Hiatus irrationalis," the same "things" are doubled by their immaterial structure because they include their own "forms." They appear to have been produced either by the material agency of a "forge" or by the "flow" of blood in human bodies.

The mention of the "forge" ushers in a second motif, the poet's desperate search for agency: the speaker begets "things" thanks to an "unceasing desire" that seems to have been born from his dreams. Once this theme has been sounded as a pantheistic hymn, it segues into a sudden downward turn, like a crash or a collapse. We now see the speaker precipitated, having fallen onto a "shore." Its hard and stony ground receives the thud of a body propelled forward by the "weight" of thought. It seems that the poet has been brought down by his own "thinking demon." Is this an echo of Descartes's *malin génie?* Such a ground appears as the site from which "evil" (*mal*) issues. This evil deprives him of the most basic senses, like sight and hearing. "Evil" is defined as stemming from an evil god, a god who is also a senseless god, for he is called "god deprived of meaning." Hence the subjects must struggle against three instances that reveal a universal absurdity: against the "ground," against the "evil," and against a god who is less omnipotent than deprived of any rational justification.

The following tercets suggest that one can rebound from the low point reached in this absolute negativity, from this utter lack of meaning. The solution is to overcome the mutism of negativity and radicalize it by dissolving fully into the totality of Nature; this entails that one is reborn if one accepts a fusion of one's being with universal desire. If the negativity of the end of the quatrain yields a moment of mutism, an inability to speak when language (*verbe*) has died in the poet's throat, there is a way out nevertheless—to accept to be a part of "Nature." The tercets show how the previous concept of "things" in the plural can be elevated and encompassed by this unifying "Nature." It is "Nature," obviously quite close to Spinoza's *natura naturans*, that is the infinite agency of nature expressing itself through creation, that allows the poet to dissolve in an elemental flux. However, in the last two lines, whereas "flux" seems to suggest a liquid, it is in fact to a "fire" that burns in the poet's body that he owes his destiny, thanks to an anaphoric slippage from *flux* to *feu* (fire). Then the poet is called an "immortal lover.". The last two words, *immortel amant*, end up rhyming outside the scope of the sonnet: *amant* echoes with the proud signature that follows the date of its composition (August 1929): "Jacques Lacan."

"Jacques Lacan" thus signs a Petrarchan sonnet in alexandrines that exhibits very little of the wild metaphors and free verse of Surrealist poems. Indeed, the sonnet's inspiration is philosophical, its main source being Alexandre Koyré's survey of Boehme's philosophy published in 1929. Close to the end, *La Philosophie de Jacob Boehme* (*The Philosophy of Jacob Boehme*) commented Boehme's famous sentence "*In Ja und Nein bestehen alle Dinge*," meaning: "In Yes and No all things are constituted" (Koyré:1929, pp. 393–394). For the German mystic, nature was a dynamic synthesis of affirmation and negation, both implying each other dialectically. This monistic theory of Nature aimed at reconciling affirmation and negation via the agency of a universal Fire. Lacan's sonnet had been entitled "*Panta Rhei*" in an earlier handwritten version dating from 1929. One can find this first version in Annie Tardits's excellent essay (Tardits:2009, p. 182). When the poem was rewritten for publication in 1933, the title morphed from Greek to Latin, as if to signify that Heraclitus had begotten Boehme. Here we catch a glimpse of Lacan writing his ode to the Heraclitean "logos" thanks to which "all things flow," but this *Logos* then rhymes with a Christian *Logos*, the *Logos* presented by saint John as the beginning (*archē*) of everything and God. Both merge into Lacan's own *Verbe*, a term impossible to render adequately in

English but that announces the *legs* we encountered in his translation of Heidegger's essay on "Logos."

"Hiatus Irrationalis" betrays one major stylistic influence, that of Paul Valéry's metaphysical style. Like Valéry, Lacan blends allusions to Greek philosophy, especially that of the pre-Socratics, with more recent problematics of desire and the sentient body. Lacan stages a dialogue between the poet and nature, both caught up in dialectical fire capable of reconciling the opposites. Valéry would also state that thought itself was a demonic invention and at times seemed nostalgic for a mute immersion in things. Another predecessor is Arthur Rimbaud who saw himself as damned, possessed by a fire that also ran through Nature: "It is the fire that rises again with its damned soul" from *Season in Hell* (Rimbaud:1986, p. 317). However, the main problematic derives from Boehme's mysticism in which a material and spiritual desire emerges as a universal principle running through nature and animated beings.

A perfect *coincidentia oppositorum*, this upsurge splices Heraclitus' stream, the sap that courses in plants, the sperm and other fluids produced by humans, with Boehme's universal fire. "Hiatus Irrationalis" manages to transform the river of endless becoming, the famous' *"panta rhei,"* with Boehme's vision of a universal conflagration. Before reaching the *Mysterium Magnum*, the subject will undergo a moment of speechlessness evoked by the first tercet when it paints the painful moment of mutism. Boehme's mystical vision foreshadows an absolute Other whose silence lets nature disclose its hidden secrets.

Lacan found the phrase *"hiatus irrationalis"* in Koyré's book on the philosophy of Boehme, but the expression was provided incidentally; it is used only twice, in italics, and without any reference whatsoever. Koyré knew that the Latin phrase did not come from Boehme's vocabulary; this was a term often used in post-Kantian philosophy. A gifted philosopher like Emil Lask, a student of Husserl, had explored it to reveal tensions among Fichte and Hegel: both tried to combine an irrational positing of the subject with the conditions of possibility and intelligibility inherited from Kant, but the discovery of the infinite yielded a perception of the "incommensurable and irrational" (Lask:1902, p. 171). Lask pointed out how, in 1804, Fichte recognized that there would always be a *hiatus irrationalis* (irrational gap) between the necessary conditions of intelligibility and the contingent facts of existence. The task of philosophy as he saw it would be to remove this gap.

In his fifteenth lecture of the 1804 Berlin series, Fichte announced that he discovered an "irrational gap" between "an object whose origin is inexplicable" and our "projection" of that object. Fichte's subjectivity occupied the position of an individual will whose actuality is irreducible to rational intelligibility. Here is the relevant passage:

> The higher maxim presented in this reasoning would just be this: to give no credence to the assertions of simple, immediate consciousness, even if one cannot factically free oneself from them, but rather to abstract

from them. What is this consciousness's effect, for the sake of which it is discarded; and therefore what is that which must always be removed from the truth? Answer: the absolute projection of an object whose origin is inexplicable, so that between the projective act and the projected object everything is dark and bare; as I think I can express very accurately, if a little scholastically, a *proiectio per hiatum irrationale* (projection through an irrational gap).

(Fichte:2005, p. 119).

In this lecture, Fichte was not abandoning rationality but paving the way to a different phenomenology. One can see how Hegel would proceed when he expanded this post-Kantian point of view. Thanks to Kojève and Koyré, Lacan knew that Hegel's concepts entailed the deployment of irrational desire. It is the *Begierde* (desire) underpinning the struggle between different consciousnesses; this appears first as a natural principle before becoming subjective and relational, and finally reaching rationality. Here is why Lacan's sonnet evokes an all-consuming desire, which calls up Hegel's analysis of blood as the condensation of irritability, as we saw with his *Philosophy of Nature*. Here, this concept is introduced thanks to Boehme's God, a God who nevertheless leaves room for an Other, perhaps a negative and evil double. Lacan also pushes Boehme in the direction of Spinoza's *Ethics* by ushering in, as we have seen, the idea of *natura naturans* underpinned by a universal desire traversing all things; of course, all subjects are submitted to the same rhythm.

One should not downplay the darker elements brought about by the philosophy of Jacob Boehme even if they have been grafted on Heraclitean images of the flux of becoming. Boehme was instrumental in bringing a new theme in philosophy, namely an intense sexualization of the generative process, which was not explicitly visible in Heraclitus' thought. Here is one example among many:

The originall of the Eternall Spirituall and Naturall fire is effected by an Eternall conjunction or Copulation, not each severally, but both jointly: viz. the Divine Fire, which is a love-flame, and the Naturall fire, which is a torment, and consuming Source...

(Boehme:1623, p. 9)

The dialectical thinking of Boehme entails a bold sexualization of nature; elements like fire and water partake of this sexual energy that elicits a material dialectic: "The fire cannot burn without the water, and the water were a nothing without the fire, and they mutually beget one another, and also do again vehemently desire each other" (Boehme:1623, p. 61). In this natural hierogamy, the fire devours, consumes, and kills its opposite; such a death is required for the regeneration of life.

However, Boehme adds a theological layer to what might have remained a naturalistic pantheism, for in his thought, the main source of fire is God, and fire embodies God's wrath. God is perpetually angry in Boehme's system, the "consuming fire of God's anger" betrays a "dark wrathful source" (Boehme:1623, p. 25). The fire of wrath emanating from the irritated divinity, in other words from an evil God, is called "wrath" in English and *Grimmigkeit* in German. Boehme's complex notion underpins the sonnet's line *"le mal aveugle et sourd, le dieu privé de sens"* (blind and deaf evil, the god deprived of meaning). *Grimmigkeit* is a term that Lacan never forgot. He refers to it in conjunction with Sade in the seminar on the Ethics of psychoanalysis, in a context where he mentions the Cathars, the French heretic sect for whom God was a Supreme-Being-in-Evil. He adds: "The *Grimmigkeit* of Boehme's God, fundamental evil as one of the dimensions of supreme life, proves that it is not simply in libertine and antireligious thought that this dimension may be evoked" (Lacan:1992, p. 215).

Boehme's *Grimmigkeit* is presented as an alternative to Kant's theological optimism in "Kant with Sade," as we have seen. It was because Kant wanted to avoid any imputation of malignancy to God that he appealed to the Law as such; his pure Law, as we saw, had to be cleansed from all "pathological" side-effects. The closeness to ataraxia Kant evinced in his wish to be "pure" and formalist derives less from the influence of Stoicism than a rejection of the mysticism he kept attacking. Kant first made fun of Swedenborg whom he derided in the 1766 essay "Dreams of a Spirit Seer." Then he included Boehme as a distant pernicious influence. Lacan develops this view: "... Kant feels pressured here by what he hears too close by, not from Sade but from some nearby mystic, in the sigh that muffles what he glimpses, having seen that his God is faceless: *Grimmigkeit*? Sade says: supremely-evil-being" (Lacan:2006, p. 652).

Indeed, the word *Grimmigkeit* remains untranslatable, which is why Lacan does not give an equivalent for it. An English equivalent might be "fierceness" or even, according to William Blake, a disciple of Swedenborg who had read Boehme closely, "energy." In *The Aurora* translated into English by John Sparrow in 1656, *Grimmigkeit* was always rendered by two terms that kept changing: "wrath or fierceness," or "fierceness or bitterness." Surprisingly, that *grimmig* "wrath-fire" would be shared by God and Lucifer: a "twofold source" of "good and evil" is the essential factor in the regeneration of life. Boehme writes: "For from its twofold source, everything hath its great mobility, running, springing, driving and growing, for meekness in nature is a still *rest*, but the fierceness in every power maketh all things moveable, running and generative" (1656, Pdf). This was a lesson William Blake learned from his reading of Boehme whose main intuitions he developed poetically in the scandalous "Proverbs of Hell" from *A Marriage of Heaven and Earth*. George Bataille was right to consider these proverbs as announcing the cult of energy as delight and jouissance that one later finds in Sade (see Baker:2015, pp. 273–289).

Lacan had read Blake, at least through André Gide, as we can verify in his essay on Gide:

> A marriage of psychology and the letter—I would like to echo here a title by William Blake that was dear to Gide, in order to designate what happens when the letter, being educated by psychology, refinds in it its own instance in a position to redirect it.
>
> (Lacan:2006, p. 629)

The syntax of this sentence is slightly clearer in French: "*y retrouve sa propre instance en position de la régir*" (Lacan:2006, p. 747); it suggests that when the letter can be schooled by psychology—or when literature is aware of its unconscious determinations—then it will understand how its "*instance,*" a term we have glossed at some length, or again its enunciative apparatus, will be determined by its position in the structure.

The staggering number of philosophical layers implied by Lacan's sonnet, Greek pantheism, Protestant mysticism, and post-Kantian critical philosophy, all hinge around a central gap, a yawn, a chasm: *hiatus* comes from the Latin verb *hiare*, which means to be wide open. In that sense, the two words of the title appear as quasi synonyms, for *irrationalis* situates the gap of the unconscious as the opposite of reason. Beyond Fichte and Koyré, Lacan might have seen the same phrase *hiatus irrationalis* used by Georg Lukacs's *History and Class Consciousness*. This classic of Marxism published in German in 1923 was a reference for philosophers on the left, like Walter Benjamin. Lacan, who was fluent in German and a voracious reader, and whose affinities with Marxism and the Frankfurt school were clear in the 1930s, as we have seen, would have heard of Lukacs's main work. At some point, Lukacs gives a political analysis of the role played by German mystics in the early modern times. He discusses the theological underpinnings of the widespread peasants' rebellions in Germany. The main revolt was led by Thomas Münzer, a radical theologian executed in 1525. Lukacs links the doctrine of the hidden god *(deus absconditus)* with the utopia of thinkers who had an impact on Jakob Boehme, who was born fifty years after the death of Münzer. Lukacs did not endorse those revolutionary theologies, for he remained critical: here is why he remarked that Münzer's actions revealed a "dark and empty chasm," the "*hiatus irrationalis* between theory and practice." Such *hiatus irrationalis* characterizes an ineffective and subjective, attitude, hence generating an "undialectical utopia" (Lukacs:1967, Pdf). Both Koyré and Lukacs had gone back to Johann Gottlob Fichte's *Wissensschaftslehre* in which the Latin phrase refers to an irreducible gap between thinking and reality; it points to a yawning interval between theory and praxis. Lacan appreciated how a visionary mysticism disclosing a truth about desire could be a substitute for a doomed pre-communist utopia.

Lacan's sonnet was contemporary with his attempts at letting the insane or the psychotic speak. Having frequented the Surrealists, Lacan discovered that everyday language is structured like poetry thanks to the "inspired speech" of raving psychotic patients. In 1931, Lacan co-authored with Lévy-Valensi and Migault a piece entitled "Inspired Writings," an essay analyzing the psychotic ramblings of a young female teacher who had been hospitalized at Sainte-Anne. She would write in a psychotic style and in a mostly invented language freewheeling verses in which one could discern a regulated system of echoes and puns. As the three psychiatrists observed, the function of rhythm was dominant, with numerous echoes from popular sayings, famous poetic quotes, automatic expressions, proverbial idioms slightly distorted. Such stereotypic echolalia was self-consciously presented as "poetry" by the psychotic patient.

In this joint paper, the ground-breaking stylistic analysis of the grammar of mad utterances acknowledges the pioneering work done by the Surrealists just a few years before. The authors quote Breton's first *Manifesto of Surrealism*, but also look for models of interpretation in Breton's and Eluard's imitations of different types of delirium, the five psychotic "imitations" from *The Immaculate Conception* (1930), a text that they quote in a footnote. In the wonderful section entitled "Possessions," Breton and Eluard reproduce types of psychotic styles, "Mental debility," "Acute Mania," "General paralysis," "Interpretive delirium," and "Dementia Praecox" (Breton and Eluard:1990, pp. 51–78). In their dazzling introduction to "Possessions," Breton and Eluard reject the idea that they are indulging in facile pastiches of clinical texts, even though they insist that they have looked at authentic archives of "alienated" or insane patients. Their aim is rather to show that the poetic faculties of normal subjects allow them to reproduce the most bizarre, paradoxical, and eccentric verbal productions of those who are deemed to be "insane." Breton and Eluard conclude by disclosing a veritable poetic program, and do not hesitate to provoke literary critics—the ravings of the insane will offer new criteria and new poetic forms capable of replacing traditional genres. Arguing that this stylistic exercise in multiple imitations was pleasurable, they recommend this practice as generating a more valuable "literature," to evoke Lacan's essay:

> Finally, we declare that this new exercise of our thought had brought pleasure to us. We became aware of new, up to then unsuspected, resources in us. (...) we would gladly suggest the generalization of this exercise, and that for us the "attempt at simulation" of the diseases of those who are locked up in asylums could advantageously replace the ballad, the sonnet, the epic, the improvised poem and other obsolete genres.
>
> (Breton:1988, p. 849)

This half-serious poetic program was shared by Lacan; it led him to formulate the thesis that the Unconscious was "structured like a language," which became a motto that he repeated in all his seminars and essays. Such a thesis would find a confirmation in countless readings of famous poems, often by Victor Hugo, Paul Valéry, or Paul Claudel. The theory of poetic metaphors had been discovered in "involuntary Surrealism," as the Surrealist poet Paul Eluard put it when praising Lacan for a dissertation in which he reproduced the crazy writings of his patient, the delirious prose-poetry of "Aimée." Poetry discloses the essence of language, therefore, there is no need to retain the distinction between prose and poetry. Both prose and poetry are formations created by a general rhetoric of the Unconscious. It is thanks to these mechanisms that one can fathom better the vital and mysterious connection between subjects as beings and "Being."

This couple of concepts derives from Martin Heidegger. As we have seen, Lacan and Heidegger shared a theory of poetic "Saying" disclosing man's relation to Truth, even if this Truth appeared as elusive as a goddess like Diana. The quester who wants to reach Truth can be destroyed in the process. In "The Freudian Thing," subtitled "or Meaning of the Return to Freud in Psychoanalysis," Lacan gave a highly rhetorical speech in Vienna in 1955 in which he heralded his "return to Freud" against all deviations of Freudian doctrine, especially the ego-psychology that prevailed in the United States. When the lecture was published in 1956, not only did it include a three-page-long prosopopeia of Truth, in which Truth speaks in the first person, saying: "I, the Truth, I speak," but also a highly wrought conclusion. Its last paragraph conceals a submerged quatrain in classically rhyming alexandrines, but hidden in extremely opaque prose. If one restores the poetic layout, one discovers this little poem:

Actéon trop coupable à courre la déesse,
proie où se prend, veneur, l'ombre que tu deviens,
laisse la meute aller sans que ton pas se presse,
Diane à ce qu'ils vaudront reconnaîtra les chiens...

(Lacan:2006, p. 436)

Bruce Fink translates accurately: "Actaeon, too guilty to hunt the goddess, prey in which is caught, O huntsman, the shadow that you become, let the pack go without hastening your step, Diana will recognize the hounds for what they are worth" (Lacan:2006, pp. 362–63). Lacan managed to produce a poem in the style of Giordano Bruno whose *Eroici Furori* he had quoted a little before. When Lacan compared Freud's passion for truth, a passion that allowed him to enter the cave of Diana, with the timid attitude of his disciples who refused to follow him to the end, he concluded with a poetic analogy: "... so the Acteon who is dismembered here is not Freud, but every analyst in proportion to the passion that inflamed him and made him—according to the signification Giordano Bruno drew from this myth in his *Heroic Frenzies*—the prey of the dogs of his own thoughts." (Lacan: 2006, p. 343)

We recognize the invocation of universal desire allied with a principle of flight and capture reminiscent of "Hiatus irrationalis." If we read the Actaeon quatrain closely, its weird humor emerges; it undermines any serious invocation of Greek myths. The sly joke, "*reconnaîtra les chiens*" (will recognize the hounds) lets us hear "*reconnaîtra les siens*" (will tell her own from the pack). The rather obscure phrasing, "*trop coupable à courre la déesse*" (too guilty to run after the goddess) contains, among other echoes, "*chasse à courre*" (fox hunting) and "*coureur de femmes*" (a womanizer). In his militant program pointedly addressed to the Viennese Psychoanalytic Society, Lacan appeared as poet-philosopher of psychoanalysis, a post-Heideggerian thinker progressing by opaque epigrams, a psychoanalyst wishing to revolutionize a whole field of knowledge.

We are now in a better position to understand Lacan's regret that he had not been "enough of a poet." This uncharacteristic admission of humility contrasts with Lacan's usual bombast. A similar idea can be found in Freud: he keeps praising poets for their brilliant discoveries (all at once, armed with their fervor and a sort of beginner's luck, they chance upon the hidden mechanisms painstakingly described by psychoanalysis) but also berates them for their shortcomings:

> In the past, we have left it to the poets to depict for us the "conditions of love." ... Poets have certain qualities that enable them to solve such a task, in particular a great sensitivity in the perception of hidden mental impulses in others, and the courage to make their own unconscious speak. ... they cannot represent the stuff of reality unadulterated, but are obliged to isolate fragments of it, dissolve obstructive connections, soften the whole and fill any gaps.
>
> (Freud:2006, p. 241)

Lacan would agree; he, too, was never one to "soften the whole" or "fill any gap," even when quoting Heidegger who repeated that man "dwells" poetically in language. This is what Lacan quotes in *My Teaching*: "In language man dwells" (Lacan:2008, p. 27). Heidegger alluded to a famous line by Hölderlin that he often quoted: "Poetically man dwells..." (Heidegger:1971, pp. 213–229). Lacan's own teaching was meant to go further, as he explained in a conversation with the philosopher Henri Maldiney. Maldiney asked him whether he agreed with Heidegger who never talked about a "subject" but only about *Dasein*, which calls up a neutral existence. Lacan responded that he had simplified Heidegger deliberately and reduced him to a "striking formula." Moreover, he was fully aware of the fact that his own "divided subject" was not to be confused with Heidegger's existence as *Dasein* (Lacan:2008, p. 52).

Rehearsing the saying that "In language man dwells," Lacan adds that we are born not only *in* language but above all *thanks to* language. What is more, such a "birth" to presence and the world does not constitute a final event: it continues throughout our lives. The birth to language continues being written thanks to the hieroglyphics, the coats of arms and the runes inscribed in our psyches, those unknown and obscure signs that we carry, the scars we owe to harsh contacts with reality. A psychoanalyst learns to read these signs, hence must be conversant with all types of poetry. It does not follow from this that she or he will automatically be able to write poetry. Like Heidegger, Lacan assumes that subjects inhabit language but that they are also divided by language, split by what remains of the lost object. Whereas Heidegger implies that poetic creation is a building or the creation of a building, Lacan presents it as a proactive or performative project.

For Lacan, poetry provides an indispensable tool for anyone who practices psychoanalysis; "interpretation" in the classical Freudian manner, that is in fact some form of translation, will be replaced with poietic transcription. More pointedly, poetry energizes the practice of hermeneutic equivocation by triggering actively dialogic games played with the signifiers presented by analysands. This practice remains in line with the way Freud presented literary competence as a key to mastering the art of psychoanalysis. In *The Question of Lay Analysis*, Freud contrasts medical training with the cultural competence he presents as a prerequisite for psychoanalysts. His ideal curriculum includes "the history of civilization, mythology, the psychology of religion, and literature (*Literaturwissenschaft*)" (Freud:1950, p. 118). That alleged "science of literature" refers to a thorough mixture of literary expertise and a knowledge of the rules guiding interpretation. Because literature and the humanities are essential to the training of analysts, such a "science of literature" will be endowed with some performative power, for it explains that one must be aware of the dialogical nature of interpretation. A general hermeneutics of the sign encompasses the entire literary field and the existential issues shared by all human beings.

Since Sophocles gave shape to the myth of Oedipus, culture has provided countless examples, characters, situations, and even jokes that help define or make sense of individual diagnoses. For instance, an awareness of the chronicles of gods and heroes can be brought to bear on the understanding of transgenerational traumas. Culture does not function as a marker of distinction, for it mobilizes a knowledge in touch with unconscious processes. If the unconscious can be defined as a knowledge that does not know itself, our dreams confirm this knowledge provided we learn how to interpret them. On the other hand, although we are not aware of the fact because we believe in our absolute singularity, our dreams belong to culture, a term combining our personal engagement with formalized modes of fiction and the values that constitute a whole civilization. Such views, shared by Freud and Lacan, will not entail, for all that, that all psychoanalysts must turn into poets.

Lacan knew too much about the inner workings of the Unconscious to let himself play at pretending to be a naive creator in poetry. His poetry is intertwined with his writing and his teaching. Too close to the *"insu que sait"* of the Unconscious, this "non-knowledge that knows" entails a certain "unsuccess" as a poet. This was the price Lacan had to pay in order to be a good psychoanalyst, perhaps because like Marquis de Sade he was too much an "immortal lover" of Truth. This eternal lover can, nevertheless, deliver a poetic truth, which it does poetically as well. Here is why the last word must be left to a poet, a poet Lacan often quoted. It is Max Jacob who wrote: "The truth is always new."[2]

Notes

1 Another version can be found in Alan Sheridan's translation of *The Four Fundamental Concepts of Psychoanalysis* (Lacan:1978, p. viii). My translation follows *Autres Ecrits* (Lacan:2001, p. 572.).
2 Max Jacob wrote *"Le vrai est toujours neuf"* in a startling account of an accident he had Place Pigalle in *"Nuits d'hôpital."* The sentence, which could figure as the motto of psychoanalysis, is quoted by Lacan (Lacan:2008, p. 17).

Bibliography

Allaigre-Duny, Annick (2001). "A propos du sonnet de Lacan," *L'Unebévue*, 17, Paris, p. 27–48.

Baker, John (2015). "A partir de Georges Bataille et William Blake," in *La Part Maudite de Georges Bataille: la dépense et l'excès*, ed. Christian Limousin and Jacques Poirier, Paris, Garnier, p. 273–289.

Barnet, Marie-Claire (2003). "To Lise Deharme's Lighthouse: *Le Phare de Neuilly*, A Forgotten Surrealist Review," *French Studies*, Vol. 57 / 3, p. 323–334

Boehme, Jacob (1623). *Mysterium Magnum, or an Exposition of the first book of Moses called Genesis…*, London, Lloyd.

Boehme, Jacob (1656). *The Aurora*, trans. John Sparrow, London, Internet Archive, https://ia800206.us.archive.org/28/items/JacobBoehmesAurora-ElectronicText-edition/Jacob-Boehme-Aurora-electronic-text.pdf

Breton, André (1988). *Oeuvres Complètes*, vol. 1, ed. M. Bonnet, Paris, Pléiade, Gallimard.

Breton, André and Eluard, Paul (1990). *The Immaculate Conception*, trans. Jon Graham, London, Atlas Press.

Fichte, J. G. (2005). *The Science of Knowing*, J. G. Fichte's 1804 lectures on the Wissenschaftslehre, trans. Walter E. Wright, Albany, SUNY Press.

Freud, Sigmund (1950). *The Question of Lay Analysis*, trans. Nancy Procter-Gregg, New York, Norton.

Freud, Sigmund (1982). *Die Frage der Laienanalyse, Schriften zur Behandlungstechnik*, Frankfurt, Fischer.

Freud, Sigmund (2006). *The Psychology of Love*, trans. Shaun Whiteside, London, Penguin.

Green, Richard Firth (1999). *A Crisis of Truth: Literature and Law in Ricardian England*, Philadelphia, University of Pennsylvania Press.

Heidegger, Martin (1971). *Poetry, Language, Thought*, trans. Albert Hofstadter, New York, Harper and Row.

Koyré, Alexandre (1929). *Jacob Boehme*, Paris, Vrin.

Lacan, Jacques (1966). *Ecrits*, trans. Bruce Fink, New York, Norton.

Lacan, Jacques (1975). *De la Psychose Paranoïaque et autres écrits*, Paris, Seuil.

Lacan, Jacques (1977). *Seminar XXIV*, 17 May 1977, Gaogoa, gaogoa.free.fr/Seminaire.htm

Lacan, Jacques (1978). *The Four Fundamental Concepts of Psychoanalysis*, trans. Alan Sheridan, New York, Norton.

Lacan, Jacques (1992). *The Ethics of Psychoanalysis, Seminar VII, 1959–1960*, trans. Dennis Porter, New York, Norton.

Lacan, Jacques (2001). *Autres Ecrits*, Paris, Seuil.

Lacan, Jacques (2006). *Ecrits*, tr. Bruce Fink, New York, Norton.

Lacan, Jacques (2008). *My Teaching*, trans. David Macey, New York, Verso.

Lask, Emil (1902). *Fichtes Idealismus und die Geschichte*, Tübingen und Leipzig, Mohr.

Lukacs, Georg (1967). *History and Class Consciousness*, trans. Rodney Livingstone, Merlin Press, 1967, Pdf http://literaturepdf2.files.wordpress.com/2010/05/georg-lukacs-writing

McIntire, Gabrielle (2008). *Modernism, Memory and Desire: T. S. Eliot and Virginia Woolf*, Cambridge, Cambridge University Press.

Nobus, Dany (2018). "Psychoanalysis as Poetry in Lacan's clinical paradigm," *After Lacan*, ed. Ankhi Mukherjee, Cambridge, Cambridge University Press, p. 72–92.

Rabaté, Jean-Michel (2003). "Lacan's turn to Freud," in *The Cambridge Companion to Lacan*, edited by Jean-Michel Rabaté, Cambridge, Cambridge University Press, p. 1–24.

Rimbaud, Arthur (1986). *Collected Poems*, trans. Oliver Bernard, London, Penguin.

Tardits, Annie (2009). "La mélancolie du hiatus, un sonnet inaugural de Lacan," *Le Genre Humain*, Paris, Le Seuil, N. 48, p. 159–183.

Woolf, Virginia (1985). *Moments of Being*, New York, Harcourt Brace.

Index

Pages followed by "n" refer to notes.